*Acclaim for Sun Shuyun's*

# THE LONG MARCH

"A beautifully told story. . . . Utterly compelling. . . . [Sun Shuyun] is an engaging writer with an excellent eye for detail."
—*The Guardian* (London)

"Powerful. . . . [The] devastating account [of the survivors], which comprehensively subverts Mao's official version, is a testament to Shuyun's old-fashioned journalistic values."
—Nicholas Shakespeare, *The Daily Telegraph* (London)

"Impressive . . . excellent. . . . Subtle [and] layered."    —*The Observer*

"A mixture of engaging, lively travel writing and impressive historical reconstruction. . . . Offers a rewarding journey into the experience of people, within living memory, who needed endurance beyond the comprehension of most of us."    —*Financial Times*

"Compelling. . . . It may well change the core of modern Chinese history."    —*Deseret Morning News*

"Splendidly researched and craftily written."
—*Kirkus Reviews* (starred review)

SUN SHUYUN

## *THE LONG MARCH*

Sun Shuyun was born in China in the 1960s. She graduated from Beijing University and won a scholarship to Oxford. A filmmaker and television producer, she has made documentaries for the BBC, Channel 4, PBS, and the Discovery Channel. For the past decade, she has divided her time between London and Beijing.

# THE LONG MARCH

# THE LONG MARCH

## THE TRUE HISTORY OF COMMUNIST CHINA'S FOUNDING MYTH

## SUN SHUYUN

ANCHOR BOOKS

A DIVISION OF RANDOM HOUSE, INC.

NEW YORK

FIRST ANCHOR BOOKS EDITION, MAY 2008

*Copyright © 2006 by Sun Shuyun*

All rights reserved. Published in the United States by Anchor Books, a division of Random House, Inc., New York, and in Canada by Random House of Canada Limited, Toronto. Originally published in the United Kingdom as *The Long March* by HarperPress, London, in 2006, and subsequently published in hardcover by arrangement with HarperPress in the United States by Doubleday, an imprint of The Doubleday Broadway Publishing Group, a division of Random House, Inc., New York, in 2007.

Anchor Books and colophon are registered trademarks of Random House, Inc.

The following photographs are included by kind permission of Chinese Archive Sources:
Mao presiding at the opening of the First China Soviet Congress
Mao's calligraphy, Zunyi Museum
Mao and Zhang Guotao at Shaanxi, 1937
Red Army at Shaanxi, 1937
Bo Gu and others, Shaanxi, 1936
Zhou Enlai, Mao, and others, after Xian Incident

The following photographs are included by kind permission of Hou Baoyu:
The Xiang River
The Red Army's road out of Zunyi
Luding Bridge

The rest of the photographs have been taken by the author.

The Library of Congress has cataloged the Doubleday edition as follows:
Sun, Shuyun.
The Long March : the true history of Communist China's founding myth /
by Sun Shuyun.
p. cm.
Includes bibliographical references and index.
1. China—History—Long March. 1934–1935.   I. Title.
DS777.5132.86 2007
951.04'2—dc22
2006052132

**Anchor ISBN: 978-0-307-27831-9**

*Author photograph © Robert Cassen*
*Book design by Pei Koay*

www.anchorbooks.com

Printed in the United States of America
10   9   8   7   6   5   4   3

*To all the men and women on the Long March*

# CONTENTS

## ★ ACKNOWLEDGMENTS

I am deeply grateful to everyone who helped me on my journey and with this book, especially RHC, ever patient, ever supportive.

# THE LONG MARCH

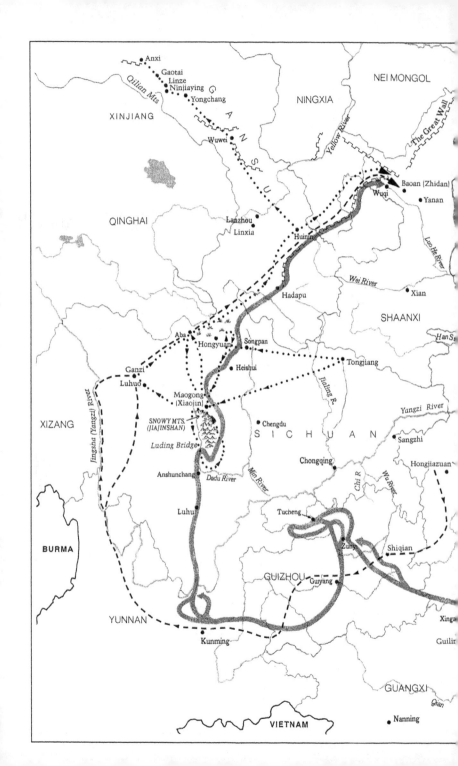

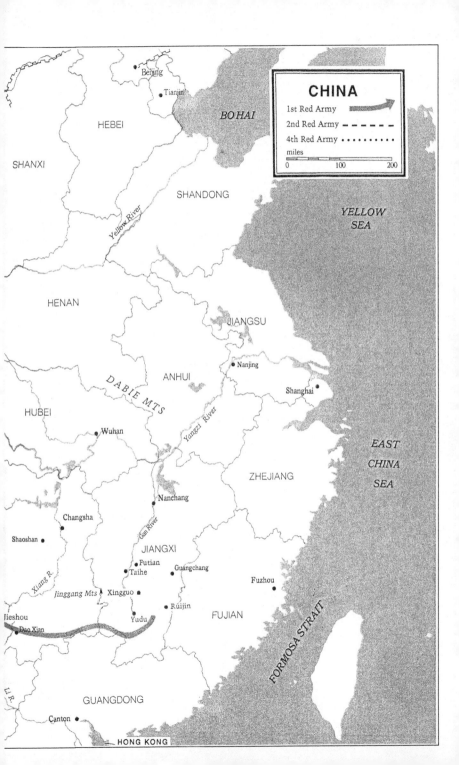

I was born to the sound of a bugle in the barracks of the People's Liberation Army where my father served; I grew up with stories of his battles. There were plenty—he was in the army for nearly thirty years. He joined up with the Communist troops when he was 16. He often said only they could help the poor in his village. He really felt for the poor. "In winter they dropped like flies," he told me.

Father fought his way across the whole of China and helped to defeat the Nationalist government led by Chiang Kaishek, whom he called "a paper tiger." On October 1, 1949, when Mao declared on Tiananmen Square that the Chinese people had "stood up," my father thought he was finished with fighting. He planned to find a wife, have children, and settle down. But he was called to the Korean War; he told me, "We had to show the American imperialists our true colors, otherwise they would shit on our heads and take over our homes." He got shrapnel in his back, and from early childhood, I saw him wearing a leather corset around his waist, like a saddled horse.

Fighting erupted again soon after I was born. The Cultural Revolution became virtually a civil war, employing every weapon except for planes. There were barricades in the streets, rifles, and cannons. Father was no longer with the army, but he was horrified to see our city turning into a battlefield, as if his former life was returning. My grandmother was just confused—she thought the Japanese had invaded again. To this day I still dream of the battles, whose gunfire I could hear outside our sandbagged windows.

It was not Father's personal stories that impressed me most. He talked about his experiences at war only when I begged him to. For him nothing was more exciting and revered than the Long March.

Father was too young to take part in it, but his senior commanders were all veterans of the March. "The battles we fought were like child's play compared with theirs; the hardships we encountered were small dishes," he told me. "The Marchers were outnumbered by their enemies one to a hundred, and they had nothing to eat but leather and grass. Yet they won! It was a miracle."

As I started school, I began to understand the message he'd tried to drill into me: "If you find it hard, think of the Long March; if you feel tired, think of our revolutionary forebears." Surely nothing compares in difficulty with the Long March. In 1934, the fledgling Communist Party and its Red Armies, some 200,000 strong, were driven out of their bases in the South by Chiang Kaishek. Pursued, blocked, and harried by their enemies, they chose the only way out—to go where no one could follow, over mountains higher than birds could fly, across rivers where all the boats had been burned, through swamps and grassland death traps. It was Mao who steered the course from victory to victory. After two years of incredible endurance, courage, and hope against impossible odds—and a march of 8,000 miles—the Red armies reached the barren Yellow Plateau of northwestern China. Only a fifth of those who set out arrived—worn out and battered, but defiant. In just over a decade, they had fought back and launched the new China in the heat of revolution. In Mao's own words:

> Has history ever known a long march to equal ours? No, never. The Long March has proclaimed to the world that the Red Army is an army of heroes. The Long March has sown many seeds which will sprout, leaf, blossom, and bear fruit, and will yield a harvest in the future. In a word, the Long March has ended with victory for us and defeat for the enemy.

The myth was born, and it remains the enduring emblem of China today. For us the Long March is a story on a par with Moses leading the exodus out of Egypt. We can hardly escape it. It is enshrined for the nation in the musical extravaganzas *The East Is Red* and *Ode to the Long March*, and feature films of battles fought during the March are cinema classics. They take the idealism, optimism, and heroism of the

Long Marchers and imprint them on our minds. The myth glows ever brighter with the help of two major adulatory accounts, both, oddly, by Americans: Edgar Snow's *Red Star over China* (1936) and Harrison Salisbury's *Long March: The Untold Stories* (1985). With the imprimatur of the Chinese Communist Party, they make the myth close to impregnable.

Decades after the historical one, which according to Mao was only the first step in the Communist scheme, the nation has been spurred on to ever more Long Marches. But not everyone could keep up with the rigor of the Marches. Mao had almost all the veterans of the Long March purged in the Cultural Revolution—they were too old, and too unwilling, to do his bidding. The Red Guards were the new Marchers.

The economic reform after Mao's death—another new long march to modernize China—saw the beginning of our newfound material prosperity. But for my father the changes were the abandonment of everything he had given his life to. How could the landlords and exploitative capitalists he had struggled against have become the new heroes, respected and admired by everyone? What he found hardest to swallow was that his generation was blamed for what had gone wrong. Still, I was shocked when I told him I had won a scholarship to study in Oxford, and he replied, "You might as well stay there; there is nothing here for you to come back to." My father died a bitter man, cremated in his Mao suit and wearing all his medals.

But whatever else has changed in China, few have ever challenged or even modestly questioned the Long March myth; it is just part of who we are. Nevertheless the questions remain: Was Communism the magnet that drew the poor in droves to the Red Army? How did the Red Armies supply themselves with food, weapons, and medicine? What happened to the four-fifths of the Marchers who did not reach the end—were they killed in battle, did they succumb to hunger and cold, did they desert, or did they fall victim to their own comrades? Was Mao the great strategist who never lost a battle? How were Mao and the Red Army finally saved? People have begun to ask such questions, but they are earthly matters. The Long March remains the sun in the sky.

Books about the March fill yards of shelves, but they rarely ask all these questions, or provide answers. In 2004, seventy years after it began, I set out over the same route, to discover as much as I could about the realities beyond the myth. There is not much documentation remaining—so many of the records were destroyed as the Armies fled. Quite a few generals have published their memoirs, but real scholarship is rare. Of the 40,000 original survivors, perhaps 500 are still alive, and they are now in their eighties and nineties. Most are just ordinary people who were left behind or managed to reach the end, but they still have much to tell us.

I traveled mainly by train and bus. It is still a daunting journey, through areas little changed to this day—inaccessible, and desperately poor and undeveloped—but I saw enough to know that nothing can possibly compare with what the Marchers endured. My challenge was to find survivors and unlock their stories. I marched to the remote corners where they lived, sometimes 10–15 kilometers in a day, and up as high as 18,000 feet. The rough territory made me appreciate what the real Marchers went through, even though I was well fed and equipped, not worn down by a heavy pack and covering great distances day after day, month after month, on an empty stomach, ill-shod and poorly clothed, ambushed and bombed, in between battles with more mobile and better-armed enemies.

I managed to find more than forty veterans, happily with their memories still fresh and their spirits undiminished. Once I started talking to them, their stories poured out. Frequently, I would come back for a second or third day; they had so much to tell, and were so keen to tell it. I was intrigued, astonished, moved, and inspired. They retain the idealism and optimism that first drove them, and also their doubts, uncertainties, and fears. They touch the heart of the Long March: its bravery and sacrifice, its setbacks and suffering, and its self-inflicted wounds. Why so many supported the Communist cause also became very clear—as well as why many did not.

I record here the voices of these men and women. This is the Long March without the embroidery of adulation, and in all its humanity, as it was lived. It is not my story. It is theirs.

# 1 ★ DRAIN THE POND TO CATCH THE FISH

*I'm sending you to the Army my man,*
*You must see the reason why*
*The Revolution is for us.*
*I'm sending you to do or die.*

*Here's a towel I've embroidered*
*With all my love to say:*
*Revolution for ever!*
*The Party you must not betray!*

The song pierced the silence of Shi Village, which nestled at the foot of a hill covered in thick bamboo groves. It was mid-October, 1935, in Jiangxi Province, southern China. The autumn harvest was already in and the land surrounding the village was yellow with the stubble of rice stalks, but some fields stood as if wasted, with grass sprouting in the dried-out paddy, already turning brown. A few water buffalo were plodding home, only stopping when they came to their favorite place, the village pond, where they drank, ducks and geese swam, children bathed, women washed their clothes, and men asked one another about their day. Nearby stood the giant camphor tree, whose overhanging branches gave ample shelter from the rain and intense heat of the South.

Today the water buffalo had the pond to themselves, and only the village ancestor shrine opposite showed signs of life, but not with pious prayers and hypnotic chants offered to the ancestors: only the revolutionary song calling on young men to join the Red Army. Through the imposing entrance topped by grey-tiled eaves, boys carrying spears rushed in and out, looking solemn, as if they had been entrusted with the most important task of their lives. Two young women were putting a table and some benches outside the gate. As the song died away, more women came out, clutching shoes they were making out of cloth, calling their children, while others gathered up firewood from outside the gate, and went home to cook.

"Nobody is too tired to sing! Keep up the good work!" called Wang Quanyuan, the young woman who had just emerged from a house nearby. She had on a grey cotton jacket, the kind every soldier wore, tied with a rope round her waist, but its simplicity made her beauty stand out even more. She asked one woman to bring more benches, and then stopped one of the boys who was running by, and whispered something in his ear; nodding eagerly, he took to his heels.

Wang noticed the slogans on the white wall of the shrine, written in black ink but slightly washed out by the summer rain. "Down with the Landlords and Evil Gentry!" "Long Live the Communists!" "Long Live the Soviet!" "I mustn't forget to tell them to repaint the slogans," she murmured to herself, remembering that until four years ago she had no idea what Soviet was. Someone had told her that it was a foreign shop, and others said he was the brother of a famous Communist labor organizer. A warlord definitely thought so: he had posted a notice throughout the villages, offering a reward for the capture, dead or alive, of Mr. Soviet. In the local dialect, Soviet was pronounced *Su-wei-ai*, which meant "we," so perhaps the Soviet was *our* government, she once thought. Now she was actually working for the youth and women's departments of the Soviet, a government of workers and peasants that had been set up by Mao and his Red Army in southern Jiangxi in 1931. Small as it was, with barely three million people in half a dozen counties, hemmed in on all sides by Chiang Kaishek's Nationalist troops, the Jiangxi Soviet had all the functions of a state. Wang was told that the Communist Party was working to turn the whole of China into a Soviet. That would be the day, Wang smiled, but then became very solemn. "Everything hangs on tonight," she muttered to herself.

As darkness fell, the bell hanging from the camphor tree rang out.

Four giant bamboo torches lit up the pond and the gate of the shrine hall. Women, and a few men, old and young, gathered with several hundred people from nearby villages, summoned by Wang's Red Pioneers. She had also sent for half a dozen militiamen from the county Party headquarters; when they finally arrived, Wang stood up and delivered her speech:

"Sisters and brothers, grandfathers and grandmothers, the Red Army is at its most critical time now, with many wounded every day. But in a war, there is always winning and losing. If we stop fighting just because we have lost a few battles, our Revolution will never succeed and we will always be exploited by the rich. You are strong. Do you want to be trampled on for the rest of your lives? If not, join the Red Army now!"

There was no reply.

Wang nodded to the militiamen who were standing close by, and continued: "Don't be afraid. We will win. Use your brain. This village has hundreds of poor people, and only one or two landlords. Aren't we more powerful than them? All we need to do is to unite, but there is a traitor who does not want this to happen. He seems to care about you, telling you to keep your men at home, but if we all stay at home, our enemy will come, taking our land and raping our women. Is that what you want?"

"Of course not!" shouted the militiamen.

"Then let's bring the traitor out." Wang waved her hand. Two militiamen appeared from behind the shrine gate, each holding the arm of a man, followed by a third with a pistol in his hand. Silence fell and the villagers looked at each other speechless. The accused was none other than the Party secretary of their district, Mr. Liu. Suddenly, a Red Pioneer raised his arm, shouting, "Down with the traitor! Kill the traitor!"

"Tell me, what do you want done with him?" Wang asked several times.

"Kill him," yelled a militiaman.

"Kill him now!" a chorus of voices followed.

Two shots at point-blank range and Liu fell to the ground. Wang announced grimly: "This will be the fate of anyone who dares to sabotage the Revolution."

It was hard to believe, when I met Woman Wang, that she had ever done such things, or suffered more than I could bear to think about. She had started as the quintessential supporter of the Revolution. Poverty had made her family sell her into a marriage which she did not want; joining the Communists represented hope. Chosen as one of only 30 women to go with the 1st Army among 86,000 men, she survived and rose to head the Red Army's only women's regiment. A year later, she was captured, raped, and given to a Nationalist officer as a concubine—a "crime" for which she was denounced by the Party, remaining under a cloud for the next fifty years. Still, she remained loyal to the Party, which she regarded as dearer to her than her parents. I remember thinking to myself after reading her biography: if there was ever a true Communist faithful, it must be Wang.

What better way to start my journey than by talking to her? I set out in October 2004, exactly seventy years after the Chinese Communist Party and the 1st Army abandoned their base in Jiangxi and began their escape from the Nationalists—the Long March as it became known. From Beijing I took the train, eighteen hours due south, and then after two hours more by bus through green-clad mountains and hills I found myself in Taihe in southern Jiangxi. It was a big town, with a grand new avenue, beautifully surfaced and complete with modern lighting—not many buildings yet, but looking for twenty-first-century growth. I wondered if I would have trouble finding Wang—after all, Taihe had a population of half a million people and all I had was her biography, which I had been rereading on the train. I took a rickshaw from the long-distance bus stop and mentioned Wang's name hesitantly; I was relieved when the driver told me to take it easy. "What a woman! How many went on the Long March from Jiangxi? Eighty thousand? I guess not many of them are left today. Three in this town, and forty in Jiangxi. If you come next year, they will probably all be gone." He took me down the big avenue and then into the old quarter. Dusty, narrow, busy, and crowded, just like the photographs of provincial towns in the 1930s. I was dropped off next to a dumpling shop with a queue of hungry customers. Behind it was Wang's courtyard, shaded by a pomegranate tree with its dark red fruit just bursting open. Beneath it, there she sat, looking gentle, serene, and elegant, belying her 91 years, and without a trace of the toughness of the Red Army commander.

She was not surprised to see me, a complete stranger, walking in off the street and wanting to find out about her past. My copy of her biography was a good enough introduction. She asked me to sit down and called, "Another visitor from Beijing!" A middle-aged woman came out. From what I had read, I assumed she was her adopted daughter—Wang was unable to conceive after the Long March. "You shouldn't ask too many questions, she gets too excited. Last week we had a journalist from Beijing, and she talked so much, it made her ill. Anyway, it is all in there," she said, referring to the book on my lap. Wang cut her short. "They think talking is a waste of breath, but they don't understand. So many men and women died for the good life we live today and I want people to remember that." She sent her daughter back inside for another biography, written by a local Party historian. "You might not have come across it."

The daughter came out with the book and a tray of sliced watermelon. "Eat now, read later. I will answer all your questions. It will take you a few days—you see, unfortunately, I have had such a long life." She took a mouthful of the melon, and smiled, as if it was the rarest fruit in the world and she was tasting it for the first time. Clearly she was keen to talk. She was quick and warm, and over the next three days she opened up like the pomegranates—I heard of the idealism, the hope, the suffering, the sacrifice, the harshness, and the courage of her life, like those of so many others. But Wang also painted in some of the shadows of her history, things that were almost against her nature to reveal, and most certainly at odds with the glorious stories of the Long March that I had grown up with.

Wang was born in 1913 in Lufu Village, not far from where she lives now. Her family barely had enough rice for six months after the landlord took his exorbitant rent. From the age of 5, she roamed the mountains with her sister to collect wild plants to eat. By the time she was 11, her parents found her a husband, who offered to pay off the family debt of 200 kilos of rice. She was in the dark about the arrangement until the wedding day, when her mother dressed her in a bright red outfit, and put her on a palanquin sent by the groom. He was sixteen years older than Wang, slightly retarded, and with so many smallpox scars he was nicknamed Big Smallpox. The villagers said a flower had been planted on a cow pie. When Wang saw him, she fainted, but her mother said the rice was in the pot, and nothing could be done about it.

Her parents' only request was that he would not consummate the marriage until Wang was 18. Meanwhile, she would work like a slave in his household. But he could not wait for seven years: he slept around and the wife of a blind fortune-teller bore him a son. Gossip spread around the village and Wang was so humiliated that she returned to her parents' house, hoping they would pity her and annul the marriage. No, you must go back, her mother told her. "When you marry a chicken, live with a chicken; when you marry a dog, live with a dog." It was fate.

When the Red Army marched into her village in the spring of 1930, she learned it was not fate. "Why do the landlords have so much land, while you have none?" a Red Army officer asked her and her family. "Why do they eat fat pork every day, while you don't see one drop of oil for a whole year? Why do they wear silk while you are in rags? It isn't fair! For every one of them, there are ten of us. If we unite, we are bound to win. What do you say? Join us! Join the Revolution!" She signed up on the spot, and her family received land, salt, rice, ham, and tools, all confiscated from the landlords.

She told everyone about the benefits of the Communist Revolution, citing herself and her family as examples. And she did so by using the most popular method in rural Jiangxi—folk songs. She set new words to the old tunes, not the usual love ballads but full of zeal for the Revolution. She was so good, she was given the nickname "Golden Throat." This was one of her favorites:

> If we save the mountain, we'll have wood.
> If we save the river, we'll have fish to fry.
> If we save the Revolution, we'll have our own land.
> If we save the Soviet, red flags will fly.

In December 1933, Wang had some unexpected news. Her devotion and success in work with women and young people brought her to Ruijin, the Red capital, as the people's representative for the Second National Congress of the Soviet.

"Have you visited Ruijin?" Wang asked me expectantly. I said I was going to after seeing her.

"You should have gone there first. It was the capital! An old lady like me can wait. You know, we had a saying at the time: up north it is Beijing; down south it is Ruijin."

She did concede later, although very reluctantly, that Ruijin could not compare with Beijing. It was a typical southern town with good *feng shui*. The curving Mian River embraced it, and an undulating mountain range shielded it from the west, with a white pagoda overlooking it from the hill to the east. No bigger than an average county town, its four gates and four roads leading in from them crossed at the center, and 7,000 people lived within its walls. Because Chiang had imposed an economic blockade with his Fifth Campaign, many shops had their shutters down. Local products such as bamboo, paper, nuts, and dried vegetables from the mountains could not be shipped out; salt, oil, gasoline, cloth, and other daily necessities could not come in. Those who broke the embargo were liable to punishment or even execution. The Nationalists reinforced the blockade with a Special Movement Corps, whose members had every incentive to catch the offenders—they were rewarded with 50 percent of whatever they confiscated.

Wherever there were profits, there were smugglers: salt, medicine, gunpowder, and other much-needed items were transported, hidden in coffins, at the bottom of manure baskets, and inside bamboo poles. They even managed to bring in an X-ray machine in a coffin, with three dozen men and women pretending to be grieving relatives, crying their eyes out. The warlord of Guangdong also defied the blockade by secretly buying tungsten that was found in abundance within the Soviet. But it was like throwing a cup of water onto flaming firewood. Ruijin was feeling the pinch. Salt was the scarcest commodity; Wang did not taste salt for months, and out of sheer desperation she and her friends scraped the white deposits from the walls of toilets, and even from graveyards, and boiled them down.

Even today she craved salt. "I think I'm making up for the shortage all those years ago. You don't know what it's like, as if your body were made of cotton, or you were walking on clouds. I often fell." I knew how deprived she felt when she invited me to join her, her daughter, and her two grandchildren for lunch. Had she not explained, I would have thought the daughter had emptied the salt pot when she was cooking. The chicken, the bean curd, the beans, and the soup were all so salty that I could barely eat them. I must have drunk a gallon of tea to wash the meal down.

All the hardship of daily life in Ruijin was forgotten when Wang attended the Congress on January 22, 1934. The Hall of Workers and Peasants, specially built for the occasion, took her breath away. She had never seen anything like it. It was not like a Buddhist temple; it was not like the mansions of rich people; it was not like shrine halls, which were normally the most impressive buildings in southern towns and villages. It was very grand, an octagon, the shape of a Red Army cap. Above the imposing main entrance was a big red star with a hammer and sickle on it, the emblem of the Red Army. The impressive scale of the interior matched that of the exterior: it was massive, with two stories, and it could hold over 2,000 people. She could not understand how they had built it, with a roof but no central pillar. And it was lit by these strange lamps that did not need oil. All it took was for someone to pull down a black handle on the wall, and the hall was flooded with brilliant light.

Wang and the 776 delegates stood inside the hall, listening as a band played a rousing song, "The Internationale." A tall, lean man with big eyes came onto the platform, and stood in front of the Communist red flag. The woman next to her whispered that this was Comrade Mao, the man who set up the Soviet. She had hardly registered the fact before Mao said, in his thick Hunan accent: "Comrades, on behalf of the Central Executive Committee, I declare the Second National Congress of the Soviet open. On behalf of the Central Executive Committee I give the whole body of delegates the Revolutionary salute!" There was thunderous applause from all, and Wang clapped so hard, her hands hurt.

Mao, founder of the Jiangxi Soviet Government, Zhu De, the Commander of the Red Army, and other senior Party leaders all spoke during the Congress. What they said was mostly beyond her—for example, she did not know where Tibet was and why Mao mentioned it in his report on the Soviet government. But she was really fired up by Mao's conclusion:

> Our Congress is the supreme organ of state power of the whole country . . . Our Congress will make the Fifth Campaign end in utter rout, develop the Revolution in the whole of China, extend the territory of the Soviet to all regions ruled by Chiang Kaishek's government, and unfurl the red flag throughout the country. Let us shout: Long live the Second National Soviet Congress! Long live the Soviet New China!

She could not get over this somersault in her life. It was like heaven and earth swapping places. One moment she was a poor country girl; the next she was a member of the supreme body which governed the Soviet. A folk song came to her mind, down to earth but true to her feelings:

> *Light from lamps is no light*
> *Compared with the brightness of the sun;*
> *Fathers and mothers are dear*
> *But the Communist Party is dearer.*

The most important day in Wang's life was April 17, 1934. With her right arm raised before the red flag, she made this solemn pledge to the Communist Party: "I will sacrifice myself; I will keep my promises; I will struggle against our enemies; I will fight for the Revolution; I will obey orders, and never betray the Party." She knew she would honor this pledge. She was even willing to die; without the Party, her life would not have been worth living. Mao's words on the Red Army Martyrs' Monument in Ruijin, built in 1932, were engraved on her heart:

In the great fight against imperialism and for land reform,
many comrades have gloriously sacrificed themselves. Their
sacrifices demonstrate the invincible courage of the proletariat
and lay the foundation for the Chinese Soviet Republic. The
worker-peasant toiling masses of all China are advancing,
marching on the blood these comrades shed, to overthrow
the rule of imperialism and Chiang Kaishek's reactionary
government and win victory for the Soviet over the whole
of China.

Wang was sent to the Party school, where they groomed future leaders,
but she had hardly settled in there before she was called to the most urgent task of the moment: the recruitment drive. For the past four years
since October 1930, Chiang Kaishek had launched five successive campaigns against the Communist base in Jiangxi. He started with 100,000
men for the First Campaign, thinking he would have no difficulty getting rid of a mere 9,000 Communist guerrillas supported by fewer than
2 million people, in an area of just 200 square kilometers. He likened
the Communists, or the Red Bandits as he called them, to a locust trying to block the way of a cart—they were day-dreaming. But the Red
Bandits gave him a taste of their ferocity and skilled guerrilla tactics—
15,000 of his troops were captured in two months.

Exasperated, Chiang threw in more men and arms, and himself flew
to Nanchang, the capital of Jiangxi. He appointed himself Commander-
in-Chief, but only to suffer more humiliating and crushing defeats—he
lost nearly 50,000 men to the Red Army in 1931 alone, and another
30,000 in early 1933. After this, he vowed to wipe the Red Bandits out
once and for all—they were obviously more than just a nuisance. In July
1933, Chiang began his fifth and biggest campaign: 500,000 men descended on the Jiangxi Soviet from three directions, equipped with the
latest weapons from Germany, Britain, and America, and supported by
200 planes with 150 American and Canadian pilots.

Ten months into the Fifth Campaign, the Red Army lost over
50,000 men. On May 20, 1934, the Central Committee of the Party
called for more soldiers for the front:

The decisive battles in the coming months will decide whether we live or die. These will be the last and most crucial moments for us to wipe out and kill the enemy. This is total war. Every member of the Communist Party, every worker, and every member of the toiling masses should prepare to shed his last drop of blood at the front.[1]

The Party called for 50,000 recruits within three months. However, this was not enough, and September saw another urgent campaign with a target of 30,000, with each village, district, and county given fixed quotas. Wang was told to go to Gangxi County, which had repeatedly failed to reach its target.

Why was she given a hard case like Gangxi? I asked.

"To test me. To try me. To encourage me. As we say, good iron should be used for the blade." I wanted to tell her that the Party chose the right person.

She walked from village to village, accompanied by Liu, the Party secretary of the district, whom she had been assigned to help. What she saw shocked her. The villages were almost haunted, with little sign of life and very few young men around; some were simply abandoned, with the peasants having fled to the areas controlled by Chiang's government. When she went up to an old man in the field for a chat, he yelled at her: "You are draining the pond to catch the fish. But you don't understand, there are no fish left in the pond!" Liu took her aside, explaining that two of his sons had joined the Red Army five years ago and he had not heard from them since. Everyone was doing their best like the old man, Liu promised. The district had about 1,300 men between the ages of 16 and 45, and over 1,000 were either in the army or working for it as porters and laborers; the rest were sick, or they were from landlord and rich peasant families and so could not be trusted to fight for the poor. He did not see how his district could come up with another 45 men this time. But he would try his hardest.

The deadline came on September 27, and out of a quota of 4,000 for Gangxi, barely 700 had signed up; Liu's district only came up with twelve. On September 28, she received an urgent message from the

Women and Youth Departments in Ruijin. The deadline was extended to October 5: "This is the last deadline and must not be one minute late or a single recruit short."

I asked what would have happened if she failed to meet the target. Would she lose face, or worse, her job?

She turned around and looked at me, surprised and almost annoyed by the questions.

"Lose face? You have no idea. People could lose their lives." One of her friends had a quota of fifteen in a previous recruitment drive, but she only managed twelve. She was put in prison for sabotaging the Revolution. Her family all thought she was going to be executed: they even prepared her funeral clothes. But she was released after fifteen days, on condition that she would make up for her crime by meeting a double quota next time.

Did she not think the punishment was a bit extreme? The poor woman must have tried.

"Trying was not enough. You had to succeed," Wang quickly corrected me. "You know what the Party said: 'Failure in enlisting equals helping the enemy!' I did not get it at first, but later I understood. If the Red Army had more soldiers, we would have been able to hold on to the base."

In their drive to reach the targets, local officials often resorted to extreme measures. Shengli County insisted that all Party officials join up. Overnight many fled to the mountains—some even committed suicide—and there was absolute chaos. In the worst areas of Ruijin, those who refused to join the army were locked in dark rooms with their hands tied behind their backs. And no food was served to them—the soldiers at the front were more deserving. Wang's department received any number of letters from the village women's associations, complaining about the rough way their men had been treated. One letter read: "The Party secretary said there was a meeting in the village hall to discuss land issues. Many people turned up. Suddenly two men locked the door. 'Sign up for the Red Army, or no one can leave.' It was not until the early hours when some finally agreed, and they were taken off straightaway." What shocked Wang even more was that some women activists promised sex to any man who would join. They did fill their quotas quickly, but she wondered how long the men would stay in the army.

I had always thought the peasants competed to join the Red Army—after all, it was to defend their land, their homes, and their children. Our literature, art, films, and school textbooks are full of stories and images of parents signing up their sons, wives persuading their husbands to fight, sisters making uniforms for their brothers, and young women seeing off their lovers to the front. I particularly remembered one metaphor: the Red Army was the fish and the peasants the water. The fish would be dead out of water, and the water would be poorer without the fish. The support of the peasants was the secret weapon of Communist success. As for forced conscription, I had always been told that only Chiang's army used it.

Wang laughed when I told her that. She held out her hands and said: "People are different, just like my ten fingers. Many had suffered like me, and they begged to join the Revolution. Recruitment was not difficult at all in the early campaigns. But as the war continued, it got harder and harder. There were not enough men around. Also people thought we were losing, so they did not want to die for nothing. That was why we had to work on them."

Wang was right. After five campaigns by Chiang's troops in five years, both the population and the area in the Jiangxi base had been reduced so drastically that a Red Army officer said it was no wider than an arrow's flight. In one year more than 160,000 men had been drafted into the Red Army just to break the Fifth Campaign. In fact, almost all the able-bodied men had already been enlisted. Mao did his own investigation in Changgang District in late 1933. Out of 407 men between the ages of 16 and 45, 79 percent were in the Red Army, very much as Party Secretary Liu reported for his district.[2] Perhaps the old man in Gangxi County was right: the Party was draining the pond to catch the fish.

"We had to defend the base at all costs. The survival of the Party required it." Wang was adamant.

She had been ordered to deliver her quota of forty-five men in October 1934. For the first time in her life, she was having sleepless nights.

But Wang quoted another saying. "A man should not be made desperate by his pee." She had an idea.

She put on her jacket and went outside. It was drizzling, dark, and silent, with not even a dog barking: they had all been killed to stop them from giving away the army's movements. She tiptoed from house to house, alert for the sound of conversation. Suddenly she heard the voice of an old lady:

"Aya, such a dreadful day! How are the three coping on the mountain? Perhaps you should take them their bamboo hats."

"What's the point? They must be soaked by now," replied a woman, perhaps her daughter-in-law.

Wang listened for a while, and then crept quietly to another window.

"Party Secretary Liu is two-faced. In front of comrade Wang, he is all enthusiasm; behind her back, he bad-mouths the Red Army. What is he playing at?" asked a young girl.

"Stupid girl! Secretary Liu is thinking of us. The Red Army has been losing for the last six months. So many are being killed every day. If your brother hadn't deserted and gone into hiding, he would have been cannon fodder by now," grumbled a man, who seemed to be the father.

Now she understood what was going on. So there were still fish in the pond and birds in the mountains. If she could persuade them to come out of hiding, she would not only meet her quota, but also send much-needed men to the front. But what was she going to do with Liu? She thought about it and decided to send a messenger immediately to the county Party headquarters. Then she launched her plan of action.

At the crack of dawn, Wang dispatched a dozen Red Pioneers to the nearby villages, requesting everyone to come to an urgent meeting that evening in Shi Village. Then she went to the house with the three deserters. The old lady and her daughter-in-law looked as if they had had a bad night. Wang inquired about the men in the family and the older woman said that her son was away as a porter for the Red Army, and her two grandsons were fighting at the front. "We all do our bit," she added, poker-faced.

"By hiding in the mountains, granny?" Wang asked.

The old lady lost her nerve, and blurted out: "Yes, you give us land, but with no men in the house, what can we do with it?" She shrieked, pointing to her bound feet and her daughter-in-law's: "Thunder will strike women who work in the paddy. When your people called on our sons and husbands to join, they promised to send men to help on the land. Some turned up at the beginning, but they were more trouble than they were worth—you had to feed them and look after them. And soon nobody bothered to come. We haven't got much of a harvest this year. We complained to Secretary Liu. He said we should go and loot, or get our men back."

Wang might have sympathized if she had not pointed to their bound feet. That made her angry. Under the Communists, women could not get married unless they unbound their feet first, yet these women refused to free themselves. She and some other activists once attempted to straighten women's feet by force, but they soon went back to their old ways. In her eyes, they were like parasites, sitting at home waiting for their husbands to work the fields. They only had themselves to blame.

It baffled her how women could fail to support the Revolution. They benefited most—unbound feet, abolition of arranged marriages, violence toward women outlawed, and more roles for them in general. Their very happiness depended on the survival of the Soviet. When the New Marriage Law came out, tens of thousands of women immediately asked for a divorce, remarried, and then divorced again. The local officials were so swamped by the paperwork, the Party had to pass a decree forbidding men and women from marrying more than three times, and they must live together for at least two months before they could register for divorce.

What surprised me was that Wang did not walk out of her own arranged marriage, as she had persuaded many other women to do. On the contrary, she promised her husband that she would fulfill her wifely duty if he signed up for the Red Army. He did so the very next day, and his happiness was doubled when he was allowed into her bed without having to wait for another two years and honor her mother's request. Why was that?

"Why not? The Red Army needed all the manpower it could get," she said in all seriousness.

"But you weren't happy with him," I said.

"What's happiness got to do with it? When so many people were suffering, how could you be happy? I couldn't," she reminded me, before she went inside to make more tea—her daughter had gone to the market to get things for supper.

A thought did occur to me, fleetingly: did Wang sign her husband up because she knew that would be the surest way of getting rid of him? As we say, bullets are blind. I was wrong. When she returned with the tea and biscuits, Wang said that her husband died from tuberculosis while she was busy recruiting in Gangxi County. He was desperate to prove he was worthy of her affection, and he exerted himself as a scout for the Red Army. His last words were: "Without seeing her, I cannot even close my eyes in death."

I was ashamed I had even contemplated such a thought. It would have been to misjudge Wang entirely. I could not think myself into the degree of dedication she had attained. For her, and many of her generation, personal happiness and physical desire did not count—they were submerged in the excitement she felt for the Revolution. Yes, she had another recruit, and would be praised for it. But her innermost feeling was devotion—to the people and ideals that promised to lift China out of the oppression she saw all around her, and had been subjected to herself. I remembered the slogans and exhortations that filled our schoolbooks: "Communism is higher than the sky. Sacrifice everything for it." For me, they were just slogans; for Wang, it was faith.

My respect for Wang increased later when I pieced together how much she was up against, from memoirs, interviews, and government archives of the 1930s—when the Communist Party was still quite open about its strengths and weaknesses. At the time, it was not unusual for women to threaten their husbands with divorce if they signed up for the Red Army. Others went a step further. Ruijin had a hospital for disabled soldiers and it became a favorite haunt for women looking for husbands. Their reasoning was simple: at least their husbands would stay at home. If all else failed, and their husbands were called to the front, they would sleep with any available man. Local women's associations constantly reported to the center about the problem of "women stealing men." One of the reports read:

> Many wives of the soldiers haven't heard from their men since they joined Mao's and Zhu's Army six years ago. Quite a few have asked for divorce, and if we do not grant it, they will make huge scenes and call us all sorts of names. Or they simply go ahead and sleep with other men and have illegitimate children. What is the most appropriate way to solve this problem?[3]

Wang would have preferred harsh measures—otherwise men would all want to stay at home. Much to her disappointment, the Party amended the Marriage Law: women could ask for a divorce if they did not hear from their husbands for three years, instead of six; and the children they bore in the meantime would be recognized as legitimate "because they are the masters of our new society."

But in the recruitment drive in Shi Village, Wang decided to be tough. She told the old lady and her daughter-in-law to bring in their men from their hiding places in the mountains—or else they would regret it. She left them in no doubt what the punishments were. "We will publicly shame you at the rally tonight. Then we will put posters on your doors, windows, and gates, denouncing you as traitors and deserters. All the benefits you have received, food, blankets, clothes, and oil, will be returned to the government. And your men will be forced to work on the Red Army soldiers' land, or be sentenced to a year's hard labor. Please think carefully."

The grandmother sat in the front row at that night's execution. After Party Secretary Liu was shot in the head, the blood trickled toward her feet across the floor. Her legs were shaking like paddy husks, but she struggled to stand up and offered her two grandsons. Many followed, including two women who signed themselves up. Wang had more recruits than her quota. For the first time in many months, a genuine smile lit up her face.

I thought I recognized that smile when Wang recounted the final moment of the story, as if she was back in front of the crowds, encouraging, agitating, and judging. There was no pity, no regret, and no apology. The confidence that the truth was with her was unshakable. The Revolution was supposed to be for the masses and they were treated like an inexhaustible mine from which the Party could dig everything they needed. It did not occur to them that the peasants could not bear any more burdens. If their support was crucial for the Revolution, as they were told all the time, perhaps their reluctance and even refusal was part of the reason why the Party and the Red Army had to abandon their base in Jiangxi and begin the Long March, to search for a new one. I doubted Wang ever thought this way. She simply did what the Party told her, and did it very well. As it was, she hardly had time to enjoy her success and report it to the Party, when an urgent message came from Ruijin on the evening of October 15: "Important event. Return at once."

She set off immediately with the messenger. It was good the moon was almost full, guiding her every step of the way, while she grappled with the mystery of why she had been called back so suddenly. Could it be her delay in meeting the deadline? She had not heard from her boss—it was as if she had been forgotten. She feared she might be thrown in prison, like her friend, or worse, executed.

"If I had to die, better to die in battle, taking a few enemies with me. That would have been worth it." Now her mind was all on battles. Suddenly the thought came to her: was a big battle coming? From the early summer, apart from recruitment, she had taken part in another government campaign to borrow or appropriate grain from the peasants. The target was 1 million *dan* of rice—almost the entire autumn harvest in the Soviet. They got there in three months, using much the same methods as the recruitment drive.

At the same time, there was a call for funds: 800,000 silver dollars were issued as government bonds. Everyone must buy them, or donate money. She thought the women's department was very ingenious in asking women to donate their silver jewelry. Perhaps they were inspired by Mao, who noticed this custom in southern Jiangxi. "Every woman has silver hairpins and earrings, no matter how poor they are, and bracelets and rings, if they are not starving." Women's associations at every level organized task forces and propaganda teams to shame those "who are still wearing the symbols of feudalism and bourgeois decadence." In the end, they collected 220,000 ounces of silver.[4]

And then, just before she was dispatched to Gangxi County, a memo went out to all counties for 200,000 pairs of extra-thick straw sandals and 100,000 rice pouches, to be delivered to the Red Army before October 10. To her amazement, there was not much resistance; perhaps the peasants would do anything rather than enlist. Some women had written rhymes on pieces of paper and put them inside the sandals; one of them read: "With this pair of sandals, you will travel 10,000 *li*. No matter how high the mountains, and how deep the rivers, you will never stop on the road to revolution."

Perhaps a big battle *was* coming. Otherwise why did the Red Army need so many soldiers, so many pairs of shoes, and so much money and grain, and all for October? "That is it," she clapped her hands, giving the messenger a fright. "As Father would say, 'The fish will either be caught in the net or they'll break it and sink the boat.'"

It was early morning on October 16 when she arrived back in Ruijin. She went straight to see Liu Ying, the Head of the Youth Department, who had sent for her. "You were quick. I didn't think you'd be back tonight," Liu said, handing her a towel to wipe the sweat off her face. The sisterly concern in Liu's voice assured her that her worst fears were unfounded. All the same, she offered her apologies for missing the deadline. "Don't worry, we're in the same boat." Liu patted her on the head. She did not fill her own quota. She was summoned back three days ago to choose six staff to go on a major operation. "So, there is a big operation," Wang cried out with joy. "Whether you can take part or not all depends on the checkup tomorrow morning. Report to the General Hospital at nine o'clock."

She was in for a shock when she reached the hospital. People were running about, dismantling and packing up heavy medical equipment, or loading medicine into panniers on their shoulders. The wounded were groaning on their beds with no one to see to them, or being carted off on stretchers or helped to hobble away. "Why are we breaking the place up?" she wondered. Wang, and the other 100 girls waiting for their checkup, only added to the chaos by chattering nervously and giggling, like a flock of sparrows that could not stop chirping.

The doctors drew blood with a needle, listened to her chest down a tube with a cold metal disc at the end, hit her knees with a wooden hammer, and then asked her to lift a 20-kilo sack over her head. All the time, her heart was beating so fast she thought she might be ill, though she had never been sick in her life. What really scared her was the big machine which they said could see her insides. Its Chinese name was pronounced *Ai-ke-si*, which meant "If you go near it, you die." It was a great relief to come out in one piece, and be told that she was strong as a horse, and they would take her. She should go and get her provisions now and then report to the Cadres' Battalion of the General Health Department of the Central Column in the afternoon. What was the Central Column? She had no idea, but she knew where to go.

She must have been overjoyed to be one of only fifteen girls chosen out of the hundred at the hospital, and of thousands more who never got that far.

"Why so few women? Why me? I have asked that question millions of times," Wang said. I waited for her to answer herself.

"Perhaps they thought we would be a burden. But I was healthy and strong," she finally said, though still uncertainly. The truth may be different. All the top leaders of the Party and the Army had their wives with them on the Long March. They wanted an equal number of other women to come along. Wang was a Party member; she had always delivered whatever was expected of her, and more; and she was known for firing two pistols simultaneously, hitting the bull's-eye with both. What she did not know at the time was that the Red Army was about to abandon Jiangxi and set up a new base elsewhere.

At five o'clock sharp on the afternoon of October 16, the bugle sounded, as the sky turned pink in the setting sun. Wang marched out of Ruijin with the General Health Unit. Now it was clear: the Central Column was essentially the government on the move, more than 10,000 people, including many Party officials from all levels of the Jiangxi Soviet administration. She wore the dark blue jacket she had received that day, with matching trousers tucked inside her socks, and a pair of new sandals. The pack on her back held a light quilt, one more pair of sandals, seven kilos of grain, and an enamel washbasin dangling on a strap. A hat made of double-layered bamboo covered the pack and would be useful in the autumn rain. Now she felt like a real soldier, ready for battle, except that she had no rifle; but there were six stretchers in her care—the 1st Army insisted that all injured officers above brigadier level be taken on the March. She had seen many battles, but this was something different. Taking the wounded to the front? She knew not to ask too many questions.

## 2 ★ TURTLE-SHELL POWER

Soldier Huang was adding frantically to the defenses of his foxhole—putting stones on the two layers of logs, and more pine branches on the stones. Everything was wet, the trees were dripping, and the mud stuck to his shoes. As he looked out nervously, he could see one of the Nationalist blockhouses, or "turtle-shells" as they called them, 600 meters away. It was a solid brick building like a round granary with gun slits, stronger-looking than anything he had seen in the villages. They had been preparing themselves for a week and he wondered when the fighting would start. But he did not want to dwell on it, so he tried humming one of the songs he had learned in the last few days:

> *Comrades! Ready with your guns!*
> *Charge with one heart,*
> *Struggle and fight to kill!*
> *Comrades! Fight for freedom!*
> *Fight for the Soviets!*

He struggled to remember the next line. A faint light on the horizon was visible through the rain, which had been falling steadily ever since they had reached the front. As dawn broke, he could hear birds singing. Suddenly they went quiet and a heavy growling noise took over. He leapt into his foxhole. A few seconds later the sky was black with planes, like huge flocks of crows, and the crump of bombing began. The din became deafening. One bomb dropped close by and his foxhole collapsed, leaving just his head free. He dug himself out and glanced round: two-thirds of the foxholes his company had built were flattened, and the trench was destroyed.

The captain ordered the men to take position. Huang put his rifle down and lay next to it in the wet soil of what was left of the trench. Looking to left and right, he could see quite a few men missing—the bombing had taken its toll. And then the artillery began. The ground shook and flowers of earth blossomed and fell on him, almost burying him. Within ten minutes a quarter of the company was dead or wounded.

When the shelling stopped, Soldier Huang was still kneeling on the sodden ground. A man rushed to pull him up, shouting that the infantry would soon advance on them. He only had five bullets. The captain shouted, "Don't fire until they are three meters away." Huang could see their white cap badges and the sun flashing on their weapons. They fired and he missed his target. A few fell, but within seconds the enemy was on them.

It was bayonet to bayonet, kill or be killed. He accounted for two of them. He was barely thinking, too numb even to feel fear, and screaming like a madman to release the panic bottled up in his chest. Before long, the Nationalists retreated, and the captain ordered his men to do likewise. As they staggered away, their feet fighting with the clay earth, the shelling began again. This was the daily pattern.

At dusk, everything fell quiet. There were piles of bodies within 70 meters of their trench, enough to form a human barricade. He shuddered to see an officer walking around, finishing off those who were still groaning from their wounds. He was told it was to stop them from surrendering and giving information to the enemy. Once they had buried the dead, they gathered around the mess tent. He had little appetite although he had eaten nothing the whole day. The cook had prepared food for over 100 but there were only 30 left in his company. After the meal, they retreated five kilometers in the dark, to dig another trench. This was Soldier Huang's first battle and he was only 14. The Guangchang battle in April 1934 lasted eighteen days and the Red Army lost 6,000 men, with 20,000 wounded. It was the heaviest blow the Red Army had suffered up till then, and it was the turning point in Chiang's campaign.

I found Huang through the pensioners' office of the Ruijin County government, which, in the Communist tradition, had excellent records of the Long March survivors and anyone they wanted to keep tabs on. "I'm not sure how much he can tell you," the clerk said slowly after he had finished the newspaper he was reading. "He is only a peasant. You should really talk to old Wu. He used to be the Prime Minister's bodyguard. He knows things, but he is in the hospital. Last year we still had a dozen. Now there are only eight left." Two lived in the mountains with the nearest road five miles away, three were in the hospital, and one was away visiting relatives. "Why don't you start with old Huang? If he is no use, come back to me."

I should have felt discouraged but I did not. I knew what he thought: it was only worth talking to the heroes and the big decision-makers; but their stories are already in our history books, told and re-told until they have become symbols, the eternal refrain. Perhaps for him, Huang was not enough of a committed revolutionary, but his ordinary life as a foot soldier on the March was just what I was missing. With luck it would tell me the unadorned truth about what the rank and file really experienced.

I took a rickshaw—there were no taxis—and set off for Huang's village on the outskirts of Ruijin. We went past the farmers' market, through the houses of the old quarter with their tiled roofs and curling eaves, and over the sandstone bridge across the Mian River, swathed in mist. There was a grace and tranquillity to the scene. Suddenly we turned a corner and the illusion was dispelled—we were in a huge square of incongruous pink concrete houses and shops, with a fountain in the middle—a giant steel ball on a tower. The rickshaw driver turned proudly toward me, "This is our new town center. Our Party secretary got a promotion for building it."

I was relieved to leave the theme-park square behind and go back to the green countryside with its endless paddy fields. It was next to one of them that I found Huang's village. All its 1,000 people shared the name of Huang, and the clan's ancestor shrine stood prominently in the middle. I was directed to find him there, listening with a huge crowd, not to the village head relaying the latest Party instructions, but to an eager salesman preaching the benefits of Heart K, which was supposed to give you more blood. Huang was a convert, taking two ampoules every day. "I want to live as long as possible," he told me, waving the small box of magic potions he had just bought. He did not look as though he needed them. He was short, hard, and lean, with a piercing gaze. He walked upright, faster than I could easily follow. On the way to his house, he introduced me to his cousins, nieces, nephews, grandnephews, great-grandnieces, three brothers, and two sisters-in-law. It was still a closely knit clan.

Huang's house was in the middle of an open courtyard, with his eldest son occupying the house in the front, his youngest brother at the back, and his two nephews from his third brother on the left and right. The house was bare apart from a bed with a mosquito net, a table with a small black-and-white TV, a few benches, and the stove. He had few visitors and spent his day listening to local operas. "I can't see properly because of the snow blindness I suffered on the Long March," he explained as he turned on the set. "Her voice is so sweet. But is the actress as ugly as my wife said?" he asked, with a mischievous smile. His wife was right: she was so ugly I was glad he could not see her properly.

"I'll keep the treat to myself then," Huang said with a good laugh, and switched off the TV. He suggested we sit outside instead to enjoy the autumn sun. He handed me a stool, and a sweet, while popping one in his toothless mouth. "I cannot complain, really. This is a good life," he said, sucking on the sweet noisily. Looking at Huang, I thought of the Chinese saying: "A wife, children, a patch of land, and a warm bed make a happy peasant." Huang seemed to be its living proof, but the pensioners' office had told me he joined the Red Army when he was only 14. He must have been very enthusiastic.

"They kidnapped me," he said, raising his voice.

"Kidnapped?" It was the first time I had heard the word in this connection.

"Thunder will strike me if I tell you one false word," Huang said. "At first they only wanted the strong and handsome ones. The Red Army deserved the best. Then they took the old, the sick, and even a couple of opium addicts. And then it was children. The Party secretary in our village forced everyone with a dick to sign up, whether they were

15 or 50. The Nationalists did not force children to join, but the Red Army did." Huang shook his head.

He was the oldest of five boys and two girls. He was 14 in 1934, three years short of the minimum age for enlisting. A woman activist visited his family every day, working on his mother. "My boys still wet their beds, and they're shorter than a rifle. How can they fight a war?" his mother pleaded. "Oh, my sister, don't worry. They can be orderlies, or learn the bugle. There are plenty of things to do in the army. They get fed, and clothed too. It takes the burden off you."

His mother was not convinced—so many men had gone to the front and never come back. And as the Chinese say, a good man is not destined for the army, just like good iron is not for nails. She sent Huang to hide in the mountains with his uncle and 20 other men from the village, but three days later she called him back. The village had a quota of 300 recruits, and the Party secretary would be thrown in jail if he could not meet his target. He had arrested Huang's father and would not release him until either he signed up or one of his sons did. After a sleepless night, Huang's mother decided to opt for her eldest son—the family had so many mouths to feed and could not do without the father. She packed his favorite rice cakes with ham and a padded jacket that belonged to his father. "Take good care of yourself. Quick like a rat and alert like a fox," were her last words to Huang.

He had only a week's training, on a winnowing ground. He practiced shooting with a stick—every single rifle was needed for the front. Holding the wooden stick, the instructor told them to aim a bit above the target, and he could not understand why. "Think of your pee. It's the same idea." He got it, but still wasted three of his five precious bullets in the first battle. And he nearly killed himself when he pulled the pin out of his grenade, and stood there watching it fizz as if it were a firecracker. Luckily, the man standing next to him saw it, grabbed it from his hand, and threw it out of the trench. It exploded seconds later.

Huang was lucky to survive his first battle. The lack of training accounted for up to 50 percent of the casualties suffered by the Red Army. The problem was so serious that Liu Bocheng, the Chief of Staff of the Red Army and the Commandant of its academy, felt compelled to address it in a series of articles in *Revolution and War*. An orderly was sent from his academy to execute a prisoner, but he misfired and shot himself. "As a veteran soldier, he was unable to fire accurately at a tied-up enemy! . . . In battle the White soldiers suffer fewer casualties than the Red Army. Why? Maybe we have braved more enemy fire, but we are also to blame: many of our soldiers do not know how to shoot accurately or use a bayonet."[1]

If he had to fight, Huang wished he had more bullets. It would give him a better chance of coming through. He had only five for each assault, with three grenades. The bullets were produced in the Red Army's own workshop in a disused temple. Local craftsmen and a few engineers captured from the Nationalists recycled used shells or melted down old copper coins and wire, molded them into shape, filed them down by hand, and then filled the cartridge with home-made explosives. Huang had trouble loading them into his rifle; when he managed to pull the trigger, it took a minute for them to explode, and even then they did not go far. Often they just tumbled out of the barrel and landed at his feet. Liu Shaoqi, the Commissar of the 3rd Corps and later President of China, called on the arsenal to do a better job. "The bullets were so useless. Over 30,000 of them were duds. The rifles were repaired but they went wrong again after firing a single shot."[2]

Huang could also have done with a better rifle, although he knew many soldiers did not even have one or, worse, a whole platoon shared one. His was a locally made hunting gun, quite temperamental. The trigger got stuck so often that he used the bayonet more. Still, it was dearer than his life, at least in the eyes of his captain. One night they were retreating in a downpour. He slipped and fell into a puddle. Hearing the splash, the captain immediately asked, "Is your rifle OK?" Huang felt really angry. Was the rifle more important than his life? He wanted to smash it, but he knew he would be court-martialed if he did.

He kept asking his captain when he could get a proper rifle. "Next time we have a victory," he said, "you grab whatever you like. That is how we always did it before. You know what we call Chiang Kaishek? Our head of supply." The captain began to reminisce about the old days. He remembered what Mao had said right before Chiang's First Campaign: "Comrades! With enemy guns we will arm ourselves. With captured enemy artillery we will defend the Soviets! We will destroy them with their own weapons, and if they will only keep up the war against us long enough, we will build up an army of a million workers and peasants! We will strip them of their last rifle, their last bullet."[3]

The Red Army lured Chiang's troops deep into their base, where the villagers had been evacuated with all their belongings. "We needed porters, but none was available; we searched for guides, but none could be found; we sent our own scouts, but they could collect no information. We were groping in the dark."[4] Such was the despair of one Nationalist general in the campaign. Chiang's front-line commander, General Zhang Huizang, was keen to prove himself and pushed the furthest, cutting himself off from the flank divisions. He was ambushed by the Red Army on New Year's Eve; he and 15,000 of his men were captured, and the spoils were enormous: 12,000 rifles, light and heavy machine guns, trench mortars, field telephones, a radio set with its operators, and sacks of rice, flour, ham, and bacon, as well as the funds Zhang carried for the entire campaign. There was enough medicine for the Red Army hospital for months. The spoils were carried back to the Red Army bases by horses and seven camels, also taken from the Nationalists. Three weeks later Chiang called off the First Campaign.

The Red Army continued to supply itself with the most up-to-date weapons from Chiang's defeats—20,000 rifles in the Second Campaign, and more equipment of every kind in the Third and Fourth. In 1933 and 1934 alone, Chiang spent nearly 60 million silver dollars importing state-of-the-art rifles, artillery, and planes from America and Europe, but most of these ended up in the hands of the Communists.

All the stories of success in previous campaigns were beginning to trouble Huang, as they had been stuck in trenches for weeks, with bombs falling, shells whistling overhead, and bodies piling up. He wondered whether the captain made them up to get rid of the gloom, or they were fighting a new enemy altogether. The Nationalists were just like turtles: they put their heads out of their blockhouses to see if they were safe; as soon as they sensed danger, they retreated. Even when they were under attack, they stayed put and waited for reinforcements.

The captain said these were Chiang's new tactics. "He has learned his lesson. Instead of chasing us and falling into our traps, he is trapping us. Think of a spider's web. He is trying to catch us with this net of turtle-shells, but we'll smash them and break through." Huang did not think this could be done. "We were ordered to launch short, swift attacks on the blockhouses as soon as they were put up." He gesticulated with both arms as if he were pointing at his target. "They were near, only a few hundred meters. I could even hear the men talking. But every time we attacked, the artillery fire from the turtle-shells drove us back, leaving the fields strewn with bodies. Our covering fire was too feeble."

The blockhouse strategy was the key. "The only task for troops engaged in the elimination campaign is to build blockhouses," Chiang Kaishek told his officers. "We build our bases each step of the way, and protect ourselves with blockhouses everywhere. It looks defensive but is offensive," Chiang wrote in his diary. "When the enemy comes, we defend; when they retreat, we advance . . . We will exhaust them and then wipe them out."[5] He turned Mao's guerrilla warfare on its head, forcing the Red Army to confront his troops in conventional trench warfare. It was a protracted war which he knew they could not win—they simply did not have the resources and manpower to compete. "The Reds' areas are only 250 square kilometers. If we can push on one kilometer every day, we can finish them off within a year," Chiang concluded confidently.[6]

Chiang insisted that every battalion build at least one blockhouse a week. Initially it was one every five kilometers, but when the Red Army broke through, he demanded that the distance between the blockhouses should be no more than one kilometer. "Anyone who breaks the rule will be court-martialed without mercy," he warned. Halfway through the Fifth Campaign, 5,873 blockhouses had been built; by the end of 1934, there were 14,000. To link them up, Chiang ordered an extensive network of roads to be built. From barely 500 kilometers of highway in a province of 110,000 square kilometers in 1928,

Jiangxi became one of the best-served places in China, with 8,000 kilometers of roads and another 1,000 kilometers under construction, and three major airports.[7] The trouble was that cars were a rare commodity in the provinces in the 1930s, and the vast network of roads did not link up with the Xian and Gan rivers, the main transport arteries of Jiangxi. This did not bother Chiang: the important thing was that all roads led to Ruijin.

One day, something came along the road which neither Huang nor his captain had ever seen—tanks. "These giant machines crawled toward us like scorpions, with guns firing." Huang remembered it vividly. "When we saw one coming, we were so shocked we did not know what to do. We took to our heels and fled, and those who didn't became mincemeat." All the same, orders arrived from headquarters every day, telling them to hold on unswervingly so that they could eliminate the enemy with disciplined fire and powerful counterattacks. "It was senseless, like throwing an egg at a stone." Old Huang threw up his hands. "We were worth nothing, pushed forward again and again just to die in waves. Then they built more turtle-shells on our bodies, advancing as we fell back."

I had seen some remains of the blockhouses on the bus ride to Ruijin, perched on the hills. I was surprised that they had not been knocked down by peasants to build houses or pigsties. "There used to be quite a lot," said Huang. "They were really well built. You have to blow them up with dynamite—not something the Red Army had then or we have now. I don't know. Should we keep them? They are like graveyards. Every time I pass them, I feel as if a lizard is pissing on my spine."

Was he not frightened then? He was only 14.

"Frightened? I was scared to death. I wet my pants every day," Huang said without hesitation. He regretted he had not run away during the training week or on the way to the front. An older man from his village slipped away when he asked permission to relieve himself in the woods. From then on, they all had to do it in public, but people continued to run away. Of the 800 who trained with him, barely a third made it to the front.

Then it became harder to leave. There was one person in every platoon whose job it was to look out for "softies," and it was old Liu in his. A strong man who was never short of a joke, Liu was almost like a father to him, always asking how he was. Once, when he was on night duty, Liu sat down with him and asked if he missed his parents, and Huang burst into tears. "Has anyone offered to take a message home for you?" Liu asked casually while holding his hand. He blurted out that Uncle Huang, a distant relative in another company, mentioned it in passing a few days back. "Good boy." Liu patted him on the head and left. He never saw Uncle Huang again. He thought he was killed in the bombing until one day someone said to him, "Trouble comes from the mouth." Then he understood.

Huang was dying to go home—only fear of being caught stopped him. He was certain they would catch him if he returned home, and after disgracing him and his family they would send him back again. He did not know where the others had gone and they were not telling him. "They flew away like birds, you could not stop them," Huang sighed. "Sometimes, a few were caught and shot in front of everyone, but they just kept disappearing in droves."

Party archives and documents from the period confirm Huang's story. In November and December 1933, out of at least 60,000 troops, there were 28,000 deserters in the Jiangxi Soviet—Ruijin alone had 4,300.[8] The political commissar of the 5th Corps wrote in his diary that in September 1934 his 13th Division lost 1,800, or one-third of its men, due to desertion and illness.[9] Even worse were the militias, who had been forced to help the soldiers dig trenches, move ammunition, and carry the wounded to the rear. An urgent memo sent to all the county governments in August 1934 showed the scale of the problem:

> Three-quarters of the militia mobilized for the recent battles in the whole Soviet region ran away within the first few days, leaving barely a quarter. It wasn't just ordinary members, but cadres and party officials . . . This has clearly weakened the Army's capacity and disrupted its operations. It is tantamount to helping the enemy. It cannot be tolerated.[10]

"You know I never wanted to be a soldier," Huang said several times when we took the stools inside—it was almost twelve o'clock and he was going to take his long lunchtime siesta. "You have to do night duty. It is much better to be a peasant, rising with the sun and resting with the sunset. And it is even better to sleep in the middle of the day. It's nobody's business what I do."

On the way back to Ruijin, I thought a lot about Soldier Huang and what he had said. He spoke plainly, simply, and honestly, with no self-glorification and no apology. He was too much the peasant through and through, open about his weaknesses, wavering, and doubts, quite impervious to the propaganda that has permeated our lives. He came across as a real person, unlike all the characters in the Long March books, who are perfect, but less believable. After all, Huang was only 14 when he started out, just a boy. In that deadly first battle, in the test of fire and blood at such a young age, he did not cry out for his mother and father, he did not run away. He held on to his gun, and did so to the very end of the Long March. Whatever fears and doubts he might have had, they were only natural. He was human after all, and a fighter.

What I did not understand was, if Huang could see it was pointless for him and his comrades to be stuck in the trenches, how could the commanders of the Red Army have failed to recognize this? Why did they insist on trench warfare instead of Mao's proven guerrilla tactics? Did it not occur to them to adopt another strategy, or was Braun, the Red Army's Comintern adviser, simply too dogmatic, regardless of the situation on the ground?

I was glad I had someone to ask these questions. I met up with another Huang, a young academic who had been examining the Red Army in Jiangxi. I had read his published articles on the Fifth Campaign and was impressed. As a distinguished Chinese historian said, far too many of his colleagues had made the study of history more like propaganda than academic research. Their task for the past fifty years has been to praise the glorious achievements of the Party, eulogize Mao, and write the history of the Communist Party from his works. They have not always been like that—but sometimes they were not appreciated, and some were suppressed or tortured. After a while, they became so cautious they lost their independence of mind. Now things are changing slowly and a young generation of historians has broken away from the old restraints and is studying history as it should be—and Huang is one of them. He was in Ruijin for field research. I told him about Soldier Huang and he told me it was merely a coincidence they were both Huangs. "In Jiangxi, there are many Huang families. Perhaps he and I had one ancestor 500 years ago."

We decided to have a quick bowl of noodles and then go to Shazhou Village over the lunch hour. It was just outside Ruijin and was the seat of the Party and headquarters of the Red Army immediately before the Long March. Set in a lush landscape of green hills and ancient trees, it looked timeless except for a couple of souvenir shops selling Red music, portraits of Mao, Mao stamps, three dozen books on Mao's talents in military affairs, poetry, leadership, interpersonal relations, and calligraphy, and a DVD about his life; there were also beautiful girls in Red Army uniforms offering their services as guides.

In the center of the village stood the imposing old clan shrine, and next to it was a long row of what had once been the lofty mansions of rich clan members. The placards outside announced their erstwhile occupants: the Politburo, the National Executive Committee, various government departments, and the residences of all the senior leaders, including Mao's at the head of the village, sheltered by a huge camphor tree.

The village was crammed with people, like a country fair. Ruijin has always been regarded as the holy place of the Chinese Revolution. Lately, Party officials have got into the habit of combining tourism with visiting revolutionary sites. Ruijin was a popular choice: to see where the Long March started, to sit under the tree where the senior leaders had debated issues of life and death, to bathe in the eulogies of the masses for the Party, at least in revolutionary songs—the good fortune of so many historical figures of the Chinese Communist Party might rub off on the visitors, whose goal was to climb higher within the Party themselves.

With a group of officials from Beijing, Young Huang and I squeezed into Mao's bedroom, bare and basic, with a bed and a mosquito net, a desk, and a chair. Over the desk was a photo of Mao, which the guide said was the only picture of him taken in Ruijin, something I found hard to believe. Mao was gaunt, slightly blank and expressionless. "What do you notice?" the guide asked. "It does not look like Mao," a plump man replied. "Why not?" "I'm not sure, perhaps he does not look his usual confident self." "You are right," she smiled condescendingly. "You are very observant. May you go high in your position." The man beamed, and the guide continued, "When he was in Ruijin, he was out of favor. They had pushed Mao aside and allowed the young and arrogant German called Otto Braun to command the Red Army. Braun was blessed by the Comintern, so he had supreme power; but he was hopeless. That was why the Red Army failed in the Fifth Campaign and had to leave Jiangxi."

Braun was not popular with the Chinese. A true Bavarian with deep blue eyes and an air of solemnity, he did not speak a word of Chinese, and had little knowledge of China. He drank coffee, not tea; he ate bread rather than rice, even though he had to make it himself; he preferred sausages to stir-fries. However, he did have military experience. He fought in World War I, and then joined the German Communist Party. Arrested and imprisoned in 1920, he escaped to the Soviet Union eight years later and studied at the Frunze Military Academy in Moscow. But he angered Mao by dismissing his ideas at their first meeting. How could this ignorant, despotic barbarian tell him how to lead his people? Mao was furious. They disagreed on just about everything, except for their love of nicotine and women. It was not just Mao who was unhappy. Liu Bocheng, the Chief of Staff, was also trained in the Frunze Academy, and was a much more experienced commander. He irritated his young boss when he dared to disagree. "You seem to be no better than an ordinary staff officer," Braun told him. "You wasted your time in the Soviet Union."[11]

However, the Chinese treated Braun with reverence; they even called him Tai Shanghung, "the supreme emperor." After all, he was Stalin's envoy, and Moscow's support was paramount for the Chinese Communists—ideologically, politically, financially, and militarily. Zhou Enlai, the powerful mandarin of the Communist Party, faced the delicate task of finding a woman robust enough to please Braun. In the end, he came up with a peasant girl, who obliged because she was told it was her "revolutionary duty." So sitting in the house specially built for him, nicknamed the Lone House, with the help of a translator and two packs of cigarettes a day specially brought in from the Nationalist-controlled areas, Braun read the telegrams from the field, and then drew up battle plans for the Red Army. His master plan combined defense and attack: trenches arranged as bulwarks against the blockhouses, and troop detachments behind and on the wings to engage the enemy in "short, sharp blows."

I was curious to know what happened to Braun's Lone House. The guide told me it was torn down long ago. "It was not worth keeping, the trouble he brought us. Had he not come, had Mao been in control, the Red Army would not have had to go on the Long March!" she said in annoyance. Then she took the crowd to another holy spot, the well which Mao helped the villagers to dig, a story we all know from our primary school textbooks. They all wanted to pay their respects, to drink the water, and be as lucky as Mao.

Watching the crowd disperse, Young Huang had a look of disdain on his face. "How can they be so irresponsible and ignorant?" he said angrily. "All this superstitious crap. This is the twenty-first century! And all the blame on Braun. It wasn't his fault really, although he did make a lot of mistakes. He was only 34. He must have thought he was another Napoleon. He gave orders and expected to be obeyed. He even told them where to put the cannons, using maps that weren't any good, and he lost his temper when they corrected him. But as things stood, there was little he could have done to turn the tide. He was not to blame for the Red Army's failures. He did not insist on trench warfare as people are always told, but guerrilla tactics and mobile attacks couldn't work anymore. We were trapped, like flies in a spider's web."

"The Red Army was stuck in the trenches for a long time." I told him Soldier Huang's story. I had questioned him in detail about his experiences in the trenches. The story I knew was that the Red Army won the first four campaigns because of Mao and his guidance, and lost the fifth because of Braun and had to go on the Long March. It seemed logical, and it had gone virtually unchallenged. I accepted it. It occurred to me that subconsciously I was trying to prove the received wisdom.

Huang and I came out of Mao's bedroom and sat down under the huge camphor tree in the courtyard. He drew my attention to the situation that Chiang had to face at the time. Chiang was the head of the Nationalist government, but he did not control the country. Much of it was in the hands of warlords who hated him as much as the Communists did. Each warlord occupied a territory where they levied taxes on peasants' harvests, even twenty years ahead; they were the largest growers and traffickers of opium, which they sold to raise their armies. In their eyes, Chiang was just another warlord like them who had tried to unify the country with the help of the Communists in 1927, but started killing them too when he realized they were going to challenge him. They pledged loyalty to him when he promised them millions of silver dollars a month, but changed their allegiance whenever it suited them.

The warlords' internecine wars, their lack of any moral values and ideals except for keeping their power and territory, and the damage they inflicted on the nation, were among the curses of twentieth-century China. I had learned all about them in school, but usually we did not associate them with the rise and expansion of Communism. While Chiang was battling it out with them—the biggest battle lasting five months, costing 200 million silver dollars and displacing 2 million people from their homes—the Communists were free to grow and grow. The Red Army in the Jiangxi Soviet expanded its territory, at its peak controlling twenty-one counties with over 3 million people, and built itself up from a guerrilla force of 9,000 men to 100,000. They even created a state within a state. Mao was grateful for the intervention of the warlords and admitted that this was uniquely helpful for the Chinese Revolution. They had a powerful impact on the energy and resources Chiang could put into his campaigns against the Jiangxi Soviet. He had to call off one of his campaigns when the warlords of Guangdong and Guangxi mutinied, almost forcing him out of office.

If Chiang had enough headaches domestically, the Japanese gave him more. Japan had set its eyes on China as if it was its due, an integral part of its imperial ambitions. On September 18, 1931, Japan took China's three northeastern provinces. A month later, Chiang had to abort his Third Campaign, and his Fourth Campaign eighteen months later, when the Japanese threatened to march on Beiping, today's Beijing. Chiang chose to appease the Japanese—for the time being at least. He knew the country was not ready for a war, but more importantly, he regarded the Japanese as a disease of the skin, and the Communists as one of the heart. "If there is no peace within, how can we resist the enemy from outside?" he appealed to the nation. To the outrage of all Chinese, he allowed Japan a free hand to run China north of the Great Wall. However necessary as a strategy, it set people against him; it would almost cost him his life, and finally it lost him China.

For the time being, though, with this decision Chiang could concentrate on his fifth and final campaign against the Jiangxi Communists in earnest. He threw in his best troops, 200,000 of them. He assembled his 7,500 senior officers in Lushan Mountain in northern Jiangxi, telling them: "The only purpose of this training is for the elimination of the Red Bandits. They are our sole target, and all your preparation, tactical, strategic, and operational, is to serve this need."[12] He gave every officer a copy of handbooks on *Eliminating the Red Bandits*, *Keys to Eliminating the Red Bandits*, and *The Principles of Training for the Army Engaged in the Elimination Campaign*.

As Soldier Huang experienced it, the blockhouse strategy was the key to this campaign. Why then had Chiang not used it earlier? It would have saved him four years, and a lot of money and lives. "Blockhouses were not his idea. Chiang admitted himself there was nothing new about his strategy—a nineteenth-century Chinese general used the very same method to put down a peasant rebellion," Young Huang said. "But for the strategy to work, it needed time and security, neither of which Chiang had before. This time he did.

"But contrary to the criticism heaped on Braun, he did not make the mistake of ordering the Red Army to sit in the trenches and wait for the enemy," Huang went on. I remembered how he had argued this so convincingly in his thought-provoking articles. The Comintern had in fact instructed the Red Army to play to its strength of mobile and guer-rilla warfare.

> From past experiences, the Red Army has achieved many
> victories in mobile warfare, but suffered considerably when
> it forced frontal attacks in areas where the enemy had built
> blockhouses . . . You should not engage in positional warfare,
> and should move behind the enemy . . .[13]

Braun agreed entirely: "As to positional warfare, whatever form it took, it was not suitable. We were all absolutely clear about it."[14] He tried to draw the enemy out of their turtle-shells and then launch short, sharp blows to wipe them out. But the trouble was that the enemy refused to come out unless they had full covering fire on the ground and from the air, often with three or four divisions together within 10 kilometers. This made it hard for the Red Army to concentrate enough men and deal them a fatal blow, hard though it tried. Even Chiang noticed this tendency: "When we fight the bandits now, they rarely confront us in positional warfare; they frequently attack us by guerrilla tactics."[15]

The battle of Guangchang in April 1934 was an exception, when Soldier Huang and almost the entire Red Army were stuck in their trenches for a month up against the blockhouses. It was the first time this happened, but the battle was not Braun's idea, as he made very clear in his memoir:

> The Party leadership considered it a strategically critical point
> because it barred the way into the heart of the Soviet area. The
> leadership also believed that unresisting surrender would be
> politically indefensible.[16]

Zhou Enlai agreed with Braun:

> Every comrade must realize, the plan by the enemy to take
> Guangchang is different from the previous four campaigns. It
> is a strategic step in their penetration into the heart of the

Soviet base; it is the key to their overall offensive. We must
fight to defend Guangchang.[17]

I had talked to the veterans and the expert, and it was clear to them why
they lost, but in seventy years, with so many books on the subject, the
same argument is still used: if Mao did not lead it, the Revolution
would fail. To support this theme, history had to be made to fit the
theory. At least militarily, even Mao learned from mistakes, as his memoirs make clear. The Party was only twelve years old, the Red Army half
that, the Soviets only three years. The guidance coming from the Comintern was often not based on Chinese reality. Naturally there were
mistakes, but a scapegoat was found on whom all the blame for losing
the Fifth Campaign was dumped.

Soon after the Guangchang battle, the Party made its decision to
launch the Long March; it knew it could no longer defend the Jiangxi
base—in fact it informed Moscow so in May 1934—but some units had
to hold the line so the preparations for the Long March could get under way. "When we moved house, it would take a few weeks. The Long
March was a state on the move, with everything it might need," Young
Huang said. "They had to replenish the troops, to find homes for the
sick and wounded, to get together food, money, and other supplies.
Also where would they go? Nobody knew for sure. That was why they
sent out the 6th Corps to blaze the trail, and the 7th Corps to divert the
Nationalists' attack."

The decision to abandon the Jiangxi Soviet was made in the
strictest secrecy. Only the top leaders and military commanders knew
about it—Mao himself did not learn of it until August, two months before the departure. There were two fears: firstly that morale would dis-
integrate, and secondly that the Nationalists would find out. As late as
October 3, two weeks before the Long March, Zhang Wentian, the
Chairman of the Soviet Government, continued to call on the people
to fight to the end:

For the defense of our regime and of our lives, our children
and babies, our land and grain, our cows, hogs, chickens, and

ducks, and for resistance against enemy slaughter, destruction, looting, and rape, we should use our daggers, hunting guns, rifles, and any sorts of old and new weapons to arm ourselves . . . Let our millions of worker and peasant masses become an unbreakable armed force to fight along with our invincible Red Army. We shall completely smash the enemy attack. We must win the final victory! Hold high the Soviet banner! Long live the Soviet regime.[18]

This is an ancient Chinese tactic known as the cicada trick: the cicada flies off after it sheds its skin in the autumn, and people are fooled by the skin, thinking it is still there.

But what did ordinary soldiers like Huang know? How far was he involved in the preparations and how much did he know about them? I was keen to find out. As if he knew I was coming, he was waiting for me in his courtyard in the afternoon, wearing a Red Army uniform, complete with octagonal cap. It suited him. "I thought you might like it. They gave them to us ten years ago to celebrate the sixtieth anniversary of the Long March. You know I never had a complete uniform until I finished the March!"

When did he know he was going? I asked. "I didn't know. Had I known it was going to be that long, I'd have come home straightaway, no matter what," he said without the slightest hesitation. Did he have any inkling that something was coming up? He took off his cap and scratched his head. "Now that you ask me, I think it was when I saw new uniforms for the first time. I think the autumn harvest was already in by then."

He and his company were pulled out of the trenches in late September 1934, and brought to Yudu, which was 60 kilometers from Ruijin. New recruits were brought in to replenish the depleted company—some were older than his father. And there were new uniforms and shoes for everyone. At last he would look like a soldier rather than a beggar. He put on the jacket—it was double layered and he felt so warm, like being by a fire. He never had one like it—it was not necessary in the South, even in winter. "Why do we have to carry this heavy stuff? Are we going somewhere cold?" someone asked, but did not get an answer. Huang was more interested in finding a jacket and shoes that fitted him. Sadly, the jacket was like a coat, and the shoes like boats. They were made for adults. Seeing the tears forming in his eyes, the captain led him into another room. His mouth dropped when he saw the huge stockpile—he had never see so many bullets in his life. He felt as excited as on New Year's Day, when he was given firecrackers. "All yours, take as many as you like," the captain told him jokingly. He loaded himself up, but the captain took away all but one bandolier and a few grenades. "You won't get very far with more than that, my son!"

Soldier Huang had his rifle across his back, a pack with five kilos of rice, a bowl, the patched jacket that his mother had given him, and an extra pair of straw sandals that the captain had made specially for him. A pair of chopsticks were thrust into his puttees. "We are going somewhere, aren't we?" he asked one of the older soldiers. "Perhaps we'll go behind the enemy lines, and take the big towns and cities. That's what we used to do after each campaign." As he spoke, all the soldiers started talking at once. "Now we'll have meat at last." "Ah, we're going to see beautiful women." "We'll bring back enough money to feed ourselves through the winter." Excitement was in the air, the gloom of the trenches had lifted.

Early one evening, when the moon was big and round, Huang and his company marched along the broad and gentle Yudu River. People came out to say good-bye. Some girls, newly wedded, were standing on tiptoe, looking about anxiously to see their husbands as they passed through. When they spotted them, they cried out with joy, only to be teased by the raucous soldiers in the company. They blushed, ran back, and watched from further off. Others, perhaps organized by the local women's association, were more bold, walking along with the soldiers, and asking, "What's your name? Where are you from? Can you win a medal and become a hero?" It was the men's turn to be shy and tongue-tied. The girls laughed and burst into song:

*A model soldier,*
*That's what I want you to be.*

*I long for your good news day and night,*
*My Red Army brother,*
*Capture a few generals and make me happy!*[19]

In the crowd, Huang spotted the mother from the family he had been billeted with, who had looked after him like a son. She ran toward him, and pushed two eggs into his hands. "Look after yourself, my son," she said, barely holding back her tears. Suddenly he felt the pain of what he had learned days before: her son joined the Red Army two years ago and she had not heard from him since. "Don't worry, Mother. We'll be back soon."

# 3 ★ WATER FLOWING UPSTREAM

*October, the autumn wind blows cool;*
*Swift the Red Army, swiftly it goes.*
*By night across Yudu's flow,*
*Old land, young blood — to victory.*

I followed the Red Army's withdrawal to Yudu, and walked by the river outside the town. Its wide expanse was placid, with tree-covered hills on the far shore stretching as far as you could see, dotted here and there with villages; close by a few old boats were tied up to stakes in the shallows. Upstream the scene is much as it was when the Red Army crossed here seventy years ago. The barges that carried the pontoons for the crossing still float on the grey-green water. But right in front of me there was something new: a white obelisk, incongruously large, its size emphasized by small conical evergreens that lead away from it on either side. Its curved sides soared to a peak, and near the top was a large gold star on a red disk. Below this was the inscription: "The first fording by the Central Army on the Long March." Downstream, some way beyond the monument, stands a majestic four-lane bridge. Large characters on a huge red arch over it announce "Long March Bridge," and smaller characters tell you it was opened in 1996, the sixtieth anniversary of the March.

Like most visitors, I came here to see the starting point of the March, but somehow I felt uneasy that the monument, the bridge, and so many commemorative sites in the town were all celebrating the start of the March. Was not the Red Army's departure also the end of the Jiangxi Soviet Republic? It was the first Communist government in China, and it had collapsed. Was there nothing to be said about that?

Chiang's military strength was one reason why the Soviet failed; it was also running out of men and materials, but the reasons might go deeper. Before I embarked on the Marchers' route, I needed to know more about what had happened here.

I first made for the house where Mao had lived. I had read in the guidebook that it was only a short walk from the river in the old quarter of town, but when I asked a young man where it was, he said, "What house?" I was puzzled. Mao's house was normally well known anywhere he had stayed, but the man seemed to know nothing about it. Perhaps he was not a local. I walked further and saw an old lady; although she did tell me the way, I still almost went past it. It was in a side street with a small entrance. There was a red placard: "Chairman Mao's Residence, July–October 1934."

It was locked, so I banged noisily on the door for some time, attracting a few passersby, before someone answered from inside: "We are not open. Go away." This was a change; I remembered the crowds that poured through Mao's residence in Ruijin. I shouted I had come a long way and could I just have a quick look? There was total silence, and then the clicking of keys. Finally, the door creaked open, an old man showed himself, and he let me in.

The house and its very small courtyard face west. In China, houses are usually built facing south to enjoy the sunshine. Those facing east or west are inferior; in a traditional compound they are normally for children or junior family members. The courtyard was bare, without the trees that normally adorned Mao's residences. He loved trees. The ancient camphor tree in front of his house in Ruijin bore a placard saying that he often sat under it to read and chat. Inside there was just a dusty portrait on the wall of the sitting room, and some drab information boards below. They carried a very brief summary of Mao's life and his activities in Yudu. A shaky staircase led to the second floor, which was where he slept. After Ruijin, this was quite a comedown.

I told the old man my disappointment. "What do you expect?" he asked, lighting a cigarette and taking a puff. "Mao only stayed here briefly, and that was when he was really down. When you are down, even dogs don't come near you." Then the man went inside and came back with a stool to sit in the sun, puffing away.

The old man had mentioned that Mao spent a lot of time in the house reading and thinking, or pacing in the courtyard. Occasionally he went out to inspect the progress of the pontoons over the river, or talked to the local people. He must have reflected on his life, what had happened that had left him out of the center of power, isolated here while hectic preparations were being made for the Long March. While his courtyard was so quiet the swallows could land undisturbed, as the caretaker put it, Yudu was a bustling place, busier than on a market day. Whole regiments of soldiers marched in and out of the town gates; mules groaned under heavy loads; orderlies dashed here and there without a minute's rest; peasants pulled bamboo poles and door planks toward the river for the pontoons.

Zhou Enlai only told Mao in August of the decision to leave the base, although it had been made as early as May. Mao had not been consulted, nor had his advice been sought about what to do: what to take or leave behind, who were to go or stay, what route should be taken for the breakout, what would become of the Jiangxi Soviet, whether they were coming back. He only knew that the Red Army was to leave from Yudu, the southernmost county of the Jiangxi Red base, and then head west to join He Long's 2nd Army near the border of Hunan and Hubei. Mao was shown the list of senior Party officials who were to leave. He looked grim as he went through it—many of his close associates were not on it, including one of his brothers. The list had been decided, like everything else, by the trio of Zhou Enlai, the Commissar of the Red Army, Bo Gu, the Party Secretary, and Braun, the Comintern adviser to the Red Army.

Many leaders and senior commanders came through Yudu to check up on the preparations, but few bothered to call on Mao. Gong Chu saw more of him than most. He was Commander of the Red Army in Yudu and of the force left behind to guard the Jiangxi base when the Long March began. He gave a graphic account of Mao's state in the days leading up to the March. Mao had had an attack of malaria and was lank and grey. Gong asked him about his health, and Mao replied: "I have not been well recently, but more painful is that I feel extremely low."[1] He invited Gong to come and see him: "I hope you can come and have a chat whenever you have the time in the evenings." He took up the invitation; Mao's wife joined them, and she would "prepare delicious suppers. The three of us would chat and drink and smoke, often . . . till midnight . . . From my observation, Mao's place was not visited by other people except me . . . It really felt as if he was isolated and miserable."

On another visit, Gong found Mao sadder still, complaining about his loss of power, how the people who had fought with him in the Jinggang Mountains were pushed aside, and how his Party enemies wanted all the power in their hands. Reflecting on the punishment meted out to him, he even cried. "Tears ran down his cheeks. He was coughing from time to time, and his face looked drawn and dried and sallow. Under the flicker of a tiny oil lamp, he was quite a picture of dejection."[2]

Mao's state of mind was understandable. He had rescued the Party and founded the Jiangxi base, and was rewarded by being removed from his position. In the 1920s, the young Communists followed every instruction from Moscow religiously. When Moscow told them to work with the Nationalist government, they did so—until Chiang decided that they were too much of a threat. The White Purge of 1927 was horrific in its butchery, and reduced the Communists almost to nothing. But gradually they restored themselves. Next Moscow came up with a plan to organize armed uprisings and take major cities, as had happened in the Russian Revolution. They tried this in Nanchang, Wuhan, and Canton—but all of them failed spectacularly.

Mao was instructed to lead an attack on Changsha, a heavily fortified city. Instead, he took his men and headed for the Jinggang Mountains on the border between Hunan and Jiangxi, where Chiang had little control—no doubt inspired by peasant rebels of the past, particularly those immortalized in *The Water Margins*, his favorite Chinese novel. The book tells of a group of rebels who rose against the emperor and became so powerful that the emperor had to yield to their demands. It mattered little that he had only 600 men. As Mao said, "A single spark can start a prairie fire." He joined with two local bandit kings and managed to set up a base there.

His reputation spread. In May 1928, Zhu De, the Nationalist brigadier who had turned to Communism, brought Mao the remains of his troops from the failed Nanchang uprising. Six months later, they were joined by Peng Dehuai, who defected from the Nationalist army with 1,500 soldiers. Together they had 5,000 men, and made up the core of the Red Army, with Mao the head. This nascent army was too big for the Jinggang Mountains to support, so Mao decided to make a move and they found a new home in the flatter hills surrounding Ruijin.

The Red base in Jiangxi grew and grew, even spreading to neighboring Fujian Province. On November 7, 1931, the Communists established the Chinese Soviet Republic, with Mao as the leader. He felt he deserved his position—he had provided a base, vision, and hope for the Chinese Revolution—but he was soon to be disappointed. With the help of the Communists' spymaster who defected to him, Chiang wiped out the Party headquarters in Shanghai. Many of those who survived decided to join Mao in Jiangxi, now the biggest Communist base in the country. Zhou Enlai arrived in Ruijin in August 1931, and all the top leaders followed; a nucleus was left in Shanghai just as a liaison with Moscow.

Mao soon began to feel the squeeze from the Party heavyweights. "After the men who had lived in foreign villas arrived, I was thrown into the cesspool . . . Really, it looked as though I had to prepare my funeral."[3] Zhou, always trusted by Moscow to obey orders, replaced him as the top man in the base. Zhang Wentian, the Red Professor, took over the running of the Jiangxi Soviet government from Mao. He did not even bother to visit Mao for a year after he arrived in Ruijin. He confessed later, "I had no idea what sort of person Mao was, what he thought, and what he was good at. I had not the least interest in finding out either."[4] The 25-year-old Wang Jiaxiang, straight from his studies in Moscow, became head of the Red Army's political department. Finally, and most importantly, after only three years' study in Moscow, Bo Gu became the protégé of the Communist Party's representative in the Comintern, and was made Party Secretary when he was no more than 25. For Mao, he was someone of no experience at all; Bo Gu did not think much of Mao either. "Marxism can't come out of country hills," he declared. Otto Braun, who was already in Jiangxi, and who never got on with Mao, threw his weight behind the Moscow-trained "Bolsheviks."

Mao's loss of power has always been presented as the Party leaders pushing him aside. In October 1932, he was stripped of his role as Commissar of the Red Army, and only retained the nominal title of Chair of the People's Committee of the Jiangxi base. From then, till the Long March began in October 1934, Mao had no authority. How had he lost everything so quickly, so completely, when the Party owed him so much—their very survival? It was difficult to understand.

The old caretaker at Mao's house suggested I should visit the Yudu Revolutionary Martyrs' Museum. "So many of us died for the Revolution. It is grand, the pride of the town," he said with his first show of animation. "You won't be disappointed there."

This museum was easy to find, directly off Long March Avenue, the town's main thoroughfare. Three heroic statues in classic Socialist Realist style—a soldier, an officer, and a peasant woman—stood in front of the entrance. The entrance hall was like a funeral parlor, packed with large wreaths dedicated to the martyrs. The exhibition was excellent, organized chronologically and replete with murals, paintings, maps, charts, and statues. They showed all the martyrs, from the founders of the Yudu Communist Party to those who died in the Cultural Revolution.

I concentrated on the first few rooms, which dealt with the period running up to the Long March. This county was always criticized as politically backward. It lagged behind other counties in recruitment and procurement, and it failed to stop people fleeing to Nationalist-controlled areas. In 1932–33, the whole county government had been removed twice. I was surprised to see that Yudu had sent 68,519 men to the Red Army from 1929 to 1934, with 28,069 in the five months before the March. The contributions were displayed in a detailed chart, each district in a column as though they were competing in Communist fervor. Most imposing of all were the gigantic murals in red and gold showing heroic battle scenes, enthusiastic demonstrations, and memorials to the dead. They more than made up for any lack of artifacts. The red color seemed to be there to remind us of the blood that was shed during the Revolution.

I was also struck by the youth of the early revolutionaries—they were nearly all in their late teens and early twenties. The expressions in

their photographs and portraits were so determined, their eyes so piercing, their commitment so visible, I could almost feel their optimism
and hope for a better future. Strangely, they almost all died in the same
year—1931.

I wondered what the big battles were in 1931 that led to the deaths
of so many local Party leaders. Could they be Chiang's Second and
Third Campaigns, both of which took place in 1931? No, they were
brief and far from Yudu, well to the north of the Jiangxi base. Besides,
the early martyrs were mostly local Party leaders who should not have
been affected by the campaigns. I could not understand it, so I asked
the staff member on duty in the room.

"Oh, they died in the purge," she said.

"Which purge?" I asked.

"The purge in the Jiangxi Soviet started by Chairman Mao," she
said a little snappily, perhaps because of my ignorance. She then took
me over to a bronze bust standing on a plinth on its own. It was like a
Rodin, a thin young man, looking slightly dispirited and even a bit lost.
All it said under the bust was his name and that he was killed mistak-
enly. "This is Xiao Dapeng. He was the Commander of the 20th Corps
and his men started the Futian Incident."

Suddenly everything clicked. I had read about the purge and the
Futian Incident, but I had no idea the leader came from here. "He was
so brave and died so young," she said with an air of pride. "If he had
lived, I'm sure he would have made it big, definitely become a general.
He was only in his twenties, a commander of a corps when he was
younger than I am now. What a waste."

It was the very first Communist purge. When Mao came down
from the Jinggang Mountains in the spring of 1929, Jiangxi already had
a well-organized Communist Committee, with its headquarters in
Futian Village, about 250 kilometers north of Ruijin. They were mostly
educated local youth, and their revolution was milder, designed not to
antagonize their families, relatives, and clan members. Mao criticized
them for being too conservative. "Leniency toward the enemy is a crime
against the Revolution," he said famously. He put his brother-in-law
in charge of them, but they deeply resented the intrusion; for them,

it was not about policy, but about power. Tension ran high between the two groups. As the old saying goes, there cannot be two tigers on one mountain. When the locals threw out the brother-in-law, Mao decided to retaliate. In October 1930, he wrote to the Party headquarters in Shanghai, denouncing the Jiangxi provincial Communists: "The entire Party [there] is under the leadership of rich peasants . . . Without a thorough purge of their leaders . . . there is no way the Party can be saved."[5]

On December 7, 1930, Mao sent Li Shaojiu, Chairman of the Purge Committee he had set up in his army, to Futian Village; Li arrested almost the entire Jiangxi Communist Committee, 120 members in all. They were held under suspicion of being members of the Anti-Bolshevik Clique, a defunct Nationalist organization. For the next five days they were tortured to make them confess. The tortures were barbaric—their flesh was burned with incense sticks, they were hung up by the hands and beaten with split bamboo, bamboo splinters were forced under their fingernails, their hands were nailed on tables, burning rods were pushed up their backsides. They all "confessed." Even so, 40 of them were killed.

Two days later, Li Shaojiu descended on the headquarters of the 20th Corps, a Jiangxi local guerrilla force. He conveyed Mao's instruction that there were Anti-Bolshevik members or ABs within the Corps and they must be rooted out. One of the targets, Commissar Liu Di, decided to stop it. As he later reported to the Party headquarters in Shanghai: "I arrived at the firm conclusion that all this had nothing to do with ABs. It must be Mao Zedong playing base tricks and sending his running dog Li Shaojiu here to slaughter the Jiangxi comrades." Liu and his soldiers elected Xiao Dapeng as the new Commander-in-Chief of the 20th Corps, as they thought the old one was too weak to protect them. Then they went over to Futian Village and set free any members of the Communist Committee who were still alive. Afterwards, Xiao took the 20th Corps to the mountains. Before they left, they held a rally, shouting "Down with Mao Zedong!" "Support Zhu De and Peng Dehuai!" This is what they said of Mao:

> He is extremely devious and sly, selfish, and full of megalomania. He orders comrades around, frightens them with charges

of crimes, and victimizes them. He rarely holds discussions about Party matters . . . Whenever he expresses a view, everyone must agree, otherwise he uses the Party organization to clamp down on you, or invents some trumped-up charges to make life absolutely dreadful for you . . . Not only is he not a revolutionary leader, he is not a . . . Bolshevik.[6]

Xiao led his men back to Yudu six months later, after he received a message that their appeal to the Party headquarters in Shanghai had worked. Little did he know it was a hoax to entice them back. One day in June 1931—the martyrs' main death year, as I had noticed in the museum—Mao called for a meeting of all the officers of the 20th Corps in a village in Yudu County; there were more than 200 of them from company level to Xiao the Commander-in-Chief. Just as they sat down in the shrine hall, soldiers pounced on them. They were disarmed and executed. The 20th Corps was abolished, with its 3,000 men killed or dispersed. Before the executions, Xiao and his officers were paraded in villages and towns throughout the Red base as a warning to the masses. As Mao told them at a major rally:

There are the men whom you followed in your blindness!
These were the leaders you trusted—men who moved amongst
us, pretended to be Communists until they were strong
enough to betray us! They used words of Revolution that
stirred your hearts, but they were like the leopard that cries in
the forest at night with the voice of a human, until men go out
in rescue parties, never to return![7]

But did Mao convince anyone? Had the purge made the base any safer? Had it rallied people, and increased their determination to resist Chiang and defend the Soviet? Was the Red Army stronger or had the Party failed to reckon with the reaction to what they had done, and achieved exactly the opposite? I had to go to Futian to find out more. Before I carried out my research for the journey, the place had been barely on the edge of my consciousness. I did not even know where to look for it on the map, yet it was the scene of this terrible purge, setting the pattern for many more to come. The curse that undermined the Revolution started there.

The journey to Futian from Yudu took me half a day by bus. I passed through undulating countryside, peaceful now, but the scene of many fierce battles during Chiang's five campaigns. I reached Futian Village by motor rickshaw from my bus stop. The place had an air of crumbling grandeur, with many large traditional houses; the name means "Rich Soil," the source of its former wealth, but the houses have been allowed to fall into disrepair, and the streets have potholes. Most of the towns and villages in Jiangxi I passed through on my travels, if not exactly rich, were moving with the times; they showed signs of money coming in, new houses, shops, motorbikes, trucks. I could feel hope in the air, toil being rewarded. In Futian Village, there was none of that. It seemed a place that time had forgotten, that history wanted to forget.

I stood for a long time outside the shrine hall that was the headquarters of the Jiangxi Communist Committee. Once a fine traditional building, it now looked sad, with layers of faded poster characters from long ago. It was locked and, thinking of what had gone on here, I was not sure I wanted to go in. I just wanted to see the place and talk to people, so I sat down against the wall opposite it. After a while, a man in his fifties came up to me, in a faded blue Mao jacket and wide trousers, as was the custom in the South. "You have been sitting here for as long as I've been smoking my pipe. Why?" I asked him whether he knew people whose families were affected by the Incident. "Is there a family that wasn't? Walk into any house, they will tell you. It was like a plague."

The Futian Incident was followed by a widespread purge which took on a life of its own. People were killed for the flimsiest of reasons. The man's father was a victim. His crime? "He said hello to the members of the Jiangxi Committee. But who didn't? This is not a big place. If you fart, the whole village hears. You greet people, it is only human. But that was not how they looked at things. People who spoke, who nodded to each other, who smoked a pipe together, whose fields were next to each other—anybody could be a suspect and taken away. They killed people like we harvest our crops. You know what happened in the end?" He did not wait for my answer. He was gushing like the river on the edge of the village. "Nobody dared to work for the Party anymore. When someone was made an official, they cried and wailed. Can you imagine that? And when people from other villages had to come here for some reason, they didn't even dare to enter. They would cup their hands together and shout their message from a long way off. They were afraid to catch the plague."

While he was talking, two more men squatted down with us and joined the conversation. "Madness! It was total madness," said one of the newcomers. "Nobody could understand what was going on. Red Army was killing Red Army! Communists were killing Communists! How could there be so many enemies anyway? If the men of the 20th Corps and the Jiangxi Committee had been bad people, why hadn't they defected to Chiang Kaishek? Nobody dared to tell Mao that. They were too scared. They kept their mouths shut like a grasshopper on a cold day."

"I would say it was paranoia," said his companion, while he paused to get out his pipe and tobacco. "Chiang Kaishek was too strong, and he scared the stuffing out of Mao. Remember, the purge happened just as Chiang was launching his First Campaign against us."

They might have had a point about the paranoia. The purge did take place at the height of tension. On top of his military preparations, Chiang also tried a softly-softly approach. Leaflets were dropped from planes, saying anyone who captured Mao and Zhu De would get a reward of $100,000. Red Army troops were encouraged to defect; they were offered $20 for every rifle they handed in.[8] Envoys and spies were sent to the Red base to persuade generals of the Red Army to mutiny. In fact, some senior Communists did defect. The Communist Party chief in Fujian Province was the first. Another very high-ranking officer, a favorite of Mao's, went over to the Nationalists with information about the Party leaders' houses, which the Nationalists promptly bombed. It only added to Mao's sense of insecurity.

Mao's purge was not copied from Moscow's tactics; it came before Stalin was to employ such means on any scale. It is estimated that over 20,000 people from the army, the Party, and the Jiangxi Soviet government died in the purge, which lasted just over a year. That was more than the casualties suffered by the Red Army in Chiang's first three campaigns. The purge weakened the Party at a time when it was most vulnerable, and it shook people's faith in the man they thought was their leader. Huang Kecheng, a top commander in the Red Army, first a perpetrator of the purge and then a victim, spoke the unspeakable in his memoirs fifty years later—historians have praised them for their honesty. "How could the Central Bureau [in Ruijin] take over from Mao so quickly? Of course, the comrades in the Red base trusted the Party. But had Mao not lost the support of the people . . . ? Otherwise it would have been very difficult to push him aside . . ."[9] At Futian, in front of that dilapidated shrine hall, I began to understand why Mao lost his power—he had himself destroyed the very source of it.

Futian was also the first open challenge to Mao. He never forgot it or forgave it. The three old men told me that since 1949 many other counties and villages in Jiangxi received favors from Beijing to compensate for their sacrifices to the Revolution, but the den of the "reactionary Futian Incident" was not on the list. The sad state of the village said everything about its neglect. The descendants of the purge victims long continued to suffer Mao's wrath. They were easy targets in each of Mao's campaigns; they could not join the Party or the army; they were not considered for university places or recruitment by factories. The villagers appealed for over half a century to clear their name. Beijing sent senior officials to investigate their case. A leading Party historian in Jiangxi spent a decade pleading their innocence. He died before he heard the conclusion that came out in the official *History of the Communist Party*: "There was never an AB clique in the Communist Party, and the so-called AB members were the result of torture." That was in 1991, exactly sixty years after the Incident. Today there is still no official apology for the people involved. That is why the shrine hall was left to rot. The villagers have not been allowed to commemorate those who died, but they will not forget them. Hopefully, the day will come when people visit the shrine hall as they do the revolutionary sites in Ruijin, and hear the stories of the dead as I did from the three old men. Then the victims of the Futian Incident will not have died entirely in vain.

In Futian, I also began to appreciate the effects of the purges more clearly. If Mao's purges were confined to the Party and the army, they now moved into wider society and helped to undermine support for the Jiangxi Soviet. The three old men used the metaphor, the first purge was like cutting a man's arm, but what happened later went to the heart. When Zhou Enlai arrived in Ruijin, he did try to limit the damage of Mao's purge and pacify people. He organized public meetings in every county, putting on trial scores of the senior officials responsible for the purge. They were charged as Nationalist spies who had penetrated the Red base and created the Red Terror.[10] They were shot on the spot, and their victims were rehabilitated. However, within a few months the purges started again, this time directed at landlords, rich peasants, traders, and so-called "class enemies." Purges seemed to have entered the Communists' bloodstream as an expression of their cardinal principle—class struggle.

The fundamental issue of the Chinese Revolution was the peasants, and what mattered to the peasants was land. By taking land from the rich and giving it to the poor, the Communist Party won their support. In the Jiangxi Red base, the practice was that rich peasants were given bad land, in swamps or on hillsides, and the landlords were not allowed any—they survived by doing hard labor. The Party determined who was a landlord or a rich peasant. In February 1932, officials were sent to villages to investigate land issues, or more precisely, to discover "new enemies of the people." Futian Village was a natural target, but after Mao's cleansing were there any landlords left? I asked the three wise men sitting with me in front of the shrine hall.

"Maybe the ghosts of the landlords," one said. "They were all killed. Even their children were gone."

"They did come up with more," the second man corrected him.

"You call those landlords?" the third one almost shouted. "None of them had more than ten *dan* of rice, barely enough for a family of five to scrape by on. But then anything could turn a man into a landlord, a pig in the pigsty, a farmhand, some extra cash, or a better harvest by hard work. It was a farce."

Watching and listening to the three men, I felt they were like a string trio, each following his part, but all fitting together. It amazed me that they talked with such vigor about things that had happened seventy-three years earlier, but they and their parents and grandparents must have pondered the same questions for so long.

So why did they think the Party trumped up the charges? I had always thought landlords were evil and deserved the punishment doled out to them. It never occurred to me that enemies could just be created.

"They were doing it to keep us on our toes. Campaigns, campaigns, and more campaigns. Each time some fellows were bumped off, the rest thought they had better behave, otherwise it would be their turn next. People lived in fear, and that was what they wanted."

I found out later that in the first five months of the Land Investigation drive, 5,680 "new enemies" were discovered in the Red base, and were punished by fines, imprisonment, hard labor, or death.[11] At its peak in the summer of 1933, when Chiang was about to launch his Fifth Campaign, another 13,620 landlords and rich peasants were identified in just three months. Their punishment was spelled out in this directive by the Political Department of the Red Army:

> Besides immediately confiscating their grain, oxen, pigs . . . we order them to hand in fines to supply the workers' and peasants' Revolution, in order to show the sincerity of their repentance and obedience . . . Also they have to write a statement of repentance. If they do not hand in the fines before the deadline and do not contact us, they will be considered definite reactionaries. Then besides burning all their houses, and digging up and destroying their family tombs, we will make a pronouncement asking all people to arrest them. Their families will be punished by death.[12]

By now, landlords and rich peasants accounted for over 10 percent of the 3 million people in the Jiangxi Red base—300,000 people. On top of this there were the alleged ABs and other suspects who were thought to be hiding inside the Party. They knew their likely fate, and the best thing was to run. The three old men used a phrase that I had heard before but was puzzled by: "The water began to flow upstream." It turned out to be a local description of the flood of people who left the Jiangxi base and went to the Nationalist-held territories. We had always learned that the people went out of their way to support the Red Army and the Soviet, as the mural in the Yudu Martyrs' Museum showed, but from the summer of 1933 hundreds of thousands of people fled. In Futian Village, very few managed to escape because the Party kept a close eye on them. Elsewhere the Party was powerless to stop the exodus.

It began with the landlords; then it was the peasants; and finally whole villages or even districts disappeared. "Shangtang District has 6,000 people, and more than 2,000 have gone to the White area, taking their pigs, chickens, pots, tools, and even their dogs. How can we stop it?" the county Party secretary asked in Ruijin.[13] The woman at the Martyrs' Museum told me that tens of thousands also ran away from Yudu County. The county and district officials were dismissed because they could not stop it. Most of them were killed. Their bodies were flung into the river at night and were still there in the morning, turning in the current.

Soon frightened officials and militiamen joined the flight too, taking more people and even weapons with them. Worse still, some people came back with the advancing Nationalist troops as scouts, guides, and spies. Chiang's overwhelming forces were already crushing the Red Army. With the additional intelligence Chiang now had, the army had even less chance. The physical capacity of the Jiangxi base was exhausted. Whatever support the Communists still enjoyed they had squandered with the purges. They could not possibly hold out and consequently had to leave and go on the March.

Incredibly, before they did so, the Party ordered yet another purge. It was to clear up the remains of the "class enemies" in the Army, to strengthen discipline and prevent desertion, and among those who would stay behind, to make sure they were loyal. Several thousands, including many Communist intellectuals, officers, and captured Nationalist commanders, were rounded up in a dozen centers in Ruijin. After interrogation, they were taken to a military court deep in the mountains, where they heard this verdict: "You have committed serious crimes against the Revolution. We cannot have people like you. We are now sending you home."[14] They were ordered to walk to a huge pit nearby, where men waited to chop their heads off, and then kick them into the pit. The killing continued for two months after the Long March began.

The gruesome history of the last purge and what had gone before in the Jiangxi Soviet was recorded in painful detail by Gong Chu. I had read his memoir *The Red Army and I* some time before; knowing he wrote it after he left the Red Army and the Party in 1934, I was unsure of him. How much could I trust the account of a "traitor," who had to justify himself and what he had done? He revealed so many shocking stories—how the Red Army burned and looted to survive, how officers walked around after a battle to finish off anyone who was still alive; how a top commander was denounced for eating meat and playing poker; and how everyone lived in total fear in the Jiangxi Soviet. I simply could not associate them with the Party. Twenty years of Communist upbringing had left their stamp on me, when all I was told, heard, and read was the good things the Party did.

But after talking to the survivors, seeing the legacy of history, finding out about events that did not appear in textbooks, and listening to tales that people would not forget as long as they lived—everything convinced me of the validity of these stories. In the 1980s, President Yang Shangkun, himself a witness of the purge in Jiangxi, asked officials to investigate and he was told that Gong's book was "fairly accurate." Rereading the book on my journey, I could understand what made Gong give up the Communist cause. This was the reason he gave:

> Every day I had nightmares. I seemed to have the images of tens of thousands of people floating in front of me. They were groaning, they were crying, they were screaming, they were struggling, and they were rebelling. I doubted they were nightmares because I had witnessed them.[15]

I returned to Yudu the next day in the early evening. The sun had, as we say, lost its poison, no longer burning with the heat of day. I strolled past Mao's residence back toward the river. His choice of that tiny courtyard now made sense. Perhaps nobody would think of leaving him behind, but he did not want to take the slightest chance. When he was told the Red Army was to leave from Yudu, he came here to wait rather than stay in Ruijin. And in Yudu he chose a house which could hardly have been closer to the nearest crossing point. He could not be without the army he had created, the revolution he had led. He was confident he would rise again, and with this army he would rebound and realize his ambition.

At about six o'clock in the evening on October 18, 1934, Mao left his house walking alongside the stretcher he had built for himself—two long bamboo poles with hemp ropes zigzagging across them, and thin sticks curved in arches over them, covered with a sheet of oilcloth to keep off the sun and rain.[16] He would need it. He had not fully recovered from his malaria, though the best doctor from Ruijin had got him just about fit to travel.

He joined the Central Column with his bodyguards, secretaries, and cook, and the porters who carried his stretcher. His wife, seven months pregnant, was assigned to the convalescent unit; she would be carried on a stretcher throughout the March. He left his 2-year-old son behind with his brother and sister-in-law—no children were allowed. This was the second child he had had to leave, and he never saw either of them again. Mao was also leaving the base which he had set up and fought for, the place where he had gained and lost his political eminence. He walked toward the river, into the dusk of evening.

# 4 ★ MIST OVER THE XIANG RIVER

Chiang Kaishek's plane soared into the air from Nanchang, the provincial capital of Jiangxi. It was October 15, 1934. The *Central Daily* headline read, "Chiang Confident He Will Get Reds." It compared the Communists to the faltering end of an arrow's flight. Chiang looked down at the land, the green hills and meandering rivers of Jiangxi, and had a sense of relief, even jubilation. For almost a year, he had been in Nanchang, taking personal charge of the Fifth Campaign, which he thought would take care of the Communists once and for all. He felt free to tour the North and to spread his ideas for running China, unaware that Mao and his men were escaping under his nose and at that very moment. Still less did he know how easily the 86,000 men and women had broken through his lines of defense.

The biggest culprit was Chen Jitang, the warlord of Guangdong, the first province the Red Army had to pass through from Jiangxi. He had defied Chiang's economic blockade of the Red area by trading tungsten with the Communists. He did not like the Communists—he killed over 10,000 of them in Canton between 1931 and 1935 because they dared to challenge his rule—but he hated Chiang just as much, knowing his ultimate goal was to finish off all the warlords. He held anti-Chiang oath sessions with his officers, when they drank wine mixed with chicken blood, shouted "Down with the biggest dictator," and then thrashed straw men or wooden sticks representing him. On October 6, 1934, immediately before the commencement of the Long March, he signed a secret treaty which arranged for a ceasefire, exchange of intelligence, free trade, and right of way for the Red Army—his troops would retreat 20 kilometers from the route of the March. He presented a parting gift of 1,200 boxes of bullets, which had been air-dropped by Chiang for him to fight the Communists. Even his nephew could not understand, saying, "Good grief, you let the Communists escape before your own eyes. I thought you hated them."[1]

His neighbors, the warlords of Guangxi, Li and Bai, were even more hostile to Chiang. They made their first bid to oust him in 1929, but were sold out by their allies, who were bribed by Chiang with a few million silver dollars. As the Chinese say, if you have money, you can make ghosts work for you—let alone unscrupulous warlords. Li and Bai openly claimed, "Chiang hates us more than he does Mao and Zhu. If Mao and Zhu exist, we exist; if they are gone, we will be gone too. Why should we create this opportunity for him? We let Mao and Zhu live, and we will live too."[2] Chiang appointed Li as Commander of the Southern Route to chase the Red Army, with an up-front payment of three quarters of a million *yuan*, and then half a million a month for his army, plus 100 heavy machines guns, 40 cannons, and 1,000 boxes of bullets. He sent back a cable to confirm his acceptance and took his payment; but he did not lift a finger to organize the chase.

Chiang was exasperated, but he came up with what he thought was a perfect plan. He had just the excuse to enter the warlords' territories and take control of them. He even became excited by the opportunity—the other half of China, from Guangdong in the South, Guizhou and Yunnan in the Southwest, and Sichuan the biggest trophy of all, might be his at the end of the day. He spelled out his plan: "We do not have to wage war to conquer Guizhou . . . Henceforward if we do the right thing . . . we can unify the country."[3] Chiang and the warlords were, as we say, sharing the same bed but with different dreams. Chiang could not wait to get into the warlords' turf and attack the Red Army at the same time; the warlords wanted to speed the Red Army on its way to deny Chiang just such an excuse.

The Red Army could not move fast. Liu Bocheng, the Chief of Staff sacked by Braun, compared the March to an emperor's sedan chair. Carrying it at the front were the 1st and 3rd Corps; behind were the 8th and 9th, with the 5th Corps guarding the rear. In the middle were the Military Commission and the Central Column. The Military Commission had over 4,000 staff from the communications, logistics, engineers, artillery, hospital, and cadet units, and the Red Army Political Department. The Central Column consisted of the Jiangxi Red government, reduced in size but with all its key functions intact, and 7,000 reserves and porters carrying files and cupboards, the entire content of the Ruijin Library, the Red Army's reserves of silver and gold in 200 battered kerosene cans, sewing machines, printing equipment, repair plant, and the cumbersome X-ray machine packed carefully in a coffin-size box which alone needed two dozen men to carry it. As Edgar Snow said, it was a nation on the move, 86,000 men and women with everything they might need in their new base. The autumn rains which fell at this time of year for days on end did not help either. The columns only managed three kilometers on the first day.

The rain and the march, even at a snail's pace, did not dampen Soldier Huang's spirits. He was excited by his first foray into the big world. They slept by day and marched at night to avoid the Nationalist planes, although there were none to be seen. At first he found it hard and kept dozing off and falling. One night his bamboo torch scorched his hair, but he soon got the hang of it. He found the march a pleasant change from battles, cannon fire, bombing raids, and the dreaded turtle-shells. "The enemy seemed to have evaporated," he said. "I wondered why the leaders hadn't got us out and marching earlier. It would have saved a lot of lives."

After a few days, the accents of the people in the towns and villages they passed through began to change and Huang became concerned. Where were they going? How long were they going away for? Were they coming back? Nobody knew. His commissar told them, "We belong to the Party. Wherever the Party points, we will go." But when the local dialect became completely incomprehensible, he was really worried. He did not know they had already left Jiangxi and were in Guangdong Province. He kept stopping and looking back, maybe trying to remember the route or just missing his home—he was not sure. He had to be pushed back into the marching column. And then after five weeks, they were in a strange land of green cone-shaped hills wreathed in mist, rearing up above gleaming rivers. To the Chinese, this was, and still is, a paradise on earth—Guilin in Guangxi Province, southwestern

China. But to Huang and his comrades, it meant they were too far from home, and they wanted to go back.

Right from the beginning, desertion was a serious problem. Woman Wang remembered the warning from their political commissar in the Central Column before they set off: "Comrades, we are entering the White area . . . You should be extra careful. Do not fall behind. Don't be tempted by the enemy's propaganda. And be vigilant about deserters."[4] But the caution had little effect on the reserves and the porters, who were the first to desert. Party documents, cupboards, costumes and sets for plays, and pots and pans were dumped. Heavy equipment such as the printing machines was carried first by eight, then six, then four men; finally it had to be abandoned or buried. There were not enough porters to carry the X-ray machine, the prize possession of the Red Army hospital. In the end, Mao persuaded them to bury it: "When the whole country is ours, you will have as many X-ray machines as you like. Chiang will have prepared them for you. Don't worry about it now."

Wang could not relinquish her wounded, not a single one. She had twelve porters to carry her six officers. She chatted with them like a sister, offering them her own ration of rice, and boiled water for them to soak their feet at the end of the day. Just three days into the March, one of them begged to be released—he was missing his wife and children. Wang told him of the importance of his work for the Revolution, but he would not listen.

"Whose revolution?" he retorted. "How can I protect my home and my children by abandoning them?" One night he complained of a stomach problem and disappeared.

"I had kept an eye on him, but I couldn't tell him not to release himself," Wang said. "Thank heaven and earth, he did no harm to the officer he was carrying. Otherwise I would have been finished." Eight of her porters ran away in the first month; finding replacements was a real headache. Few were willing to go for more than two days while they could still return home easily. Later she found a solution. "In many provinces we passed through, the people were opium addicts. I begged them to help us and they would yawn and ask if we had opium.

When I said yes, they immediately perked up. After they had their fixes, they got up and carried the stretchers as if they were feathers."

But she was often reduced to tears. One day, two porters ran away, and by the time she noticed the missing stretcher, it was dark. She found the abandoned officer not far from where they had started that morning. She carried him on her back to the camp—it was already early morning. "I don't know how I managed it. So many times, I thought I could not get up and face another day," she recalled. "But the Party had trusted me to take care of these men. If I had one breath left in me, I had to make sure they were safe and sound." It was the soldiers from the fighting units who came to her rescue.

The soldiers, however, began to desert too. The Commissar of the 5th Corps, Chen Bojun, kept one of the most detailed and accurate diaries of the Long March. He noted his concern in many entries. "Today over 100 soldiers dropped behind on the march," reads one. Another says, "Today two men went missing with their rifles, it is most worrying. Our ten-man units must keep up their vigilance to stop this happening again."[5]

The ten-man unit consisted of the most loyal Party members, selected one from each platoon. Its task was to work on the new recruits and anyone who was thought not to be sufficiently committed, and prevent people from lagging behind, deserting, or surrendering to the enemy—they were to kill them if they could not stop them. They needed no permission from the military officers, and were responsible only to the Political Protection Bureau—the secret police. The head of the bureau had absolute power; the Bureau was answerable only to the Party Central Committee; it could kill without recourse to the commissars or any other authority. He called a meeting of all the ten-man units, instructing them:

> This cannot go on. It will destroy the army. We must
> strengthen the activities of our ten-man groups . . . Generally,
> the deserters first pretend to be ill, or too feeble to walk, and
> then purposely lag behind; then they leave their units. Finally
> they sneak into the houses of the locals and hide there, and
> find their way home. We must stop them.[6]

The Political Department sent out urgent orders:

> From those who desert on purpose, who harm the welfare of
> the masses, and who refuse to return to their units, we must
> choose examples, and carry out widespread struggle within the
> Red Army. We must punish them severely. The most serious
> offenders will be executed.[7]

And then the propaganda teams set to work:

> Comrades, bear the hardship without any grudge. We are go-
> ing to take big cities soon, where there are lots of spoils and
> treats. Be brave, don't lag behind, and march on resolutely!

But the cascade of deserters continued. The numbers from the 2nd
Army were very telling, as we know from the frank and thorough diary
kept by its commissar. They started with 10,068 people; in six months,
698 died in battle, 300 were wounded and left behind, 137 were missing but unexplained, 208 defected to the Nationalists, and 4,004 deserted. Of the latter, 1,012 were caught and convicted of frequent
offenses, and 857 were executed.[8] A dozen from Huang's company ran
away. One of them was caught, for the second time. He was made to
confess as the men stood by and then he was ordered to kneel. He was
shot in the head. Huang remembered how the man's brains splattered
all round him. If he ever thought of desertion again, he never tried it.

Huang talked very honestly about his frequent desire to quit. Desertion was as much a reality as bombing and pursuit by the Nationalists, but there is no mention of it in the history of the Long March. Red
Army men were made of steel. How could they desert? That was what
Chiang's men did. The drastic reduction of the 1st Army from 86,000
to barely 30,000 in the first six weeks of the March was attributed to the
Xiang River battle. It was the first big one the 1st Army fought. This is
the general description of it in the official history of the Long March:
"The battle on the Xiang River was the longest and the most heroic on
the Long March. It involved the largest number of soldiers and the
fiercest fighting, with the heaviest casualties for the Red Army, a loss of

almost 50,000 men in five days."[9] Of course, we were reminded that the tragedy was the fault of Braun and his followers.

I remembered watching the battle in the *Long March* series made by Chinese Central Television. The director placed himself and two other men on the riverbank, and said to the camera that if the 50,000 bodies lay like them, they would stretch for 20 kilometers. I was amazed. What was the river like that swallowed 50,000 men? I wanted to see for myself.

The Xiang River, a tributary of the Yangzi, winds through Hunan and Guangxi provinces, and pours into the South China Sea. I joined it in Xingan, which has the Monument to the Martyrs of the Xiang River. Built in 1996, it is the biggest revolutionary memorial in the country. I was stunned by the giant sculptures that greet the visitors: first, huge faces 11 meters high, five times life-size, carved in grey granite—a grim-looking soldier, a serenely smiling young woman, an old man—and then friezes depicting the Red Army, and peasants and workers supporting them. The effect is powerful; they cry out to you as if they were the souls of the tens of thousands who died in the battle. The monument is at the top of a long flight of stairs, as though they want us to climb and experience the hardship of the March. It is made up of three giant concrete guns linked together, seeming to pierce the sky, and symbolizing Mao's dictum "Power comes out of the barrel of a gun." On my way up, I saw a large group of army cadets making pledges in front of a red flag held by two people, their arms upraised. "We owe our life today to millions of martyrs like those who died here. Let us walk on the bloodstained path left by them, hold the red flag high, and continue our revolution."

The vault beneath the three guns was the exhibition hall. I felt disappointed—after the imposing façade, it is a letdown. The exhibition hall itself is just one small room, and there is very little in it: the usual photographs of the main leaders, a couple of dusty glass cases with a pistol and a grey uniform, and a crude model of the battle plan. The inscription could not be briefer, just a few lines repeating what the textbooks say. I knocked on the door on the way out to see if I could find a guide who could tell me a bit more. A young man with big round glasses invited me to sit down after he heard my inquiries. My first question was that I could not see any river. Where was it?

"You're right. The real battleground is too far, 15 kilometers from here. Nobody would go. This is on the way to Guilin, so it is a must for everyone."

Perhaps he had a point, considering how little I knew about the battle when I started out on my journey.

"I didn't know the Red Army fought here either until I got this job in 1991," he said. "I grew up here. We all learned about the Long March in school. Still, I had no idea they passed through my village. And they had the toughest battle of the entire March on my own doorstep."

He was not the only one who did not know. When the Propaganda Ministry in Beijing decided to make a film to commemorate the fiftieth anniversary of the Long March, it gave the program on the Xiang River battle to Hunan, the province next to Jiangxi. They said they had not heard of it. It was passed to Guangxi Province, but the Guangxi historians knew nothing about it either. They asked the experts in Beijing, and finally got an answer. I asked the young man what he thought was the reason for our ignorance.

He thought for a while. "So many people died here—50,000 men. It was a big defeat. We are used to talking about victories. Who wants to broadcast their failures?"

He then went on to explain why they decided to build the monument. "The Red Army had 86,000 men when they left Jiangxi and there were barely 30,000 after they crossed the Xiang River. Fifty thousand men were dead. We have to explain to the people what happened. We have to respect history, but it takes time to admit a terrible loss such as this. Ours is the last of the Long March monuments, though it is the biggest. I think it has to be the biggest because here lie the souls of 50,000 martyrs."

But why was there so little information here about the battle? I asked.

"You ask too many questions," he said, suddenly becoming irritated. "What do you expect? The battle took place seventy years ago.

Most survivors have passed away. Our museum is new, there aren't that many objects left from that time. We are still looking for things."

After Jiangxi, I felt the urge to question everything I read or was told because nothing was what it seemed or what I had been taught, but I did not think I was going to get more answers here. Before I left, I told him about the army cadets on the steps, and asked what he thought they would get out of coming here.

"They will learn three things," he said crisply. "How did the Red Army preserve the Party even though it was ten times weaker than Chiang? How did defeat in the Xiang River battle prepare for Mao's comeback? Braun commanded the Xiang River battle and the last campaign in Jiangxi, and the Red Army lost. Only Mao's military strategy was the sure way to victory."

I was glad that the museum was built to commemorate the martyrs, and that the defeat was admitted. At least that was a step forward—a large one in the history of the Communist Party. The monument is so big, so splendid, no doubt costing a lot of money and considerable thought, but why is it so empty of explanations, of the lessons drawn from the battle? We are offered just one sentence: ". . . as a result of the erroneous military command and the escape policy adopted by Braun and Bo Gu, the Red Army was reduced from 86,000 to barely 30,000 after the battle at the Xiang River." Is this really true? I was thinking of the desertions that Huang and Wang mentioned soon after the March began. Were those deserters accounted for? Were they included in the missing thousands? Perhaps the truth is far too complicated, but whatever it is, this one-sentence explanation is too light to bear the weight of the tragedy. Or, as an English playwright has said, the best way to forget an event is to commemorate it.[10]

On the way out, I asked if there were any survivors in the vicinity. "Ah, there is an old man called Liu who lives in a village. He is from Jiangxi, and stayed on after the battle. He tells a good story. The most important thing is, he hasn't lost his marbles like the others. Unfortunately, he is not the right type for us, if you know what I mean. But you might like to talk to him."

I thought I would go and see the river first. I could not wait. It was almost dark when I arrived in Jieshou. The town had been the front-line headquarters and the main fording place for the Military Commission and Central Column across the Xiang River. There were no streetlights, just feeble glimmers from a few houses filtering through the evening shadows. A couple of restaurants were open, to animals as well as humans: dogs and chickens strolled in and out, sniffing here and there, picking up a morsel or two. I bought myself a packet of biscuits from the shop next door—only to find its sell-by date was eighteen months earlier. The one hotel in town was shut. I waited half an hour and a man emerged from the Internet café behind it to let me in. He gave me a most charming welcome—"No towel, no toilet paper, no hot water, no breakfast"—and went back to his cyberworld, locking the door on his way. There was nothing to do but sleep.

I walked out in the morning. The air was clear and fresh, with a faint trace of sweetness. The mist was receding to reveal the gentle water, flowing imperceptibly; there was more movement in the ripples from a woman doing an early morning wash. It was not as wide as I had imagined, perhaps 50 meters or so. On the far side there were trees and paddy fields; this side was the old town: a cobbled street a mile long, lined with old houses and shops. At the end of the street, standing on its own facing the river, was a small but gracious temple called "Three Lords, Heaven, Earth, and Water." This had been the headquarters itself, commandeered by the Red Army.

Not far from it I came to a street stall, where an old couple were stoking their oven and bringing out bowls and chopsticks ready for breakfast customers—there was rice porridge, soy milk, steamed buns, wonton soup. I bought two buns and asked them if they had lived here all their lives. "Yes, we were born and bred here," said the woman. "I've never been more than 10 kilometers away."

Was the river always this wide? I asked.

"Now is the low season. In the summer there is more water, and the river flows more rapidly." Seventy years ago, the Red Army crossed it in the same month—November 1934. I asked the couple what they remembered about the big battle.

"When the Japanese bombed us, that was a big battle. The place was turned to rubble," they said together.

What about earlier, in the winter of 1934? I asked. They looked at each other, then at me. "Another big battle?" Had they forgotten? I waited and finished my second bun. "Wait and have more buns. I'll go and get someone who knows everything," the man said.

He ran down the lane and a few minutes later he came back with a man who was much older, with white bushy eyebrows and the air of a wise Kung Fu master. He turned to the pair. "I think she was asking about the Red Army. You were still stuck on your mothers' tits, that's why you don't remember. Most people were scared and ran away. My family made cotton quilts, we could not take them and run, so we stayed. I was 12 at the time. When the Red Army arrived, we found them very nice. They told us a big battle was coming."

What did he see? I asked.

"Oh, chaos. Chaos everywhere," he said quickly as he took a stool and sat down. "It was not so bad at the beginning, but after a few days everything was thrown into uproar, as if someone had overturned a beehive. You can't believe it. They put up pontoons over the river but there were so many people waiting to cross it. The horses were too frightened to walk on the pontoons, and men were pushing them, then they fell into the water themselves. They dropped stuff everywhere. I even found a pen later."

The old man's account confirmed Huang and Wang's experience at the Xiang River. Huang crossed it on the evening of November 27, 1934. He had an easy time. There was no fighting, no chase. "It was as if we'd entered no-man's-land," he recalled. "We had the river to ourselves." He did not know that the warlords of Guangxi had moved their troops south to avoid the Red Army, while Chiang's crack force was still 150 miles behind. For five days a 40-mile stretch of the river had no defense, but the gigantic Central Column with all its core personnel could not walk fast enough—they covered barely 6 miles a day. Meanwhile, Chiang found out that the local warlords were not doing what he had asked them. While putting pressure on them, he ordered his crack force to speed up, and brought his planes into action.

When Wang arrived at Jieshou with the Central Column four days after Huang, the scene had changed. Nationalist reconnaissance planes had discovered the pontoons and started bombing. Wang saw equipment abandoned in the middle of the road; the wounded on stretchers were crying in pain; mules which had lost their handlers were knocking men down and treading on them; dazed soldiers asked if anyone knew where their units were. "Nobody was following orders. Officers even had to fire into the air to calm people down," Wang said ruefully. "The units behind us kept pushing; the people in front hardly moved. One of the porters fell and nearly threw his charge on the ground. I had great difficulty getting all my stretchers onto the pontoons."

Further up the river, a commissar saw a scene he would never forget: "Scattered in all directions were books and papers—military manuals, maps, books on strategy, the agrarian question, problems of the Chinese Revolution, works on political economy, on Marxism, Leninism, books in English, French, and German. The library under which Red Army bearers had staggered all the way from Ruijin lay here, pages torn, books muddy, bindings crushed. All our ideological armory, all our military literature had been tossed aside."[11]

The old man said there was no fighting in the town, and the casualties were mainly due to the bombing. He heard that 30 kilometers north of Jieshou, the Red Army had some really tough battles, but he could not give me more details. Those were exactly the battles fought by Soldier Huang's division—Division 2 of the 1st Corps. After they had crossed the river, they took up positions due north of Jieshou. Their task was to hold off the Hunan warlord's troops, who were fighting hard to keep the Red Army out of their territory. But after three days, the tail end of the Red Army was still east of the river. After midnight on November 30, Huang and his comrades were woken up to hear the latest order from headquarters:

> Today's battle will affect the fate of the whole army. To be able to move westward will open the path to future development. Any delay will cause our army to be cut up by the enemy. The leaders and commanders of the 1st and 3rd Corps must go to their companies and give them pre-battle motivation. Make all soldiers and officers understand the significance of today's battle: either we win or we lose.[12]

At dawn the mist on the river was so heavy it almost swallowed it. Huang thought it was good for defense. There were odd shots here and there, but the enemy could not really see their targets. Soon, though, the cannons started to roar, their fire slowly dispersing the mist, revealing the mountains, the fields, the soldiers, and the banners. The real battle began.

"The worst was the bombers, they seemed to turn the sky black. The best we could do was to use the craters the bombs made as trenches," Huang remembered with a shudder. A bomb landed 100 yards from him, creating a whirlwind that lifted him like a straw, and the whole earth shook. Thick smoke shrouded everything for a moment, and then he saw some thirty bodies, or their limbs and torsos, scattered around the crater. The trees had been stripped of their leaves, even the wind seemed to be baked by the bomb's heat, and the air was filled with the burning of flesh and blood. That was when Huang lost some of his hearing. After the bombing came wave after wave of enemy troops. They fought ferociously, often hand to hand. Slowly they fell back, and Huang saw many of his comrades die.

There was a strange sunset at the end of the last day's fighting. In the distance, crimson mountains edged the horizon, draining the last color from the sun. Everything turned redder and redder, until sky and mountains were one. That was when Orderly Liu came to the river. He could hear shots from behind him going off like popcorn: it was the rear guard in its last struggle with Chiang's troops. The pontoons were gone; the soldiers stood there, shocked by the color of the river and the bodies floating on the water. He was so frightened he cried and wanted to turn back and run away. But his commander told him to jump in or they would all be dead. He shut his eyes and took the plunge. He was among the last of the 1st Army to cross the Xiang River.

I had tracked Liu to a village 10 miles away. The landscape was all green, the mountains right in front of me, the intricate forests of bamboo, the orange and pomelo trees the peasants planted around their houses. It was like walking into a painting. I found it hard to imagine that a ferocious battle to cover the river crossing had taken place nearby. There was nobody about—the harvest was in and people had gone to the cities for work. Liu's house was tucked in at the foot of the mountain, where you could go no further—it was as if he did not want to be found. The courtyard had chickens and ducks running about, trees growing, pigs in the pigsty. The walls had all sorts of tools hanging up, side by side with strings of bright red dried chilies. It was a picture of self-sufficiency.

Liu was 86, but looked much younger in his bright yellow and orange sweatshirt; he was still fit, lean, and agile from his work in the fields. He reminded me a little of Soldier Huang—he was also from Jiangxi. When I told him the staff at the monument had given me his address, he looked puzzled. "That's odd. They used to invite me to give talks there, but they stopped. I guess I annoyed them by always starting the talk saying the Long March was very different from what they knew. For example, I didn't want to go on it at all, but the Party forced me into it just before the March began."

I could see he was not the veteran to instill a sense of loyalty and devotion to the army into young cadets. No, he did not think that he was a good model, then or now. After he joined the Red Army, they made him a bugler—he was too small for anything else. He screamed for days to get out of it. "In our village, that's what you do when people die, blow trumpets and bugles," he said grimly. "It made me feel the dead were my fault. I didn't mind getting up early to practice. I wasn't bothered by having to learn the codes either, dozens of them. But I couldn't bear the thought of more people dying because of me. So I screamed and screamed. They didn't know what to do with me. In the end, they made me an orderly instead."

Liu could not remember which regiment, division, or corps he served in. It was all a blur, except for the battle on the Xiang River, the first and the last he experienced—the battle that changed his life. "It was unbelievable. The river was like a bath full of blood. There were so many bodies floating on the water, like dead locusts." He stopped to wipe tears from the corners of his eyes. "I dropped my rifle. It was too heavy and I had to use my hands to push the bodies aside to swim across. I was so exhausted, I almost sank. I could have ended my life then and no one would have known, but I held on to a floating body like a log, paddled for a few minutes, and then took a rest. It took me ages to cross."

After he reached the other bank, he could not find his battalion commander. "Perhaps I took too long and he thought I was dead, so he left without me," Liu said, shaking his head. His clothes were soaked in blood; he threw them away, put on an outfit stripped from a dead soldier, and picked up a rifle nearby. Now he had to make up his mind where to go. He stood there lost, while men rushed this way and that. In the end, he decided to follow the biggest group he could see. They walked in the night till they reached a village, then they were awoken by a huge explosion. The men ran in every direction, but straight into machine-gun fire on every side. He ran too, but a soldier just in front of him was hit and fell on him backwards, knocking him out. When he came to, he found a Nationalist soldier standing over him with a rifle. "I was terrified. I could do nothing but hand over my gun and surrender," Liu said. He thought they were the only Red Army soldiers caught, but when the Nationalists walked him to the nearest town, he saw hundreds if not thousands of captured Red Army men. They were put in a school where they were fed twice a day. "But there were so many of us, the Nationalists ran out of food after a while. So they let us go," Liu said with glee. Some went back to Jiangxi, but he could not remember the name of his village. So he stayed on, scraping a living as a shepherd.

How many did he think died in the Xiang River battle? I asked.

"I think more people ran away than were killed," Liu said straightaway. "Take my battalion. As we were marching, the unit became thinner and thinner. It was not clear whether they went astray, fell behind, or deserted. Whenever we passed through a village, some would disappear into the houses and were never seen again. If I had been a soldier, not an orderly so close to the battalion commander, I might have run off," he said, with his voice lowered. When he came to the river, there were barely two dozen men left in his battalion. He was not sure how many of them crossed and how many turned back.

The number of deaths in the battle has become something of a statistical game. The few descriptions in the history books speak of fighting on two days, November 30 and December 1, 1934, involving mainly the 1st and 3rd Corps. The official story says the Red Army lost two-thirds of its 86,000 men, but it is implausible that they could all have died in battle. Harrison Salisbury, who was given every access to the sources by the Communist Party, was unable to find an exact figure. He estimated that at most 15,000 died at the Xiang River, the heaviest casualties—6,000—occurring to the 1st Corps that Huang belonged to. But that still leaves over 30,000 men unaccounted for. Nobody wants to admit it but the majority almost certainly deserted.

From the few things that Liu could recollect, it seems that he belonged to the 8th Corps. It had been formed hastily with over 11,000 new recruits right before the Long March began. On the March, it was cushioned between the tough 1st and 5th Corps. As Liu remembered, he hardly experienced any fighting until the Xiang River; even then, his unit was mainly running rather than fighting. Only 600 of nearly 11,000 men in the two divisions of the 8th Corps made it across the river, and the commander was court-martialed.[13] Three other divisions—the 15th, 22nd, and 34th, belonging to three other corps—also went missing east of the river without crossing it—they too were entirely new recruits. As Braun pointed out, all five divisions, over 25,000 men, had been drafted in the months before the Long March. They received little training and I thought they might have contributed to the heavy casualties, but we also know from Braun that they were mainly used for cover or in the rear, and almost never engaged in major battles.[14] As with the porters and the 7,000 reserves in the Central Column, their disappearance had to be explained mainly by desertion, lagging behind, or death from disease.

Before I left, I asked Liu about the photo on the altar table in his sitting room of a youth in military uniform, like a younger version of himself, next to a large poster of Mao. He said it was his grandson. Why did he join the army? "Totally different story." He gulped down a big mug of cold water from a barrel, and wiped his mouth. "Now it is good to be in the army: no battles, no risk, plenty of bullets, and all the fancy equipment. They even give him regular pay. It is like a pancake falling into your lap. They are spoiled. If it was like it was in my day, I would never have let him join up." I could see in his eyes both pride and re-gret: regret that his brief army career, however reluctant he had been to join, ended in humiliating capture; pride that his grandson would in-herit the Red Army tradition and maybe become an officer with stand-ing in the village and a good life. That had been his own dream.

I went back to the river and took a long walk, watching the clear, placid water and the reflections of the houses along the bank. It was a beautiful evening scene, but slowly mist rose up, gradually swallowing the river. I could no longer see how wide or deep it was. Very appropri-ate, I thought—like the mystery surrounding the Xiang River battle, one that I did not know from my schoolbooks, that was now said to have finished off two-thirds of the 1st Army, but that some claimed never took place. A fierce battle did happen here, and the river did run with blood, though surely not the blood of 50,000. Too many burdens have been put on the river.

I had not thought much about desertion before; it was not some-thing I connected with the Red Army, but for the veterans I talked with it was just a natural part of the experience of the March; some of them contemplated it themselves. And when I thought of how hard Woman Wang had to work to meet her quota of recruits, I could understand why the commitment was not there for so many. It was the iron disci-pline of the Red Army that kept the rest going through so many thou-sands of painful miles. The Long March was a kind of selection, like panning for gold: the water and the sand run off, and the gold remains. Many good and brave men died or were left behind, sick or wounded, but those who reached the end of the March out of the tens of thou-sands who started, really were heroic. They endured so much, over-came so much. They were invincible. They paved the way for the Revolution. Every single one who came through was proud of what they achieved. I had to respect them, admire them.

## 5 ★ HUNGRY SOULS

"The Reds are coming! They are coming!" a peddler shouted as he ran toward the town of Shiqian. The market outside the city wall was thrown into panic. People grabbed their things and started to run. Inside the wall they put up the shutters of their shops and barred the doors of their houses. Some grabbed a few clothes, poured onto the streets, and surged toward the south gate, but it was too late. The vanguard units had already blocked it, and turned them back. Two German priests from the church turned around and headed for the north gate, while a third on a mule was still pushing ahead toward the south gate. He made it outside the gate but was pulled off the mule by a band of soldiers; his hands were tied behind his back and he was led away.

Meanwhile, each unit swiftly picked out its target: the *yamen*—the magistrate's courtyard, the Catholic church, the Confucian temple, the chamber of commerce, the post office, the biggest houses, the smartest shops. The soldiers who surrounded the magistrate's residence pushed open the gate and started searching for plunder: money, clothes, food, grain, opium, anything valuable. They carried it all off, and led away the magistrate and his family. They had even more of a field day with the shops, carting off rolls of cloth, cartons of cigarettes, boxes of medicine, sacks of rice and sugar, stacks of paper, barrels of opium, ham . . . The loot was taken to the Catholic church, which was commandeered as headquarters for the army, and the Committee for Confiscation. The rich people who did not manage to escape—there were plenty of them—were led to the town's prison as hostages.

Hygienist Chen was busy putting up posters on the shops which had had their contents taken away—by now he had done a shoe shop, a teahouse, a grocer's. His mind was buzzing, and his mouth was watering. He could hardly wait. His platoon would receive their share of the spoils from the Confiscation Committee. They were in luck; the Spring Festival was coming and many households had saved for it all year and were filled with provisions. He could hear pigs squealing. He looked at his bare feet—perhaps a new pair of shoes! And he would be allocated space in a nice house and have a few days' rest—just eat and sleep, with three meals a day, and every meal with pork or vegetables at least. That was what they always did after they took a town.

Chen still had an almost childish happiness on his face when he recalled the taking of Shiqian. He was 83, one of the youngest of the survivors I interviewed, and in a special rest home for senior army officers, but he looked younger than all the others. His face had a pink glow and a ready smile; his voice was gentle and often choked with emotion. He burst into sobs so many times while we talked that I felt I should not continue. I was worried about his health—he had just come out of the hospital. A hygienist on the March, a medic ever since, and running a big hospital prior to his retirement, he had seen a great deal of death, and thus he appreciated his life. He kept a note of all the comrades he saw die, many in his own arms. There was little he could do to help them—medicine was scarce, particularly on the Long March. "If I had just had enough cloth, or simple injections like quinine, or even salt to disinfect the wounds, they would not have died." His voice was trembling again, but when I asked him about taking towns like Shiqian, he was as lively as a 13-year-old. "That is the most exciting thing, much more than battles, because I knew we were going to get plenty to eat. Just imagine: medicine, salt, sugar, meat, cloth, shoes, paper. What could be better?" I could imagine how a 13-year-old boy would react seeing all those things after a childhood of poverty.

I asked him how they knew who the landlords were.

"The Political Department gave very clear and clever instructions about how to target the landlords and extract the maximum from them. Each regiment had a special task force to find the landlords and the rich families. People with big houses, with mailboxes, or with dogs that barked the loudest. You know the Chinese saying that dogs take after their masters. We also asked the locals—not directly because they wouldn't tell us. But if we asked them, 'Who would you borrow money from when you had to?' then they would tell us who the rich families were."

Did many flee?

"You know the saying, Even if the monks flee, the monastery stays. The rich could not possibly take much with them, especially not their silver dollars. They were quite heavy. Often they buried them. We would search in the dirtiest places, like the pigsty, or we would pour water on the walls or the ground—wherever it soaked in fastest, it meant it had been disturbed recently. That's how we found things. That's how we got most of our supplies on the Long March. The Nationalist propaganda called us Communist bandits, looting and killing everywhere. They were liars. We only took from the rich. It ensured our survival and victory." Then he added apologetically, "We got it wrong sometimes."

Chen served with the 2nd Corps, headed by the flamboyant He Long. He made his money and reputation by taxing the opium caravans coming from upstream of the Yangzi River and helping the poor. He did not smoke it himself but always offered it to his guests after sumptuous banquets of Western and Chinese cuisine prepared by his own excellent chef. Both the Nationalists and the Communists had tried to win him over. He joined the Nationalists, but decided they were no better than the warlords. Then he switched to the Communists and became commander-in-chief in their first armed insurrection against Chiang in Nanchang, on August 1, 1927. The uprising failed miserably. The Communists were unprepared and Chiang's forces were overwhelming. He Long went back home to the mountains of Hunan, regrouping his men. Within weeks, he had thousands of men, many from his old days. Later, he joined up with another guerrilla force and his reputation just grew.

Chen was intrigued by He's reputation—it was reputed that no bullets could touch him, no enemy could catch him, and he was such a good speaker that he could "raise the dead to fight." When He Long's troops passed through his village, they killed a landlord, and his pigs. They boiled the meat in a big pot right in the center of the village, and the fragrance spread everywhere. They told him when he joined the

Red Army, he could eat pork every day. He was only 13, but said he was 15 so they would take him. He left without telling his parents. He was too small to carry a rifle, so he was selected as a messenger, and then became a hygienist after only four weeks' training. To his surprise, the army was not as big as he had heard. "I joined it at its smallest," Chen said proudly.

But Chen soon found out about something terrible—the purges in the Red Armies and the Communist bases. He's army was badly weakened by some of the worst of them. The Party chief in He's base had no trust in his bandits turned Nationalists turned Red Army soldiers. "The Party [here] has been corrupted by the KMT, and the Red Army is no different from the KMT troops," he reported to the Central Committee. He had 90 percent of the officers in the 2nd Corps above company level executed as Nationalist spies and Anti-Bolshevik cliques. The purges were not confined to the army either. Over 10,000 people were killed in a month in one district in the Honghu base. This was a conservative estimate. The killing was so rampant and so careless that an officer said of his boss, "If we executed people without getting his permission first, he would grumble, 'You are utterly clueless,' but if you killed a pig without his permission, he would scream, 'Fuck your mother!' He would get you sacked for that."[1]

They killed so many people, they did not have to wait for Chiang's campaigns; they had to leave their base in 1932, two years before the Central Army went on the Long March, because they lost the support of the local people. But the purges did not stop even when the 2nd Corps was on the run, and the way they got rid of the suspects, mostly officers who had survived earlier purges, was particularly cruel. They were put in death squads for the toughest and the riskiest battles, with only three bullets apiece. Those who died—more than half of them—would be replaced by new suspects for the next battle, but the survivors still were not to be trusted. "The reactionaries were only brave because they wanted to deceive the party so that they could carry on their activities," the Party chief declared.[2] "You would think they were possessed, or doped," Chen said, shaking his head. By the time the 2nd Corps reached Guizhou, barely 3,000 men were left of the original 30,000, and there were only five Party members. When they had to replace the head of the Political Department, one of the top jobs in the Red Army, they could not find even one person who could read or write. They had to make do with the man in charge of food supplies.

It was on such an army that the Central Army placed its hopes after abandoning Jiangxi. The plan was to join up with He Long's army in their new base in the border area of Hubei, Hunan, Sichuan, and Guizhou provinces, but there had been no contact between the Jiangxi base and He Long for two years. In August 1934, two months before the Long March began, the 6th Corps was dispatched to find He Long, and to scout the route for the main Red Army.

The 6th Corps was headed by the 26-year-old Xiao Ke, a Hunanese like He Long. A Whampoa cadet, he soon became one of the youngest generals in the Red Army. Xiao Ke looks out from his photograph, young, smiling, and confident. I am always astonished by the youth of these commanders—their average age was in the mid-twenties. When I think what I was like at 26, I can hardly believe what they did. If they made mistakes, it was only understandable. But whatever their background—Xiao Ke came from a scholarly gentry family—they had the passion, the vision, and the commitment that drove them to sacrifice themselves for the Communist cause. Xiao Ke was particularly known for being careful and meticulous, as well as very determined. That was why he was given the hard task of leading the 6th Corps on this crucial mission. To guide him from Jiangxi to Guizhou, he only had a general map of China torn from a school geography book, which showed nothing but provincial capitals, mountain ranges, and big rivers.

In the maze of mountains in Guizhou, Xiao Ke had no idea where he was or where to look for He Long's 2nd Corps. They kept going in circles and ending up in the same place. The locals they found often knew nothing about the next valley, let alone beyond. But most of the time they could find no one—hearing they were coming, people had fled to the mountains. Once they even had to carry an old lady with bound feet, who directed them by sign language. Another time, they found an addict who could not stand up straight because he had not smoked for days. The soldiers gave him some opium but could not afford to wait for him to absorb his fix, so they carried him while he chewed his wedge of opium and told them where to go. Eventually they were ambushed by the pursuing Nationalists and lost half their men. They were on the edge of despair when a Nationalist newspaper they found in a small town reported the threat from the "Red Bandits led by He Long." Well, at least he was alive! Now the question was to find where he was.

I knew where I was going, but getting there proved to be more difficult than I had imagined. My destination was Shiqian, near where the 2nd and 6th Corps finally met, and where they had hoped to set up a base. The fourteen hours by train and then by bus were the worst of my entire journey. Before we departed, the driver asked all the passengers to buy some food for the journey. "Guizhou is very poor. There are only a few dirty restaurants on the way. I don't want you to get sick and vomit all over the bus." Seeing the camera around my neck, he asked me to put it inside my rucksack or in his toolbox. "There are gangs working the route. Every day they do a few buses." On his bus too? I asked. "Why not? I'm no different from the others. But so far, there's been no blood. They want money and luxuries like your camera. You know, you are in the poorest province of the whole country—70 percent of the people here have no jobs. Many are on drugs and they need money badly. If the police arrest them, they are pleased to have a bed for the night and a meal. But the prisons are too crowded. They are on the road again the next day."

I was worried, and clung like glue to the bag with my camera in it. I felt even more uneasy when we passed road signs saying "Incident Black Spots," with police and hospital phone numbers in big red characters. I did not suppose they meant road accidents. But I soon forgot the gangs. As a saying goes, in Guizhou there are not three inches of even ground, nor three days without rain. Only now I realized how true it was. The green, steep-sided mountains went on and on. The locals were known as good singers, and no wonder; they used to sing out their messages from one mountaintop to another. It was raining, of course, and the road, much of it narrow and unsurfaced, wound like a tangled rope. I was thrown this way and that way like a puppet. I tried to hold on to the back of the driver's seat, worrying all the time that the slightest lapse of attention on his part could send the bus tumbling to the bot-

tom of the valley, and my journey would end in the mountains of
Guizhou. But the driver did this road every day—what a brave man! I
told him as much.

"Today was good. Fifteen years ago, there was no road. I remember
that when there was a mist someone had to walk in front holding a red
lantern for the bus to follow."

Perhaps it would have been safer to walk. The Red Army did find
safety in the mountains of Guizhou. The ancient forests were so dense,
once they were inside nobody could find them. Despite heavy felling
the region is still quite thickly wooded. The driver said there were tigers
here as late as the 1960s coming out onto the road. I could only imagine what it must have been like in the 1930s. I simply had no idea how
Xiao Ke and his men managed without maps or guides.

Fortunately for them, the solution came when they took a small
town, and found a large-scale map of China in a church. Xiao Ke almost jumped for joy, but the map was in a language they did not understand. His staff reminded him that the foreign missionary they had
caught that day might be able to help. Xiao Ke and the missionary sat
down after dinner; by the light of a small candle, the missionary read
out the names and together they worked out the Chinese equivalents.
Only then did Xiao Ke know he was less than 100 miles from the man
he was searching for. Three weeks later, the 2nd and 6th Corps met on
October 22, 1934, just one week after the main Red Army set out on the
Long March to join them.

The foreign missionary who came to Xiao Ke's rescue was Rudolf
Bosshardt of the London-based China Inland Mission. He and his two
fellow missionaries, one man and one woman, and their wives and two
children were caught by Xiao Ke's troops on October 1, 1934. They
were accused of being imperialist spies, and were sentenced to eighteen months' arrest; their ransoms were set at more than $100,000 each.
The women, the children, and the other missionary were released one
by one, but they held Bosshardt for 560 days, while trying to shake off
the Nationalists on their tail and find a base to settle in.

Bosshardt's day-by-day account of his captivity, *The Restraining
Hand*, is perhaps the most complete and truthful report of the Long

March. It is factual, detailed, and unemotional, nothing like the doc-
tored official versions. It recounts daily life, the food and lodging, the
marching and rest, the battles and retreats, the discipline and the
drilling, the looting and killing, the hostages and their ransom, the faith
and despair of the Red Army. In particular, the elaborate negotiations
for the missionaries' release displayed the resourcefulness and the cruel
reality of the Red Army's methods of supplying itself. He also gave a
vivid impression of his captors' good qualities: their idealism, their vitality, and the self-belief which pulled them through the unspeakable
hardships of the March.

When I arrived in Shiqian, all my tiredness evaporated. I had not
known of its existence until recently. It was one of the best-preserved
towns I visited. The cobbled main street is lined with two-story wooden
shops from centuries ago. As I looked up, I saw the families who lived
above them on their balconies, hanging up dyed cloth, feeding babies,
engrossed in their embroidery. On the road, people ambled along carrying sheaves of grain, vegetables, or heaps of freshly caught fish in
pairs of baskets hanging from poles across their shoulders. Only an occasional rasp from a motorbike whizzing by disturbed the scene. Old
men and women were sitting in twos and threes, the men in turbans
and the women with blue-and-white scarves tied in their coiled hair;
they smiled at me as I walked past. In the center of town stood the magnificent Palace of Ten-Thousand-Year Longevity. It dwarfed every other
building in town, including the Catholic church, whose tall roof stands
out against the town's pleasing green landscape of paddy fields and
hills. Built in 1909 by the Catholic Sacred Heart sect from Germany,
the white front is an odd mixture of ecclesiastical arched windows and
Chinese roof ornaments. It is now a museum commemorating the Red
Army in Shiqian.

Chen remembered Shiqian with pleasure. It would have made a
wonderful base, but it was too small for the newly combined 2nd and
6th Corps, which were now known as the 2nd Army. Still, they rested
here for a week, the first time in many months. He ate pork or duck
most days. He bathed in the famous hot springs among the rocks outside the town, which Bosshardt described as a distinctive feature of
Shiqian. And he was given a pair of shoes confiscated from the shops.

"Shoes!" he exclaimed, with a warmth undiminished after seventy years. "They were what I desired most on the Long March." His first pair of sandals was worn out within a week, and he treated the spare pair as if it was his life. Without shoes, he could easily lag behind, and he knew he would be killed by the pursuing Nationalists. He only put them on when he was climbing a mountain or going through very tough terrain. Even then, he protected them by wrapping his puttees round them. But the sandals were made of straw and before long they fell apart. He had to rely on his "personal leather." He laughed when he saw my perplexity: "Our skin is a kind of leather, isn't it?" But wherever he could find cloth, he would wrap his feet with it.

The need for footwear drove the soldiers to extreme measures. Bosshardt noted: "Their eyes were trained through much experience to detect anything which is good to tear up and make into their sandals, regardless of whether they were wool or silk, expensive garments or any cloth available."[3] Some missionaries returning to their stations after evacuation found their curtains, sheets, or garments all gone. But the soldiers usually grabbed more than they could handle. The roads immediately outside towns taken by the Red Army were often littered with clothes as if the town's laundry had been dropped there—as soon as the soldiers hit the road, they began to unburden themselves of meters of cloth or sheets that they were too tired to carry.

In Shiqian, Bosshardt's hopes were also raised. It was over a year since he had been taken hostage and zigzagged with the Red Army in the mountains of eastern Guizhou to escape the Nationalists. One day he saw He Long, who shouted to him while riding past: "Unless you pay the ransom quickly, we will chop off your heads. Don't think your beards will save you; I killed a Roman Catholic priest with a beard many times longer than yours."[4] However, he was told that they would reduce the ransom considerably if they could have antiaircraft guns, electrical accessories for their wirelesses, and a long list of foreign medicines. The Mission sent half a dozen middlemen, each carrying at least one load of medicine, maps, transmitters, semiconductors, and 200 silver dollars, which was the precondition set by the Red Army for negotiation. Time and again, they were robbed on the way; one was even dressed like a beggar, with a little outfit for mending old shoes, but he was thought too suspicious to be let through the Red lines. Then came Ting, the Communists' own middleman, who had acted for a rich landlord and had gained their trust. He negotiated the other missionary's release for 20,000 silver dollars, and then it was Bosshardt's turn.

The two middlemen who joined Ting in Shiqian finally struck a deal with the Red Army. Bosshardt would be freed for $10,000, but only if the Mission would apologize to the Communists, take messages to another Communist base, and purchase more medicine and electrical equipment for them. Consequently, 2,000 soldiers went off to collect the booty, but they were fired on by Nationalist troops and lost four men. In their eagerness, they had gone two days before the agreed-upon time. Bosshardt was dragged along for another two months and almost died of a fever on the way. Eventually, the middlemen managed to locate the Red Army again, 700 miles away in the mountains of western Guizhou, on the border with Sichuan. On Easter Sunday 1936, eighteen months to the day from his capture, Bosshardt was a free man.

Xiao Ke gave Bosshardt a farewell banquet, complete with wine and coffee—the first time he had tasted it in eighteen months. He had felt so deprived he had been mixing burned rice with water, which at least looked like coffee. The young commander gave the missionary a piece of his mind again about God: "I cannot understand how one educated abroad as you have been can possibly believe in God. Surely you know we come from monkeys? I suppose that anyone with any brains at all knows that evolution is a fact."[5] Despite the taunts, Bosshardt received these parting words from the Red Army: "When you report to the newspapers, you must remember we are friends. You have seen how good we are to the poor, how we work on principle, and are not common bandits as we are slanderously reported to be."[6]

Most hostages were not so lucky. Throughout his captivity Bosshardt saw hundreds, even thousands of them—landlords, rich gentry, magistrates, shop owners, traders, doctors, teachers, and their wives, concubines, and children. With each town or village the Red Army took, there was a fresh lot. Anticipating a big catch in a prosperous place like Shiqian, the Red Army released quite a few to make room for new ones. They were detained for three days to three months, and when no ransom could be extracted from their families, many were executed, often at the roadside in full view of the troops. It was almost a daily occurrence.

Bosshardt kept a meticulous account of the hostages and their deaths. He was particularly sad for an old man of 75 from a not-so-rich background. His family came to negotiate for his release but they could not afford the ransom. One evening, they saw him being carried out, hands and feet tied to a pole like a pig being carried to market. "We heard the women asking the captain of the guard if they could take him home and give him a decent burial," the missionary wrote with unbearable sadness. "He showed his callous heart by asking them: 'What is he to you?' He refused to grant their request. Three or four wrangled for the swordsman's privilege, but the eldest of the hagglers, a youth of about 20, carried the day. Borrowing a sharp sword he dragged him away, followed by a second comrade carrying a hoe to act as sexton. Soon they returned smiling, and as indifferent as though they had done nothing more than kill a chicken for dinner."[7]

It was the first time I learned in such vivid detail about the hostage-taking and ransom demands by the Red Army. Shock is too weak a word to describe my reaction. I knew confiscation from the rich and powerful was routine—it was one of the three tasks for the Red Army, together with fighting and propagating Communist ideas to the masses. But kidnapping for ransom was different, especially when many of the victims were women, children, and old people. Xiao Ke admitted years later that the desperate need to feed such a big army in such a poor place required desperate measures: "To be frank, we had been on the march for fifty days in very hot weather. The wounded and sick increased by the day, but we had no medicine. We knew the missionaries could get hold of medicine and funds."[8]

When I asked Chen about the ransom and the hostages, he did not hesitate. "That was one of the best things on the March. Particularly in Hunan, the landlords were very rich, and once we extracted over 40,000 silver dollars in three weeks. It kept us going for quite a while! We had steamed rice three times a day, and pork and vegetables every day," he recalled with a broad smile. But he did not think too much of Guizhou. "It was so desperate the poor had a saying: 'If you want to eat rice, you have to wait for the next life.' Little girls walked around with nothing on because they could not afford trousers. The landlords there were poorer than many of the poor villagers in my hometown," Chen recalled in disbelief. "But they were better off than the rest. So we had to target them. Someone had to pay for the Revolution. How else could we survive?"

Chen thought highly of the medicine, opium, salt, sugar, meat, flour, rice, and other goods confiscated and received as ransom along the way. "In many areas we passed through, even if you had money, there was nothing to buy," he recalled. That was particularly true of medicine and electrical goods, the two commodities the Red Army would take in lieu of ransom. They even told Bosshardt that if the money spent in securing them exceeded the ransom, they would pay the difference. When the Red Army took a town, ordinary soldiers were not allowed to confiscate from medicinal and electrical shops—they were the responsibility of a special unit. Chen's happiest memory of the March was when they sacked a big town along the Yangzi River. The Nationalists did not know, and continued to air-drop food, cloth, and medicine for three days. "It really fell into our lap from heaven. I never saw so many drugs in my life."

It was during this attack that they acquired the services of a captive who became one of the top doctors in the Red Army. He saved Bosshardt's life. "The Reds were making full use of his professional skill. He gave me a hypodermic injection, and several doses of medicine to take which proved very effective. From this time on I rapidly improved." Bosshardt was curious, as I was, about how hard the Red Army tried to win over the technical staff they caught. In his company there were two doctors, an engineer, a wireless operator, a general, several commissioned officers, and two dozen petty officers. They were always treated with courtesy, given the best billets and the best food. "They were hot properties," Chen said with enthusiasm. "Like the doctor we caught from the Nationalists: he was a kind man, a brilliant doctor, and he also spoke English and German. Whenever we confiscated foreign medicines, he was the one who could tell us what they were.

We'd have been lost without him. He helped to train so many of the Red Army's own doctors, nurses, and hygienists. I owed my training to him. If only we had had a few more hostages like him, we could have saved more lives."

As the March went through uninhabited areas later, the problem became more serious. Iodine, gentian violet, and Vaseline were precious, and Chen applied them sparingly. Injections were only for senior officers, although Bosshardt, with the highest ransom on his head, enjoyed the privilege too. Traditional Chinese herbal medicine was easy to find—tree bark, dandelions, orange peel, dragon eye lychees, cicada skins, turtle shells, snake gall, and scorpions are just a few of the common ingredients. Bosshardt was prescribed dried orange peel, herbs, roots, dried licorice, and Chinese dates for his stomach trouble. They came in a dozen small packets, and required five or six hours of brewing. For a huge army on the move, it was not as convenient as Western medicine, but many traditional Chinese doctors were kidnapped and brought on the March. When a colleague of Bosshardt's, another captive, complained of severe pain caused by the dampness, he was given acupuncture, and it proved very effective.

The panacea for Chen was *jiuji shui*, or "charitable water." I thought how appropriate the name was until he told me what it was— opium dissolved in water. Opium was believed to be a remedy for diarrhea, cough, heat stroke, headache, fever, vomiting, indigestion, rheumatism, typhoid fever, malaria, and plague. It could also dispel chills and preserve energy. And it was one thing that the Red Army was never short of. While marching from Guizhou to Sichuan, the 2nd Army confiscated 67,827 ounces of it.[9] Chen gave it to any soldier who did not have a wound but complained of discomfort. "Everyone had some, as medicine, as a bargaining counter, as currency. Even if it did not cure, at least it relieved the pain. Patients were given it for major operations like amputation, but you had to get the amount right," Chen said. There was a story of a tiger that killed a horse, the most desirable transport in Guizhou, and ate half of it. The farmer was so angry that he put opium in the carcass. When the tiger returned the next morning and finished the horse, it died of opium poisoning.

In Guizhou, and in Shiqian, the other opium which the Red Army found plenty of was religion, the "poison of the mind." The remote and inaccessible mountains of Guizhou had became a target of Christian missionaries at the end of the nineteenth century. Bosshardt's Mission was the most successful in converting the locals, particularly the tribal people. Created by a young Englishman in 1865, their goal was to spread Christianity to the remotest and poorest parts of China. In their first thirty years they converted fewer than 100 Chinese. The Chinese were frightened of them, thinking the missionaries were devils, and their grey and blue eyes were due to their lack of nourishment, which they made up for by eating the eyes of Chinese children. They stoned the missionaries, set fire to their houses, and petitioned local officials to throw them out. Cholera and plague killed many of them. One missionary died after eight years of traveling in Hunan, without finding a foothold—but failure and rejection made them more determined. Their breakthrough came with the Miao tribe in Yunnan and Guizhou provinces in the early 1910s. The Han Chinese disdain for "barbarians" brought the Miao and the foreign devils together. By the early 1930s, the China Inland Mission had more than 1,300 missionaries, over 100 centers, and 95,000 followers, mostly in Guizhou and Yunnan. As their annual report proudly declared, "Professionals, spies, members of secret societies, opium addicts, prostitutes, rich and poor, bandits and scholars were finding Christ."[10] Their hospitals, schools, opium refuges, and leprosy clinics were particularly popular with the people. Other missionaries followed.

When the 2nd Army arrived in Shiqian, only a small county town, it had a rather grand Catholic church, where three German priests and several nuns served a large Catholic community. The army took over the Catholic church as its headquarters, not the more grand and spacious Longevity Palace. After all, Christianity was regarded as the most deadly poison of all since it had brought with it all the humiliation of the Opium War. The Red Army had made it clear to Bosshardt they did not take him primarily for ransom. "The purpose is to show the foreigner that they do not want the Christian doctrine in China. It is opium for the people. They want to show that they will not have this foreign doctrine that he brings to combat theirs in their own land."[11] Two of the German priests in Shiqian escaped when the Red Army entered it, but the third one who was caught, Father Kellner, met a sad end. He died of hunger in captivity, and his coffin was left on a hillside unburied—the corpse was eaten by wolves.

The Catholic church still stands in Shiqian. I did not need to ask where it was. From anywhere in town, you can see its spire beckoning to believers. I can imagine that 100 years ago, when the houses were low and thatched with straw, it must have struck awe into the locals with its exoticism and its grandeur in this impassable mountain region. I thought of Bosshardt and the German priests, young, quiet, fair-skinned, well educated, and living comfortably, coming all this way to spread the Gospel. What devotion must have driven them to this remotest corner of China, spending time with lepers, tending to opium addicts, traveling for days to a hamlet for just one convert.

The church was spacious, airy, and unadorned except for a painting of Christ over the altar table, not unlike many village churches in the West. There were two or three worshippers there. Outside where the priests used to live was an exhibition about the activities of the 2nd Army in and around Shiqian. A group of tourists were following a guide who was trying to make her talk more interesting by adding a story here and there.

"The people of Shiqian loved the Red Army. Eight hundred signed up; over 1,000 joined the local Communist guerrillas. But it was not just us; even foreigners were impressed." Here the guide stopped to clear her throat. Everyone in the group looked up with surprise. She was rather pleased with her oratorical skill and continued, "When the missionary Bosshardt saw how brave and disciplined our soldiers were, he was sympathetic and keen to help . . . He wrote to Shanghai and Nanking to buy medicine and raise money for the Red Army. When he returned to England, he wrote articles praising the Red Army's bravery and iron discipline." The group nodded in approval. Of course, she left out that the Red Army kept Bosshardt hostage. I wondered how long it would be before a guide here told the whole truth.

I was bored by the half-truths and returned to the church. The people had finished their prayers and were sitting outside enjoying the sun. I sat down with them and asked one man if he had heard of Father

Kellner. "How do you know about him?" He looked at me in surprise. I said I had read about him in a missionary's account. "Ask any old people in this town, they can tell you the story. It was so tragic." He looked to be in his sixties, too young to have met the missionary himself. "My parents listened to his sermons. You know he spoke Chinese better than you and me. And he was so kind, caring for lepers abandoned by their own families."

Their priests were gone, and after 1949 the church was pretty much closed. During the Cultural Revolution, the statue of Christ was pulled down and the believers were forced to trample on it. The old man could barely recall the stories. "You know we bow to give thanks for the food we receive before each meal. Even that was a crime in those days. The officials said Jesus was a god of the imperialists, the priests were spies, and we were all American lackeys. They asked my parents who they really believed in: Chairman Mao or Christ. They said both—on earth they relied on Chairman Mao, but for heaven they relied on God. The cadres slapped them in the face and shouted. But what was wrong with that? Even today, I cannot see what's wrong with it. We all want to be happy. The Party wanted to bring happiness to the poor. Catholicism is dedicated to relieving people of their suffering too."

There must be a big difference between the two, I said.

He thought about it. "We Christians do not talk about hatred, only about love. But since 1949 there have been so many campaigns in China. People were told to struggle against landlords, feudalists, imperialists, the capitalists, reactionaries, opportunists, conservative rightists, radical leftists, capitalist-roaders within the Party, liberals, and so on. With each campaign, thousands, hundreds of thousands, sometimes millions died. I remember my parents and many other Christians refused to denounce the so-called enemies of the people. In the end, my father was accused of being 'an imperialist spy'—he had learned how to read and write from missionaries—and he was thrown into jail. The jail was full of Christians, but they did not repent. Our Lord taught us to love and forgive. Why can't we forgive our enemies? What do we achieve by hatred? It only increases our sins."

What the old man said reminded me of Bosshardt's response when he was ridiculed by the Red Army soldiers. Whenever they took a town, they made him sit in a chair with a placard on him describing him as an imperialist; meanwhile, loudspeakers broadcast to everyone to come and see the spectacle, as they might when a circus hit town. His nose seemed the main eyesore for the Chinese. Often the soldiers teased him, asking if he would not like them to cut it in half and make it into two. For all the humiliation he was put through, Bosshardt said he would look at the soldier taunting him and think: "The Lord loves you and died for you and then I felt that I could love him too."

But it was not just compassion. Perhaps he sensed a kindred spirit and zeal in his captors. "Their revolutionary fervor, their aspiration and hope for a new world, and their steadiness in their faith, is unprecedented and shocking . . ." he noted. "They are young, and are fighting for their cause, full of bravery and vitality." On their day of rest, apart from washing, singing, watching plays, and playing basketball with a ball made of leather filled with cloth, they listened to lectures on Communist principles and learned to read, or write confessions of their thoughts or their understanding of Communism. Gambling, the ever-popular Chinese pastime, was strictly forbidden. The political discussions in the evening reminded him of church meetings. At the end, a senior officer would call them to attention for a song. To his surprise, "One or two of their songs were set to hymn tunes. To the tune 'Jesus Loves the Little Children,' they sang 'Kill, kill, kill until the world runs with blood.' "[12]

Still, he could also find them inspiring. "A vast multitude have heard the doctrine of Communism, and have read their slogans painted in every conceivable place, even on farmhouses far from the main roads, as well as on the busy mart; or received tracts from the zealous propaganda squad. How one desires to see similar bands of young Chinese Christians buying up the opportunity of going through the length and breadth of needy [Guizhou]; yea, and throughout China, with as great a zeal employing popular methods! Oh, for such a company of men abandoned to do the will of Christ!"[13]

If the Red Army men were kept busy by their studies of Communism, Bosshardt was sustained through his long captivity by his faith.

"For faith that brings triumph when defeat seems strangely near! Oh, for faith that brings triumph into victory's ringing cheer—faith triumphant, knowing not defeat or fear." He recited these lines silently every day. He spent his time memorizing all the psalms alphabetically, although later they did give him a copy of the Bible after they ransacked a church. On Christmas Day 1935, he cheered up when it dawned on him that Jesus had been born in a place even poorer than the house where he was held. Only once did he seriously think of giving in because he could not see the way out. The ransom was too much for his Mission to pay. In 1932 alone, thirty foreigners were taken hostage and eight were murdered because they failed to deliver the ransom asked. If that was to be his fate, he would rather die sooner. Then he reflected and became more positive. "How often as missionaries have we felt unable to get low enough to appreciate the poverty and sufferings of many of the people to whom we have come to minister?" he asked himself. "The Lord has given [me] the opportunity to live in the closest contact with the Chinese and to experience their sorrows, anxieties, and problems besides getting firsthand knowledge of their depravity and poverty."[14]

The soldiers also began to like Bosshardt. They took good care of him: he was always given the best food, pork, beef, stewed chicken and eggs, pomelos, oranges, and sugar cubes, even occasionally cheese and condensed milk confiscated from churches. His shoes were worn out: one day a soldier took his off and gave them to him, and walked the whole day barefoot. When they broke camp in the evening or when they had a few days' rest, they would sit around and ask questions, like how many countries there were in the world. Bosshardt asked them back. "Five," they shouted. "China, imperialist country, foreign country, alien country, and Japan." When they found out he could knit gloves, socks, and sweaters with sharpened chopsticks and confiscated wool, orders came in thick and fast. He Long's six-month-old daughter even had a tunic made by him. When the soldiers became really friendly, they asked him about his faith. One day, a hygienist asked him what benefits England received from the Gospel. His reply must have sounded familiar to the confused soldier: "Care for the sick and the poor, education for the masses, the uplift of womanhood, and individual rights are all fruits of the Gospel."[15] They also requested psalm readings, and Bosshardt happily obliged. They listened with great interest, but he knew very well that for them the psalms and the stories of Christ were like fairy tales. They had their own beliefs.

I asked Chen how much the young soldiers knew about Communism. It was a question I posed to all the veterans I interviewed. He pondered for a minute, and said: "My commissar once asked me the same thing. I was not sure what to say. I said, 'Communism is the Soviet Union.' So he asked me what the Soviet Union was. I hadn't a clue. All I knew was we had to overthrow Chiang, drive out the Japanese, take power, get rid of the landlords, and distribute their land. What else could there be?"

What Chen said reminded me of the answer given me to the same question by a top general in the Chinese army, a Long March veteran. "Can you tell me? I had no idea then or now. I doubt even Mao knew the answer. Does anyone know what it is? For me, it is a dream, a beautiful dream that kept us going." Coming from extreme poverty and oppression, the Communist ideal gave them hope for a more just and fair society, courage to face their ordeals, and strength to strive on. Perhaps no one knew or could know how much suffering would lie along the path, how big the sacrifice would be, and how great the difference would be between the vision and the reality.

But the Marchers were not all so ill-informed about Communism. The founders of the Party were all well educated—many abroad—and their leaders, Chen Duxiu and Li Dazhoo, were among the best-known intellectuals in the country. Many were from well-off families, against whom they rebelled. They had a sense of destiny. They believed that Communism was the answer for China, just as it had been in Russia. But they were few in number, and their knowledge, skills, and dedication were so essential to the Revolution, they quickly rose to be natural leaders. In the Red Army, someone with only a few years of primary education would soon become an officer, but they often suffered; they died in purges because they were not "proletarian" enough, or they reached high positions but then lost out in political intrigues. They would have been ten or more years older than my veterans, who were mostly in their teens when the March started. Very few of them were still alive; access to them was more difficult for me than my journey round the whole Long March route.

I left the church and strolled back to my hotel. Some of the things that the old man said lingered in my head: "Belief is a necessity, not a luxury. Without it life has no flavor. It's like chewing wax." I stopped and looked back, and the spire of the church was still visible. Under that soaring roof were two faiths, as incompatible as water and oil in the new China. Some seventy years ago, here in this remote corner of China, two groups of hot-blooded young men fought for their faiths, and many died. Despite his ordeal, Bosshardt never gave up. He continued to preach, to educate the poor and cure the sick; he was convinced the Gospel would bring solace and salvation to the Chinese. Similarly, the young Red Army soldiers who had kidnapped him were confident that Communism would save China; they fought their way through and won the Revolution.

During his captivity, Bosshardt often protested to his captors that he had as much right to his faith as they had to theirs. But they warned him: "If you say another word about religion, we'll have you shot." They did not shoot him but threw him out—Bosshardt was the last foreign priest to leave Guizhou after the Communist takeover. Afterwards he had these kind words about his captors: "I understand them. If all the Communists are like the Red Army I had encountered, there is no reason for fear."

Half a century later, in 1985, General Xiao Ke, who as a young man had taken Bosshardt hostage, asked for a search to be made for the missionary, and Bosshardt was found living in England, strong and healthy at the age of 88. Xiao Ke wrote to him, regretting that they were both too old to travel and meet each other, and wished him a long life. Then he wrote a Preface to the Chinese translation of the missionary's account of his life with the Red Army: "Bosshardt was taken prisoner by us, but he forgave our sins. His magnanimity and forbearance are most admirable."[16] I found it touching. The two young men and their extraordinary faiths had been diametrically opposed. Now they seemed to have accepted each other. Was old age bringing them wisdom, or was there now a recognition that China had room for more than one faith?

Soldier Huang stood in a stream doing his best to wash his mud-spattered trousers. It was the first time in weeks he had been able to clean himself up. The 1st Army hoped to take Zunyi, the second-biggest city in Guizhou Province, and set up their base there. Everyone was ordered to make themselves presentable. "You have no idea how shabby we were," Huang recalled cheerfully. "Many of us had no uniforms, only the clothes we picked up from landlords, peasants, or even monks and Nationalists. We were a rabble, but at least we could be a tidy one. We had to impress the townsfolk."

The commissar of another unit was urging his soldiers to put on their shoes. They saw no point and would rather walk barefoot—their shoes were only going to get soiled on the muddy road. "No, you don't understand. We are going into a big city. You can't go in like that." The commissar was losing his patience. Someone teased, "We must be at our best. There are lots of beautiful girls in the city. They won't like country bumpkins without shoes." Finally, everyone had their shoes on. They moved on, faster and faster toward Zunyi, the big city, the center of civilization. Excitement drove away the tiredness and numbness in their legs.[1]

The 1st Army took the city without a battle—Guizhou was out of Chiang's reach, although not for long; the local warlord Wang Jialie had kept his troops in the capital Guiyang, 100 miles to the south. The Red Army vanguard regiment caught a battalion of local militia outside Zunyi and ingeniously bribed them to call out to the guards and open the city gate. At last, for the first time in three months since they left Jiangxi, they could rest without being harassed, and enjoy what Zunyi—the biggest city they took on the Long March—could offer.

The speed of their advance left the shopkeepers and rich gentry with no time to flee. From one landlord, they confiscated several hundred pumpkins, 500 kilos of opium, and great quantities of silk and furs. Another yielded a seemingly inexhaustible supply of salt and cigarettes — soldiers could take as much as they wanted and the remainder was sold to the locals for profit. That was when Woman Wang learned to smoke. The smaller shops were ordered to stay open and their goods were gone in no time — toothpaste, soap, face towels, Wellington boots, pencils, ink, and notebooks, just about everything. Many who still had a penny or two left in their pockets clubbed together to have their first-ever dishes in a restaurant, hot pot, chili chicken, twice-cooked fat pork, sweet and sour fish, duck-blood soup, Sichuan pickled vegetables . . .

Huang had his most luxurious billet on the March, a large house in the old town, although it was only for one night — his division left the next day to guard the city from the north. He saw young girls in skirts for the first time, but their novelty could not compare with the lightbulbs. "The one in our room was brighter than the moon," Huang recalled with almost childish delight. "We kept looking at it. When it was time to go to sleep, we did not know how to turn it off. We thought we had to wait for the morning for it to disappear, like the moon. Wasn't it wonderful, they could light up a whole room without oil? Some tried to light their cigarettes from it as they did from oil lamps, but they could not. They slapped the bulb and broke it, causing a huge panic. The next morning, we took the few that were left, thinking maybe we could use them on the March."

It was also in Zunyi that officers found Nationalist newspapers and learned the fate of those they had left behind in the Jiangxi Soviet. Ruijin fell on November 10, a month after their departure, without much resistance. Whole regiments of the rear guard threw down their weapons and fled in total chaos and anarchy. Chiang wanted a peaceful victory, to turn Jiangxi into "a crucible for the New China." But sweetness and light did not prevail. Ferocious revenge was taken, not only by the Nationalist army, but more by the landlords who had been forced to flee. Men were beheaded, cut in half at the waist, or had their living organs taken out and eaten. Bodies lined the riverbanks. Many women were raped and then sold to the brothels of Canton, or taken by KMT officers and soldiers. "There is not a dwelling that has not been burned," said a government report, "there is not a tree that has not been felled, there is not a fowl or dog that has not been killed, there is not an able-bodied man remaining, no smoke rises from the kitchen chimneys in the alleys and the lanes, the only noise in the fields is the wailing of ghosts."[2]

Zunyi was to be their new base, they were told. The news from Jiangxi was horrifying, but it must also have told the Red Army that they needed to work hard to win over the people of Zunyi if they wanted to be welcome. Wang threw herself into rallying their support with her usual enthusiasm and ingenuity. At a mass rally she put on a bowler hat, dark glasses, and a long gown, carrying a stick in one hand and a whip in the other. She was playing Wang Jialie. "I am appointed by Chiang Kaishek. You must pay your taxes due for 1998!" Woman Wang mimicked with a giggle, recalling her most popular acting role on the March. "The audience collapsed with laughter." When she took off her bowler hat and her fake mustache made with cotton and ink, she called on the men in the audience to join the Red Army. "They were amazed that I was a woman — so much so that 500 men signed up on the spot," Wang said proudly.

Wang had also caught the attention of another man, the 29-year-old Wang Shoudao, Mao's old secretary and fellow Hunanese. He now headed the Liaison Committee on Local Work to galvanize support for the Red Army, and Wang was seconded to him from the Convalescent Unit. That evening, he called her to his room and declared his love for her. Instead of a wedding ring, he presented her with a pistol for her protection. "I could have said no," Wang said hesitantly. "Remember we only had thirty women in the 1st Army, and so many senior commanders wanted a wife. As Mao's man, he was out of favor. But the Party secretary of my unit said he was a good and capable man, and I should marry him. So I said yes." But Wang did not know that in Zunyi her husband's fortunes, like Mao's, were to change for good. She only heard this a month later, when the decisions made during the Zunyi Conference were relayed to the grass roots.

If the Long March is the defining event of modern Chinese history, the Zunyi Conference from January 15 to 17, 1935, is often regarded as the most crucial moment of the Long March. "The turning point of life and death in the Chinese Revolution" is how it is described in the standard Chinese textbook. Harrison Salisbury joined in with his accolade: "Many would say in the future that it was the single most significant event in the whole Chinese Revolution."[3] Braun and Bo Gu, the young Party Secretary, were blamed for the failures of the Red Army that led to the Long March and the fiascoes on the Xiang River. They were removed and Mao, who had been sidelined for two years, returned to power and steered the Red Army, the Party, and the Chinese Revolution from despair to hope, from defeat to victory, and from victory to the ultimate prize of the Revolution.

When I came to Zunyi, I could understand why so many veterans sang its praises in their memoirs or in their interviews with me. It is a city of great charm, with a population of half a million. It is laid out in a gently curving crescent along the banks of the Wu River. The old town, dating back to the twelfth century, occupies the west bank, housing the government, the bureaucrats, the scholars and schools, and the churches. Many of the streets are still lined with two-story wooden houses and shops with carved red panels. The river gives the people fish, and the encircling fields and mountains supply them with food. It is calm, clean, orderly, and not too crowded. As the Chinese say, it is a place where your stomach will be full and your heart will be content. A stone's throw away across the river is the "new" town, which goes back to the eighteenth century. The main feature is the commercial thoroughfare which runs along its entire length. The shops and restaurants seem like old family affairs. Grannies sit outside feeding their grandchildren and chatting to the neighbors. They have been there a long time, and they know their customers will come. There is no need for hard sell.

In a lane off this street is the house where Mao, Zhang Wentian, and Wang Jiaxiang stayed; it is a small two-story building with only a small courtyard in front. Initially it seemed an odd choice for a place to stay, some distance from all the other senior leaders in the old town.

Then it dawned on me how much these unassuming quarters said about Mao's bid for a return to power. Zhang was one of the five members of the Secretariat of the Politburo, and Wang was an alternate member. Together they held considerable influence in the Party and the Red Army. It did not bother Mao that Zhang had failed to call on him for a year after his arrival in Ruijin, or that Wang had little respect for his knowledge of Marxism and Communism. They were just the men he needed. The Party was controlled by Moscow-trained Bolsheviks, and as insiders and fellow Bolsheviks their challenge would carry weight. More importantly, Mao knew both men were jealous of Bo Gu, the young Party Secretary, who had been their classmate in Moscow. Zhang admitted years later, "I felt I was put in a position completely without power, which I resented bitterly . . . I remember one day before the departure, comrade Mao Zedong had a chat with me, and I told him of all my resentment without holding back. From then on, I became close to comrade Mao Zedong. He asked me to stick together with him and comrade Wang Jiaxiang—so that way a trio was formed, headed by comrade Mao."[4] Mao had made sure the three traveled together during the March.

But they were not drawn to Mao simply by his persuasiveness. The situation was dire. At the start of the March, they had set out to join He Long's army. The success of the 6th Corps in finding He Long seemed to validate the plan. It gave them hope that they could all join up. Then, suddenly, this was no longer possible because the warlord of Hunan blocked their way; he deployed 100,000 troops to make sure that they could not meet and become a threat in his territory. It did not help that all links with Moscow were cut, as the communication cell in Shanghai had been destroyed by Chiang's secret police back in October 1934. The desertions and the heavy defeat at the Xiang River worsened the panicky feelings among the rank and file. Even the usually gentle Zhou Enlai lost his temper with Braun, telling him to forget about his ideas and accept Mao's proposal to go to Guizhou.[5]

Mao had gauged the mood accurately. On the March, much to Braun's concern, he went backwards and forwards in the column, chatting with the soldiers and officers, sympathizing with their difficulties, and finding out how they felt. As a result, when he proposed the area around Zunyi as a new base, nobody vetoed it, despite the fact that Guizhou was the poorest province in China and the 2nd Army had not been able to build a base there. After all, Mao was the only senior leader who was not tainted by the withdrawal from Jiangxi and the debacle at the Xiang River. Perhaps he would lead them out of the mess as he had done in the past; at least he should be given a go since nobody else knew what to do. Mao certainly gave them confidence in this poem he wrote while in Guizhou:

> Idle boast to say the strong pass is a wall of iron;
> With firm strides we are starting afresh.
> Starting afresh,
> The rolling hills sea-blue,
> The dying sun blood-red.

So they followed him to Zunyi and accepted his request for a postmortem discussion of what went wrong in Jiangxi and what should be done to correct it. This was to be the subject of the historic Zunyi Conference.

The Conference was held in the military headquarters which stands in the heart of the old town. It is the grandest building in the place, the former residence of a minor warlord who became rich trading in opium as well as everyday products — old photographs show the shops on both sides carrying signs saying "soy sauce," "pickled vegetables," "ink and paper." Built of traditional grey brick with carved timber columns, it has verandas on both floors running from end to end, enclosed by semi-circular arches, like a Spanish hacienda. On the ground floor were the bedrooms used by Zhou Enlai and Zhu De; on the first floor near the landing was a hall with dark wood flooring, a kerosene lantern overhead, and some twenty rattan chairs around a heavy table. Here on the evening of January 15, 1935, a week after the Red Army took Zunyi, the Politburo members and the commanders and commissars of the main corps gathered. The Conference continued for the next three evenings.

They debated the causes of the loss of the Jiangxi Soviet base. Bo Gu spoke first, attributing it to Chiang's overwhelming military superiority; next Zhou Enlai detailed the Red Army's tactical errors in the Fifth Campaign. But then came Zhang Wentian, delivering the bombshell of a speech prepared with the help of Mao. He pointed out that the Red Army had defeated Chiang's First, Second, Third, and Fourth Campaigns, despite the overwhelming superiority of the Nationalist troops in terms of numbers and weaponry. In the Fifth, he said, Braun and Bo Gu had used the wrong tactics of defense versus defense, blockhouses against blockhouses. This assessment of the failures in Jiangxi and the reasons for the Long March has lasted till today. Zhang also criticized the preparations for the Long March and the cumbersome way it started, making it all too easy for Chiang to pursue. The key military figures joined the chorus of criticism.

Mao, ever the astute politician, went out of his way to insist that the failure was military, not political. Otherwise Zhang Wentian and Wang Jiaxiang, who had been essential members of the Jiangxi Soviet government, would have been implicated. Zhang confessed later: "The Zunyi Conference did not mention the political mistakes of the Party at all. On the contrary it confirmed its correctness . . . But Comrade Mao could only do it that way. Otherwise, our union would have been impossible, and the Zunyi Conference could not have succeeded."[6] This has always been praised as Mao's generosity, thinking of the big picture and striving for Party unity at a time of crisis. The supreme irony is that ten years later, when Mao was secure in power, Zhang was one of the first senior Party leaders to come under fire. Mao denounced him for his political mistakes before and after the Zunyi Conference. Zhang's confession, running into tens of thousands of words, was distributed by Mao to other Central Committee members for them to see and to learn the lessons.

Throughout the Conference, only one man, the head of the Communist Youth League, defended Bo Gu and Braun, and turned the heat on Mao. "You know nothing about Marxism-Leninism," he said. "All you have read is Sun Zi's *The Art of War*." "You don't even know how many chapters *The Art of War* has," Mao retorted. It could not have brought much comfort to Braun, who sat near the door, as if he was not sure he should be there at all. His interpreter only translated the odd sentence here and there—it would have been too much for him otherwise. Still, he got the message. "He showed his anger in the changing color of his face. It grew red as he listened to Bo Gu and turned white when Mao began to attack him. At no point did he lose physical control, but he smoked cigarette after cigarette . . . He looked more and more depressed and gloomy."[7]

Had I not learned what I had on my journey, I would have agreed with Mao's analysis—as most people still do. The loss of the base was a defeat, and someone had to be blamed—and Braun was an easy target. As Edgar Snow admitted after his interviews with Mao and Braun: "He is the arrogant foreigner, the black sheep, the scapegoat: and it is somehow comforting to be able to cast most of the blame on him. Actually, it is almost impossible to believe that under any genius of command, the Reds could have emerged victorious from the Himalayan obstacles which faced them."[8]

As for Mao's criticism of the chaotic organization and the slow speed of the March at the beginning, everyone knew that speed was essential. Initially, the Red Army was not there to fight, but to carry and guard the "emperor's sedan chair," the two gigantic central columns. Could the sedan chair have been thrown away? And whose idea was it for the five corps to carry it as they did? It was Mao's, to preserve the Party and government officials. As long as they survived, the Revolution could start again. The 1st Army did preserve them, and they were to play a crucial role in building the new China. Zhang Wentian admitted it many years later: "Before the departure, the three-man group [Bo Gu, Braun, and Zhou Enlai] wanted us [the Party and government officials] to be integrated into the army proper, but Mao suggested not, so we were not dispersed."[9] But, again, all the blame landed on Braun.

I came downstairs feeling slightly depressed. The same old story was on display in the museum, the one that everyone knew, while there was so much more to be said. I really needed someone to talk to. Everywhere I went I tried to seek out local scholars or experts; a Party historian in Beijing had suggested the ex-curator of the museum, Fei Peiru.

I had tried to ring him before I came, but did not reach him. I asked the woman in the museum shop if she knew where Fei lived. "Right at the back of the museum," she said. Did she think a stranger could call on him? Her answer was reassuring: "He is very friendly. I'm sure you could call on him. But maybe you should look at his book first." She handed me a copy of *Record of Daily Events of the 1st Army*. Collecting books along the way was becoming an expensive and burdensome habit, but they were very worthwhile. Local writers were often extremely good scholars and, as the Chinese saying goes, in the provinces the sky is higher and the emperor is further away. Fei's book was factual, even dry, but clearly a distillation of a huge amount of information. I paid for the book and went to find the author.

When I knocked on the door of his house, Fei called "Come in" and led me to his study. From floor to ceiling along the four walls were books and more books—memoirs and biographies of key Party and military leaders, Party documents, local archives, oral histories of ordinary soldiers, monographs and general histories of the Long March for each army. He was grey-haired, about 70, but looked younger; he was very genial, and very brisk. "I cannot say I have every single book published in this country on the Long March," he said proudly, as he watched me surveying his shelves like a hungry traveler who had walked in on a banquet. "But I think I have most of them, and all the important ones. I started collecting them before you were born."

"No wonder your book is so full of interesting details." I took out my copy. "I have not eaten them all. I have digested them," he said with a gentle laugh.

Fei was trained as an engineer, which is perhaps what gave him his meticulous attention to detail and a scientific approach to history. After he joined the museum staff, he witnessed the fervor of the Red Guards toward Zunyi during the Cultural Revolution. He explained that Zunyi was regarded as one of the five Red holy places, together with Shaoshan, Mao's birthplace, the Jinggang Mountains where Mao made his reputation, Yanan where Mao built up the army again, and Beijing, where Mao sat on the throne and where he died. "Our museum was like a shrine," Fei recalled with evident pleasure. "Every day hundreds, even thousands of young people poured in from all over the country. They walked the whole way with their backpacks, their red flags, and Mao portraits. They said they were the new Long Marchers. They vowed to carry on his Revolution to the end of their lives."

Yet for all the glorification and worship of Mao in this sacred place, Fei said we did not know the most basic things about the Zunyi Conference, and are still not sure of many details such as the participants, the proceedings, and the resolution. Fei was the man who corrected the dates of the Zunyi Conference from January 7–9 to 15–17. For almost fifty years it was marked as January 7–9, based on the recollection of a senior leader. I was rather shocked. How could the facts not be known about such an important event?

"The truth is that the Zunyi Conference was perhaps not as important at the time as it was made out to be later. Otherwise we would have answers to such questions," he said. This was something completely new to me. I pressed him for more. "There were so many battles, so many meetings on the Long March; Zunyi was only one. It was just one step on the way for Mao. Mao did not become the leader of the Party or the army at Zunyi, although he was made a member of the Secretariat of the Politburo. You know Edgar Snow had the longest interview with Mao that he ever gave, shortly after the Long March. Zunyi was not even mentioned. So clearly at the time Mao did not regard it as the turning point in his career, let alone in the history of the Chinese Revolution. Also the Zunyi Resolution did not appear in Party documents until well after 1949."

Fei made me understand something I had failed to grasp before. When I read the history of the Long March, and when I was on my journey, often I could not make sense of the explanations I was given. I was also puzzled why some basic facts were ignored or hidden. When the details were studied, as Fei had done on the date and participants of the Zunyi Conference, they could point to rather different conclusions. That was why such attention to historical detail was not encouraged, as Yang Shangkun, President of China and a Long March survivor, made clear to Party historians on the eve of the fiftieth anniversary of the Long March: "Historical problems should be studied in general, not in detail . . . We should only describe the great importance and the decisive role of the Red Army's Long March . . . Once we go into detail, we will run into numerous problems which cannot easily be solved."[10]

The Zunyi Conference ended abruptly on the evening of January 17, 1935. Chiang's troops had pushed aside the local warlord and were advancing toward them; the Red Army had to pull out the next day. Mao's plan to build a base here had to be abandoned. Fortunately, the 1st Army had a new destination: Sichuan. Quite a few top commanders of the Red Army were Sichuanese and thought the fertile land there was good for feeding a big army, and that the vast population would make it easy to recruit. More importantly, another Communist force, the 4th Army led by Zhang Guotao, had already established a base in the northern part of the province. The two armies could join up and usher in a new phase of the Revolution in a new base. It was an inviting goal.

What happened next has always been described as the most brilliant example of Mao's military talent. Mao himself also regarded it as his *tour de force*. For four months he led the Red Army zigzagging between Guizhou and Sichuan, crossing the Chi River that divides Guizhou and Sichuan provinces four times, to get rid of Chiang's 200,000 pursuing troops. A feature film was made about the maneuver; I could still sing the theme song.

I made a special trip from Zunyi to the famous Chi River. It was drizzling, and the road was treacherous—narrow, winding up and down, and slippery. One Marcher remembered this stretch as one of the worst on the Long March. He watched Mao climbing a hill, stick in hand, with mud up to his knees, and dirt covering him from head to toe, trudging heavily toward Tucheng, the small town on the east bank of the Chi.[11] From here it would be only a day's march to the Yangzi, and then they would be able to make their way up north to join the 4th Army. I reached Tucheng after a six-hour bus ride—it was so tough I did not know if I could face the journey back. The town was swathed in mist from the mountains; it did not seem very different from an old photograph I had seen in a book. There were still traditional wooden houses built on the hills and hidden amongst trees. The Chi River was muddy, placid, shallow, and not very wide.

I found it hard to link this small and sleepy town with one of the hardest battles fought by the 1st Army on the Long March, with over 3,000 casualties. Harrison Salisbury recorded it, believing he was the first to do so. In fact, I had read an earlier account of it by a local scholar,[12] but it is still not in the history books. Now an interview I had with a veteran in Jiangxi made sense.

I had met Zhong Fazhen in his village home. He was 85 and hard of hearing, but sprightly and forceful. I could barely keep up with him when he walked. He was recruited when he was 14; all the young people in the village had to join after Mao spent a week there, talking to the villagers and looking into rural conditions for a report he later wrote. The village had its own museum commemorating Mao's visit, and Zhong took me to see it—he is still proud of it. Having had two years' education, he was selected for the propaganda team. Later, when he showed himself to be quick, alert, and disciplined, he was made a wireless operator. He vividly described a battle to me, only saying it was in Guizhou, but not exactly where. I now realized this was the one.

On January 28, 1935, ten days after the 1st Army pulled out of Zunyi, it faced the best of the Sichuan warlords' troops outside the town of Tucheng. "I fought at the Xiang River with the 5th Corps, but not in the front line," Zhong said. "I'd never seen anything like this. It began just after dawn and went on all morning. We were in a narrow valley. We had no shells and our artillery gave out after firing just a few shots. They kept shelling us. And so many men, I don't know where they all came from, I never saw so many. We were right up close, I could see their faces. It was really fierce."

There had clearly been bad intelligence. Mao had expected just two regiments; instead he had engaged two brigades—four regiments; and four more arrived as the battle went on. By the afternoon, the Red Army's losses were getting heavier and heavier, and Mao had to call in the 1st Corps which he had positioned 20 miles away. They would not arrive until it was dark. By 3:00 p.m. the fighting was even worse. Zhu De's wife was nearly captured in a surprise assault on the headquarters just above the town—they grabbed at her rifle and her backpack; she let the backpack go and ran for her life. The Military Commission held an emergency session, an extremely rare thing to do in the middle of a battle. The top commanders' lifeguards, the Cadres' Regiment, was sent into the fray, but there was no way to win. The Military Commission gave the command to stop fighting at dusk, and ordered bridges to be thrown over the Chi.

"They broke through us, captured a hilltop, and cut our corps into several segments," Zhong continued. "They poured bullets down on us. It was terrible, we didn't have a chance. We kept retreating toward the town. The shooting only stopped at nightfall. We were the rear guard and I didn't get to the bridge till the early hours the next day. We were lucky to get away."

The Tucheng battle was the first Mao initiated after he took partial control of the Red Army. He was keen to score a big success to show he could lead the Red Army to victory; also to deal such a hard blow to the local warlords that they would leave the Red Army alone, and to take much-needed supplies. Halfway through the battle, when Mao realized the enemy was much bigger than the intelligence had suggested, he still did not withdraw his troops. In the end, it was a resounding defeat: not only were there terrible losses, but it stopped the 1st Army from carrying out the original plan of crossing the Yangzi; it was too heavily guarded for them to contemplate it.

The fiasco of Tucheng was firmly blamed on faulty intelligence. I asked Operator Zhong what would have happened to him if he had made a mistake like that. "I would have got shot, of course," he said firmly. "Whoever it was, because of him, thousands of soldiers died. Normally we were very careful, very careful. It was a big responsibility. That was why I was chosen, though I didn't want to do it. Remember, I had only two years' schooling. My Chinese wasn't that good, and then I had to learn this thing called English. I told my commissar, but he said it was a political task. I had to do it regardless." He paused, and then said with his voice lowered, "You know we were better fed than the officers. Our captain received more money than the commanders."

The Red Army gave extreme importance to the wireless service and intelligence after a very expensive mistake. During Chiang's First Campaign against the Jiangxi Soviet, the Red Army caught his field commander and strong supporter, General Zhang Huizang. His wife pleaded with Chiang to rescue him, and envoys were sent to the Party headquarters in Shanghai to negotiate for his release. The Nationalists offered the Red Army the 4,000 men left from General Zhang's division, a donation of $200,000 guaranteed by three Western banks, twenty cases of Western medicine, ammunition enough to arm two battalions, and the release of 100 Communist prisoners. The Party headquarters accepted the offer and sent its messengers to the Jiangxi base, but by the time they arrived it was too late. Mao had already had Zhang's head cut off, put in a bamboo case tied to a raft, and sent down the river.

Starting from one receiver captured during the First Campaign in 1930—the transmitter was smashed by the soldiers who did not know what it was for—the Red Army built up its own wireless service; their communication school eventually had hundreds of students. The captured officers were its core staff. They knew all the Nationalists' codes, so even if Chiang changed them each day, they were able to decipher every message between Chiang and his field commanders. After defeating Chiang's Second Campaign, Mao and Zhu De rewarded the operator who deciphered the messages with three silver dollars, with which he bought meat and chicken, and gave his friends a treat. Before the Long March started, Mao asked what the essential component of the receiver and transmitter was. When told it was the valve, he said he would carry it personally on the March. But it was too fragile, so he took the keyboard instead and gave it to his bodyguard to carry so that nobody could leak any information. The Red Army made sure that its wireless operators abided by a strict rule of confidence—anyone who was suspected of breaking it would be shot. The 6th Corps had twenty-one wireless staff; four were executed and five disappeared mysteriously.[13] When I asked Operator Zhong about his work, he refused to talk about it. He would not answer my questions about his training or how he learned the codes. "It is a secret," he said curtly. I told him I had read a book about the Red Army's wireless service, so discussion of it must be allowed. "Not for me," he replied. I was annoyed, but I respected Zhong's discipline. The Party had chosen the right man.

Zhong attributed his survival on the Long March to the extraordinary protection he and his colleagues received. They traveled with the headquarters and the leaders; each of them had two armed guards with them, to carry the batteries and equipment and also to keep an eye on them as many operators were Nationalist captives. Sick wireless operators would be carried on stretchers, while soldiers would be abandoned. After the Tucheng battle, the 5th Corps left a wounded operator behind with some money and opium because they could not find a porter to carry him. When a senior commander found out, he ordered a whole battalion to go back, break the enemy's siege, and bring him out.[14]

After the defeat at Tucheng, the 1st Army abandoned the original plan to cross the Yangzi for the time being; it would try to set up a base in northern Guizhou. That probably suited Mao as he seemed reluctant to take refuge with Zhang Guotao and the 4th Army, especially so soon after he had returned to power and was not yet fully in control. A success was now crucial for him and the 1st Army if they were to stay in Guizhou. Three weeks after the Tucheng battle, Mao led the 1st Army back across the Chi River and took Zunyi again, wiping out eight regiments belonging to the local warlord—this was the first victory the 1st Army had won since the Long March began. Mao was greatly encouraged—and ready for more. This time he set his sights on one of Chiang's crack forces. The soldiers were told: "This will be a decisive battle. Either we win, destroy the enemy, stay put, and turn the whole of Guizhou Communist; or we lose, negate our victory in Zunyi, and be forced to move again."[15]

For two weeks, the 1st Army ran, chased, and feinted attacks to draw the enemy into combat—but they would not join the battle. Chiang had ordered them to avoid another defeat like that in Zunyi. Finally, when it made no sense to run further, they dug in and started building blockhouses in the hills to face the Red Army. On March 15, 1935, in Luban, a day's march from Zunyi, there was a pitched battle—not the Red Army's forte even though Mao threw in almost his entire force. They had to fight uphill under heavy fire from above, suffering heavy losses, and eventually had to withdraw and go back across the Chi a third time.

I was baffled by this coming and going across the Chi River. I was not the only one. Operator Zhong was very confused; why between battles had he crossed the same river and passed through the same villages so many times? One minute he was told they were going to Sichuan, the next they were staying in Guizhou, and then they headed for Yunnan. "The propaganda team even made a song about it: 'One mountain after another, we turned a corner from Hunan and found ourselves in Sichuan. Hardly have we stood still in Guizhou, we are in Yunnan.' We plodded about in that poor and mountainous place for four months. It was not as if we got plenty to eat; and there were no places to stay. We slept under the sky most of the time in the damp and cold." Zhong sighed. "In four months, we could have got anywhere. Remember, it only took us six weeks from Jiangxi to Guizhou."

Braun left a vivid account of what many must have experienced: "The troops were showing increasing symptoms of fatigue . . . When planes buzzed over us, we simply threw ourselves down on the side of the road without looking for cover as we used to do. If bombs began falling in a village or farm where we slept, I no longer woke up. If one landed close to me, I just turned over . . . The number of deaths, more from disease and exhaustion than battle wounds, increased daily. Although several thousand volunteers had been enlisted since the beginning of the year, the ranks had visibly dwindled."[16]

Desertion again became a big problem. The political department issued this warning after the Tucheng battle: "Recently all the Corps have found soldiers lagging behind, many on purpose . . . We must select a few examples, struggle against them among the soldiers, punish them duly, and even execute the serious offenders."[17]

Zhang Wentian, the new Party Secretary, could not make sense of Mao's plan and complained bitterly about "the catastrophic military predicament engendered by Mao's reckless strategy and tactics ever since Zunyi."[18] Lin Biao, Commander of the 1st Corps and one of Mao's trusted lieutenants, was so frustrated he wrote to the Military Council: "This way, the troops will be dragged to ruination! We absolutely cannot have him in command like this!"[19]

Mao must have realized that his idea of a base in Guizhou was simply not viable. The two defeats—which are still not mentioned in the history of the Long March—dealt heavy blows to the 1st Army, in terms of morale, men, and material. The forced march, exhaustion, disease, and desertion also took their toll. From 30,000 men when he took over at Zunyi, he had now just 22,000 left, without taking into account the 5,000 new recruits in Guizhou—a loss of almost a third of his force. Unlike the losses at the start of the Long March which were mainly of new recruits, this time it was the core of the Red Army that suffered.

Finally, Mao was ready to go to Sichuan. On March 21, 1935, Mao led his men across the Chi for the fourth time. He feigned an attack on Guiyang, where Chiang was staying to supervise the chase. Frightened, Chiang had to call for reinforcements from the warlord of neighboring Yunnan. That left Yunnan empty of opposition. The 1st Army now swiftly moved southwest and then swung north to the Jingsha River, as the Yangzi is called upstream. They covered nearly 1,250 miles in just five weeks. Finally, they crossed it on May 9, 1935. This was Mao at his best, dazzling Chiang, the warlords, and even his own men. He achieved his aim.

I returned from the Chi to Zunyi, just as Mao and his men did, but in my case to take the train to Sichuan. I went to the photocopy shop near the Zunyi Museum to pick up the three books that Fei had kindly had copied for me. I dropped in at the new museum which Fei had mentioned. It was a magnificent temple-like building in the traditional style. It could almost compete with a palace in the Forbidden City. It was built to commemorate the seventieth anniversary of the Zunyi Conference. It was locked, but through a gap in the door I could see a vast empty space. Fei told me last time that he had been called out of retirement to curate the exhibits for the grand opening on January 15, 2006, the exact date of the seventieth anniversary of the Zunyi Conference. I understood why he found it a challenge. "It is so big, and there is so little material. I don't know how to fill it, not yet anyway," he said.

Then out of the blue, Fei had said: "You know, Mao never came back to Zunyi. He visited the Jinggang Mountains after 1949, but not Zunyi. I have been wondering why. His wife had a very tough time in Guizhou. She gave birth to a baby girl and they had to leave her behind in the care of an opium addict. It was the third child she gave away. You can imagine how sad it must have been for her. Then she was hit by a bomb and seventeen shrapnel splinters lodged in her skull and back. I think she never recovered from the physical and emotional pain. That could be the reason."

But perhaps the reason for Mao staying away from Zunyi was simple. As Fei had told me, perhaps Mao knew better than anyone else that, despite all the propaganda, Zunyi was not as important as had been made out. I remembered a brilliant article I had read later on the Conference by a Western sinologist. He summed it up perfectly: "This turning-point in the history of the Chinese Revolution has been an embarrassment for nearly everyone involved . . . for Mao because his rise was never as dramatic and final as he and his supporters would have liked; for Chinese historians, because they cannot write an accurate account of the Conference; and for Western historians, because they have published so many inaccurate accounts of this historic event."[20]

Fei had his consolation prize, though. "Mao may not have come back, but he did give us a piece of his calligraphy. You may have seen it over our entrance; it says 'Zunyi Conference'—it is the only one in the country he wrote as a nameplate. It is beautiful." I agreed with him. It is unique, forceful, and imposing. Calligraphy is an ancient art form in China, with schools of writing styles established over 1,000 years ago. Mao's belongs to no school; it is in a class of its own, and held in high esteem by the greatest calligraphers. As we say, the handwriting displays the man. But perhaps the six characters in gold are a little too big for the modest entrance.

## 7 ★ DON'T LOVE BOYS, LOVE GUNS

Woman Wang woke up on a bright morning in May, feeling a rare moment of happiness. She was in Luhu, southern Sichuan, in May 1935. Wang had just spent a second night with the man she loved. It was not like her first husband who had been forced on her by her family. This time it was arranged by the Party, and she had quickly become fond of him.

She knew how privileged she was. There was the "Saturday Night Rule"—the only night married couples were allowed to see each other. But the chief of staff had kindly allocated her and her husband the same house, as they had not been together since their wedding night in Zunyi four months earlier. It was such a beautiful place—she only had to walk out of the wooden house and she could see a calm blue lake surrounded by long flat fields of barley with tall snowy mountains rising up behind them, taller and whiter than anything she had ever seen. There was no snow where she came from and she thought it looked like white sugar.

Wang would have taken even more pleasure from her surroundings had she known that this was the land of the Mosuo, a tribal people known for the freedom of their women. Unlike the Han Chinese, whose men treated their women practically as slaves and a means of reproduction, Mosuo women were in charge of their lives and their community. They took their men freely and as many as they liked, without marrying them, and sent them away if they were not pleased with them. When they had babies, they cared for them—the men had no rights over their children. They were models of emancipated women.

For the next four weeks, what was uppermost in Wang's mind was her period. She waited anxiously for it like the sunrise. Before, she had dreaded it, since there was no paper, and cloth was a luxury, though she occasionally had some after "confiscations." She made do with stuffing leaves in her trousers, but sometimes she just had to let it run. It was so distressing that initially she envied the women whose periods had stopped—because of hunger, exhaustion, extreme cold, and the forced marching, sometimes over 40 miles a day. She longed for a horse, which they were supposed to be allowed to use once a month, despite the men's angry protests at such a privilege. But it was not to save women from walking, but from embarrassment. One day a woman in her unit was wading in a river and the water went bright red, as if she had been wounded. A young soldier shouted urgently, "Sister, sister, you're bleeding." Her blushes were redder than the blood. Now Wang prayed it would happen to her. At least it would mean she was not pregnant. The day her period came again, Wang felt a millstone had been lifted from her neck. She promptly climbed up a tree and picked a wad of mulberry leaves. She bore the nuisance with a grin.

"We dreaded pregnancy more than the plague," Wang recalled, with obvious feeling. "It was tough enough to walk without any extra burden. Imagine having a belly twice as big as a watermelon and trying to keep up with the troops at the same time?" They had a motto, "Don't get pregnant, don't get captured, and don't get the eight silver dollars!" (The last was the money for the wounded when they were left with a local family.) She did not want to follow the example of the six pregnant women in her unit. They were all wives of senior commanders, including Mao's wife He Zizhen, who had become pregnant before the Long March. Sometimes they insisted on walking, but it was a joke—by the time the rest had reached their destination for the day, they were still waddling not much beyond where they had started. They had to be carried on stretchers, and when the porters ran away, other women had to step in and take turns carrying them. Wang remembered Zizhen well: "Five pregnancies in five years. She spent most of her time getting pregnant and giving birth. But there was nothing to take to stop it; it was as easy to get pregnant as it was for a man to put his little thing in."

There is a Chinese saying that childbearing is like entering the gates of hell, from which no woman is sure to come back alive. But giving birth on the Long March was like being in hell and looking for a ray of light that was not there. Zizhen gave birth to a baby girl in the early spring of 1935, in Guizhou. As she had done twice before, she had to leave the baby behind. When she was asked to give the girl a name, she shook her head: she doubted she would see her again. Wrapped in a jacket, the baby was handed to an old woman living alone in a hut in the mountains. At first, she refused, saying she had no milk and could not possibly look after the creature. But when she saw the handful of silver dollars and a few bowls of opium, she changed her mind—she could do with the opium.

Mao compared the ease with which Zizhen delivered to "a hen dropping an egg," a remark which pierced her heart—the gates of hell was much more like it. One woman had gone into labor while marching, with the baby's head dangling out, and she fainted the next day when they had to cross an icy river. There was no spare stretcher and she was carried on a tabletop. But the most difficult birth was by the wife of Deng Fa, the head of the secret police. Chang's troops were in hot pursuit, with planes dropping bombs like rain. As if afraid of the violent world, the baby refused to come out; the mother was in terrible pain, and swearing at her husband. A whole regiment of the rear guard was ordered to put up a fierce fight for over two hours. As soon as the baby was born, it was left in a clump of grass, and the mother was carried away on a stretcher. When the regiment caught up in the afternoon, and found out they had lost a dozen soldiers for a child who was left to die, they were enraged.[1]

Wang felt that after all the pain women had to go through, they should be allowed to keep their babies; they could face anything after that. But rules were rules: a crying baby could betray the army's position, and hunger on the March was bad enough without children to feed. She did not know that the 4th and the 2nd Armies allowed their women to keep their babies on the March. He Long, the Commander of the 2nd Army, brought his three-week-old daughter Jiesheng with him. He explained: "I'm 40, and I only have you, a daughter. Even though you're not a son, I still love you. If there are no fish in the river, the shrimp become precious."[2] Her mother said carrying her was hard work. "This baby was heavier than a machine gun! If I were a man, I would rather carry a gun. At least I could fight if the enemy caught up with us." Little Jiesheng did cry a lot, which was rather amusing for the soldiers. "Little Girl, what are you crying about? You are full of shit and piss . . . You stink. Twenty years from now, when you will love to be pretty, we will tell you about this! We'll see if you think it's funny."[3] In the end she survived, the youngest person to complete the March.

As if to compete, Xiao Ke's wife, the younger sister of He Long's wife, also gave birth on the Long March, and in the worst possible place, the grassland. On that day, she walked from early morning until three o'clock in the afternoon when her water broke. Her sister, who had never delivered a baby before, cut the umbilical cord, while Xiao Ke held her from the back. The next day she set off again, with her sister by her side. Her boy, Baosheng, which means "precious life," was carried out of the grassland by Xiao Ke's bodyguard and a groom.

I wondered whether Wang's story was typical of the women on the March. After all, she was relatively privileged, one of only 30 women out of 86,000 men in the 1st Army, protected by their huge force, and rarely engaged in direct battle. I wanted to find out how her life compared with the majority of women on the March, like the 3,000 and more who were in the 4th Army. It was to that army's base in Tongjiang, northern Sichuan, that I was now headed. Wang's fate was linked with them—she was to become Commander of its Women's Regiment, who were mostly women from that army.

I boarded a train for Tongjiang. The landscape was pleasing to the eye. The vast plain of Chengdu floated by, an image of fertility, with miles upon miles of paddy fields, interrupted only by bamboo thickets sheltering the frequent houses and villages—unlike Guizhou where you only passed a village every 10 miles. Sichuan really is China's "rice bowl," and because food is plentiful here, the population grew and grew, from 50 million in the 1930s to over 100 million today.

There were four girls sitting opposite me. Two of them were dressed up in cheap chic, one in a low-cut pink tank top, the other in a white T-shirt with a pair of big red lips stretched across her breasts and

"Kiss Me" printed in English underneath; the other two wore trendy blouses and skirts. They perked up as soon as the train hit the Chengdu Plain. From their accent I knew they were Sichuanese. They had been working for three years in a cloth factory in Chongqing, the biggest city in the province and the second biggest in the country. Because of the large population, men and women from Sichuan sought work all over China. These four girls were part of the migrant force. They seemed content earning about $70 a month; back home they got less. They spent some on themselves and sent most of their money home to their families. The girls were discussing how hard it was to save—a new outfit for the homecoming cost $16, while the other complained that a $1 bracelet made her think twice before she made up her mind.

Looking at them, cheerful, spirited, but also hardened by their jobs, I thought of the young women who joined the 4th Army from northern Sichuan. They were of the same age, in their late teens, also from villages, and wanting a better life. I asked them if they were going home for a holiday. "I wish," one of them said chirpily. "You see those women in the fields. We are going to help our families with the planting." We were going past flooded rice fields. It was beginning to rain, and the big drops danced on the water. Women worked in the downpour like machines, taking a handful of seedlings and putting them in a few at a time. It was backbreaking work, and they hardly looked up— but they left perfect straight and symmetrical rows behind them, beautiful to look at.

"We're all going home to help. It's a busy time," the girls said in chorus. Have you got leave? I asked. "That would be nice. We work really hard six days a week and we are given money or days off for overtime. That's what we're using." They said they would not actually plant rice, but they would feed the pigs and the poultry, do housework and cook, and take food out to their older relatives in the fields. It sounded like a lot to do, but they were obviously used to it. "My mom tells me people may die from laziness but never from hard work," said the plainest of them.

I took a bus after the train and arrived in Tongjiang in the late afternoon. I immediately knew I was in the right place. Red was dominant: "Red Square" in the center of town, "Red Army" hotels, "Red Army" restaurants, Red saunas, Red karaoke bars. The locals were certainly exploiting their Red heritage. When I checked into a small family hotel, I mentioned this to the manageress, a friendly woman in her thirties, and a cousin of the bus driver. "Why not? It's high time. Everyone is making money. One in five men and women in Tongjiang joined the Red Army. You can say every family has a Red history. My two great-uncles died for the Revolution. What did they get in return? Nothing . . ." Perhaps they would be angry that you are a capitalist, I joked. "Oh, they sacrificed their lives so that we could live a better life. That's what they wanted—a good life."

She talked quickly, as if she did not have time to spare, as Sichuanese women do. She told me how to have a good time in Tongjiang. The Museum of the 4th Red Army was a must. "Many visitors have no interest in the exhibits," she said with a little displeasure. "But it is in the old Confucian temple. It is a fine building, going back to the Ming Dynasty." The Red Army cemetery was also worth a visit, the largest in the country. "Again, if you don't fancy thinking about the dead, enjoy the scenery. It is on a hilltop, commanding the best view in the country." In the evening I could enjoy a Red banquet, the kind of things the soldiers used to eat, wood-ear mushrooms, wild plants from the mountains, sweet potatoes. "They are all fresh, fantastically good and tasty. No punishment at all. Who needs meat and fish?" After dinner, I could go to a Red karaoke bar and sing the songs the women used to sing for the soldiers to fire up their revolutionary enthusiasm. This was the Red Tourism program.

I had found someone who seemed to appreciate what I was after. Perhaps I should push my luck. I told her I was also interested in talking to the veterans. "Are you a journalist?" she asked. I shook my head. I told her about my journey, and she looked at me with her eyes wide open. "You mean you are doing the Long March again?" I explained that was not quite true. I was not walking every single step and I had come to Tongjiang by bus. "That's still quite something. How brave you are! And what a brilliant idea! Could I come with you and carry your bags?" she said. "That is really great. What can I help you with here? I am descended from Long Marchers. It is my duty. So what do you want?"

I told her I just wanted to talk to one or two veterans. Access to them was a hit-and-miss affair. The local pensioners' office which had all the data did not give out their names and addresses easily unless you had a letter of introduction from some government organization, which I did not have. Even if you had one, it was not always straight-forward; local officials might worry that you were a journalist exposing problems in their work, such as switching pension money to other uses. I felt like a scout on the Long March, using whatever means I could to trace the veterans. "No problem. This is a small town," she said confi-dently. "As my mother says, in the old days, when a husband and wife quarreled, the whole town knew. It hasn't changed that much. You go to the museum first and I'll see what I can do."

The 4th Army had certainly commandeered the best place in Tongjiang for its headquarters. The old Confucian temple sits against a green hill, with the Nuo River flowing softly past its entrance. It is a tranquil place, one courtyard succeeding another with a temple or me-morial hall in each, fronted by neatly tended grass, and shaded by old pines and beeches. There is a statue of Confucius, and finely carved tombs and tomb guardians. Every town used to have such a temple, the nearest we came to an indigenous place of worship in a culture with no gods of its own. It was where scholars congregated in the old days, where they learned and memorized the teachings of Confucius, and where they took the exams that would propel them into the establish-ment if they were successful. Wooden plaques from centuries ago painted with these scholars' names are still hanging from the roof beams.

In the main hall, where Confucius' portrait used to hang, was the history of the 4th Army. For a long time I knew little about it because the official history of the Long March was so dominated by Mao and his 1st Army. The 4th Army was created in January 1931 out of the Red armies formed during peasant risings in the Dabie Mountains of Hubei, Henan, and Anhui provinces. It was a strategically impor-tant area, surrounded by mountains, bordering on the Yangzi, and controlling much of the Yangzi plain. The army grew, alarming Chiang, who launched a series of campaigns against it at the same time as he attacked the Jiangxi base. The biggest battle came in October 1931. The 4th Army put up a heroic fight for more than a year, and lost 35,000 soldiers. Of those who lived, over 400 were later made generals in the Chinese army, more than from any other place in the country. In the end they could not win. On October 12, 1932, 20,000 men and women abandoned their base and set off to find a new one elsewhere. This marked the beginning of their Long March.

They were thwarted by the Nationalist troops in their attempt to settle in the fertile plain south of Xian in Shaanxi. They were criticized by the Central Committee for abandoning their base and escaping. They were ordered to go back to their original base and carry on their guerrilla warfare. "If you continue to escape West, we will openly denounce you."[4] There was no turning back, though; their base was like a lemon squeezed dry. But just then the top commanders learned from the Nationalist newspapers that in northern Sichuan around Tongjiang the warlords were engaged in an all-out battle for control of the province. That meant they could take advantage of the situation and settle there. Also it was fertile, and the steep mountains made it easy to defend it. It was a lucky find. On December 26, 1932, they took Tongjiang and the surrounding counties without much of a fight. They distributed land to the poor, who in turn joined the Red Army, 50,000 in Tongjiang alone, and 65,000 from neighboring counties. In no time, the Tongjiang Red base became the second biggest in the country after Jiangxi. It was on here that the officers and men of Mao's 1st Army set their sights. They were hoping to join the 4th Army and put an end to what seemed like eight months' pointless erratic circling and several failed attempts to establish a base of their own in Guizhou.

But there was someone missing in the exhibition at the Tongjiang museum—the 4th Army chief Zhang Guotao. Knowing his history, I did not expect any eulogies, but no mention at all was almost unbelievable. Born of a rich landlord family, Zhang rose up in the Communist Party echelons much faster than Mao and became one of its most senior leaders in his twenties. He was known for his intellect, his talent as an organizer, his independent mind, and his experience with the labor movement. In 1931, he was sent by the Party to head the 4th Army and the base in Hubei, Hunan, and Anhui. It was a difficult year: the base, like all the regions along the Yangzi River, was hit by one of the worst floods in history, affecting 180 million people. Crops were ruined, dykes collapsed, houses were swept away, and prisoners drowned when their cells were inundated.[5] Zhang rose to the task. Food was rationed right away, and everyone was asked to plant at least one pumpkin—five for Party members—with vegetables and rice covering every inch of land. The pumpkins were ready in a few months. The locals were stunned: when all around them were starving, they had one of the best harvests in memory. And Zhang was pleased with himself. "I naturally became the focus," he said. "People came up with many far-fetched notions about me. Many thought they had a new 'emperor.'"[6]

He was rather too like an emperor—as soon as he arrived at the base, he replaced most of the 4th Army's top commanders with his own men, and started a frenzy of killings of the officers and others thought to support them, all in the name of getting rid of Nationalist spies and traitors. "If we kill 10,000 or even 20,000 of these men, it is not a big deal," Zhang declared at a mass rally. People competed in denunciations to earn his favor. The victims had their throats cut and were laid in alternate layers of firewood and bodies, and burned in the dark. The 25th Corps, the elite force of the 4th Army, lost half its men in these purges—6,000—in little more than a month. Its commander was strangled with a rope, while the rest were killed with machine guns when they could not get rid of them fast enough. Xu Xiangqian, the capable Commander-in-Chief of the 4th Army, could not even protect his own wife. While he was at the front repelling yet another Nationalist attack on the base, she was tortured and killed for refusing to denounce him.

In Tongjiang the purge did not stop entirely but it was less lethal. They concentrated on building up the base and strengthening the army to prepare for a concerted campaign by the premier warlord of Sichuan, Liu Xiang. He had emerged as the winner from the warlords' competition for supremacy that had lasted over a year and left 2 million people homeless. He would not tolerate the Red Army on his territory and he asked help from Chiang, who was only too happy to oblige—at last he had an excuse to go into the most populous province in China. He offered nearly 15 million silver dollars and ammunition; in return, he had a staff regiment stationed in Chongqing, not only to supervise Warlord Liu's campaign, but also to prepare his own take-over of the province. When all was ready, Liu threw 200,000 men from the various minor warlords under his command into a campaign that lasted from October 1933 until September 1934, while Chiang ran his last campaign against the Jiangxi base. To further boost his chances, Liu sought the blessing of a Taoist priest who decided the "auspicious days" for battles. It did him no good—he lost to the Red Army, and then to Chiang, who finally gained a foothold in Sichuan.

To help with the war effort the 4th Army selected the most promising women and formed the Independent Women's Regiment. Its main tasks were looking after the wounded, making clothes, repairing roads, building bridges, carrying the silver and medicine reserves for the entire army, and protecting the army headquarters. On display in a prominent position in the museum was a black-and-white photo of Zhang Qiuqin, Commander of the Women's Regiment, who later rose to be head of the 4th Army's Political Department, the highest-ranking woman in the Red Army. She was known as a Red beauty, with elongated almond-shaped eyes and high cheekbones, which are unusual for a Chinese. She looked like a film star, and was a brilliant commander as well. Once she and her women were carrying three wounded soldiers to safety when they ran into a regiment of the local warlord's men. She organized attacks from several directions to confuse them. Then she told the women to call out and plead with the men to turn their guns on their officers. To their complete surprise, the firing stopped and white flags came up—the regiment had mutinied, roping all their officers, and surrendered. "Five Hundred Peasant Women Defeat Regiment!" ran the headline in the local newspapers. The Women's Regiment was famous.

The exhibition whetted my appetite for more on the 4th Army, and in particular about its Women's Regiment, both of which I knew little about. I had been told that Tongjiang still had quite a few veterans left, so I was hopeful I would be able to talk to some. When I returned to the hotel, the manageress was waiting. "I have some good news for you." She asked the waitress to bring me some tea, and told me she had found two woman veterans, one very well-known one who was always being interviewed, the other a member of the Women's Regiment who was from Tongjiang and was home for a visit from northwestern China where she now lived. Instinctively, I opted for the latter. I had talked to more than one veteran who either because they were very senior, or because they were well trained, got wheeled out for visiting journalists and on ceremonial occasions. They mostly told me things I already knew. I am sure they had their private memories; but they had learned their patter, and probably thought I did not want to hear anything else.

I ordered my lunch of rice and sweet potato porridge and fried bamboo shoots from the Red Tourism menu. It was not much of a contribution to her business. I wished I could do more. While I was waiting for my dishes, the manageress turned on the TV. This was classic Chinese hospitality, the purpose of which completely escapes me. There was a costume soap about some princess falling in love with a common man. "What do they know about love? They fall in and out of love as frequently as they change their shoes," the manageress said. "You know, there is a woman here who really knows about lasting love. Her husband joined the Long March, and she has been waiting for him ever since. We call her the 'Crazy Woman.' She's a real character. You should write about the women left behind, not just those who went on the March. To me, they are equally extraordinary."

She was right. When people talk about the Long March, they talk about the soldiers, mostly men but also a few women. But they were not the only ones to suffer. For every man who left, there was a loving wife or mother who stayed behind. I thought of Xingguo County in Jiangxi, where whole villages were full of widows. The locals do not call Xingguo "Model County," but "Widow County." I had talked to some widows there, but I was glad to have another chance in the home county of the Women's Regiment. But first came the veteran, Wu Yuqing.

I could hardly believe she was 82 when I saw her. She was small and slender, like the women of Sichuan, with a kind expression. She always smiled, and her voice was gentle, but it was firm and decided in tone. She was born in Tongjiang in 1922 and was sold into marriage as a child by her father who, like so many men there, was an opium addict and a gambler. "You cannot imagine. In this little town, there were more than 200 opium dens," Wu told me. "Every family grew opium and just about everyone was an addict, including the children. When the children were sick, their parents would blow the powder up their nostrils as a cure; when they cried, the mothers would give them a little sniff to quiet them down. The rich smoked the first round, and the poor smoked the ashes. Women smoked too, but not as much as men. When the 4th Army got here, they had no choice but to change their rules and recruit women. As they say in Tongjiang, 'For a good life, women take the lead.'"

Wu had a cousin who worked for the Red Army and the local Soviet government. "You have nothing to lose but the rope around your waist," she told Wu one day. "She made me see the absurdity of my life," she recalled. "My mother-in-law tied a rope round my waist and just pulled it tighter when I said I was hungry. She worked me from dawn till dusk, with only one meal in between. And then she complained I ate too much. They treated their pigs better. Why should I put up with it?" Wu was only 11—too young to fight or carry heavy loads—so she was put in the propaganda team, together with forty other girls, all roughly of the same age. As soon as she mentioned this, she asked if she could sing a song for me. She sang every note in tune, not looking at me, but gazing steadily forward.

> Before, women suffered like being fried in a pan;
> Our fate changed with the Red Army:
> Feet unbound, hair cut,
> We became the same as men.
> As men, we follow the army and conquer the world.

"We sang all the way on the March. Songs to spur the soldiers on while they were marching, to cheer them up before battles, to entertain them while they rested, and to add to their joy in victory. For example, when they were tired and flagging, we would sing: 'Come on, big brothers. We are half your size. If we can do it, you can go faster too.' It is hard to describe but you only needed to say a little thing like that and it really pushed them along. Maybe they felt ashamed but certainly we had a big effect."

"Were the men attracted to you?" I asked. I had read in the memoirs of Xu Xiangqian, the Commander-in-Chief of the 4th Army, that he was quite concerned about senior officers who liked to visit the Women's Regiment, with the obvious intention of picking them up. "Yours is a fighting unit, not a reserve unit for wives," he warned Zhang Qiuqin. "From now on, men should not visit your regiment without a reason. Your women should not fall in love and should not marry. Anyone who wants to marry must leave."[7]

"I was too young. But the rule was very strict." Wu paused and lowered her voice. I had to crane my neck to hear her. "Only important men like Mao or Zhu De were allowed to have their women with them. Senior officers also took their pick. But nobody else was permitted. A handsome company commander tried his luck, and we never saw him again. You know, the leaders were clever. They knew that if a man had a woman at home, he wouldn't want to leave. We even had a song about that: 'Fluttering the red flag, and carrying five-foot rifles, we're up before sunrise. Sisters of the Revolution: don't love boys, love guns!' " She didn't have to sing that one for me—I learned the song at school and can still remember it.

Soldiers were frustrated. Many of them had their first intimate experiences with the opposite sex immediately before the Long March. They were in a hurry to get married and keep a wife and, possibly, an heir at home, or they were bedded by the women who recruited them. Zhu De told Edgar Snow's wife in 1936 that for the 1st Army, rape had been something of a problem in the early days of the March; but it was brought under control as discipline improved.[8] In the 4th Army, the rule was tightened after complaints from local people. Soldiers found guilty of rape could be executed; those who committed other unlawful acts against women would be punished appropriately.[9] But after a while, within the 4th Army, if an officer picked up a girl in the Women's Regiment, they let it be, as long as the woman did not complain or make too much noise when they were making love, and the man kept it quiet.

The strict rules did protect the women and won their hearts. Many in the Women's Regiment, including Wu, were caught and raped by the enemy later on. "When they got us, we heard them saying, 'The Red Bandits really look after their women well. Every single one of them was a virgin.' She said nothing more. This almost inadvertent testimony touched me more than any propaganda about Communist virtue. I had an image of Wu shuddering in a corner after the fact, with these dreadful words reaching her ears.

Given the risks, I wondered whether the Red Army should have taken women at all. All the men I had talked to on the journey thought not. They were afraid of what would happen to the women if they were captured. Hygienist Chen was more perceptive. He said the enemy would fight harder if they knew they were fighting women—it was shameful to be defeated by them, and if they won, the women would be theirs to have their way with.

Wu did not agree. "We are as good as men, if not better," she said with a force that was almost overwhelming after her usual calm and quiet words. She believed the Red Army would have been much the poorer without its women. There were three crucial jobs to be done that they were more skilled at: recruiting soldiers and porters for the army; collecting information from villagers about wealthy families to confiscate supplies; and, hardest of all, persuading families to take in the army's sick and wounded—dangerous because they could be punished by the Nationalists when the army left. "I pleaded, I begged, I cried. You name it and I did it," Wu recalled. "I cannot imagine a man doing it. People normally obliged, either because they pitied us or wanted to get rid of us. But it meant we saved one more soldier."

But even women could not always get their way. One day, after a battle, Wu and two other women had to find homes for two dozen wounded soldiers. "My lips must have been worn thin from begging, but in the end we managed to place only ten men, and the rest had to be left in a cave, each with a few silver dollars and two bullets. One soldier who was wounded in the leg held on to the corner of my trousers, pleading for me to take him with me, but he could not possibly keep up with the troops. Just after I tore myself away, there was a loud bang. He had shot himself in the head, and the blood spattered over me. I felt so bad, I could not eat for days. Even today, his beseeching eyes haunt me."

I was silent, unable to say anything. After a time, I asked her how else she thought women's experience on the March differed from men's.

"You could not easily tell us apart on the outside," she said. "We all had our heads shaved so the enemy wouldn't know they were fighting women. And we all wore caps. Women without hair would have frightened the local people. But some of our own men were very naughty. They would take our caps off from behind, and shout, 'Nuns! Nuns! Welcome, nuns of the Red Army!'"

For Wu, the biggest difference was that fewer women died on the March. She knew they were not in combat as much as the men. But on the Tibetan Plateau, the hardest stretch of the March, there were no battles, and still more women survived. I asked her the reason.

"Women knew how to look after themselves," she said without hesitation.

Like keeping their four treasures? I asked. She nodded eagerly. I had read about them. The first was a washbasin, which they used to wash their faces, soak their feet, cook food, and keep the rain off; and they could turn it over and sit on it. "Every night, wherever there was a washbasin, it would be the center of the camp. The women divided the work among themselves, finding firewood and clean water, digging a hole in the ground, and boiling the water and cooking the food. When it was ready, we sat around the basin, eating the porridge, and feeling the warmth of the fire. It was such a wonderful feeling. Long live the washbasin!" When the marching became tough, she threw away some of her possessions but never the washbasin.

The second treasure was a stick. At the beginning, Wu did not have a rifle, and the stick was her weapon, at least against landlords' dogs. At night the women put their sticks in the ground and a sheet of oilcloth over it and it became a tent. In the grassland, it was indispensable. "You never knew where to put your feet. A wrong step could have been the end of your life. The stick turned into my third leg." The third treasure was animal skin. Some older women in her team collected it whenever they could, and Wu did not understand why at first. "It makes the best shoes; all you have to do is wrap it around your feet," they told her. "We ate those shoes when there was a real food shortage, and it saved my life." The fourth treasure was a needle, which she kept under her cap. The women even made a rule: whoever lost their needle or broke it would be punished.

Wu had one more treasure, a beautiful black silk nightshirt which she requested after a confiscation from a particularly rich landlord. She fell in love with it the minute she saw it. Everyone thought she was being foolish—she could get money for it, and it was far too big for her— but she kept it. She meant to give it to her mother, who had never had one square meal and never known new clothes. Whatever her hardships, she carried it all the way. Sadly, she did not see her mother again; she was killed by the Nationalists before Wu could rejoin her.

Wu thought nature helped women too. They were smaller, and needed less food and less oxygen when they were on the plateau, thousands of meters up. "The men were much bigger and stronger than us. But one day I'd be chatting with them, encouraging them, they seemed all right, and then the next day I'd see the same ones lying by the roadside. I thought they were tired and resting. I shouted to them cheekily, 'Hey, my big brothers, on your bottoms again? Time to move on, otherwise you won't have your dinner tonight.' They did not respond. I bent down to give them a shove. Their hands were cold as ice. They were dead, or dying—they were too weak with hunger to go on, or couldn't breathe anymore. Thousands of men died like that. A few women died too; but most of us had what was needed to keep going. We were just luckier than the men really."

Luck had little to do with it. She survived the March, like all the veterans, because of her hope, her will, and her resourcefulness: 20 and more miles a day for a 12-year-old was tough, and many of her comrades lagged behind or deserted. Sometimes they went for days without food and she grew so hungry she could hardly walk, but she preferred the hardship of the Red Army to being treated like a dog by her mother-in-law. The rigors of the March were no worse than that. On the contrary, she had food when there was food, and occasional treats like pork and ham that she had never known before. She had her beautiful silk night-shirt, and four silver dollars in allowances for three years—undreamed-of things. The commissar told her that when the Communists won—when they had killed all the landlords in the country—she would enjoy all the things that only they had now.

Wu had an enormous willpower that her small frame and soft voice belied. She had learned not to sit down for a rest; if she did, she might never stand up again; she had seen it happen too often with the men she tried to cajole and keep moving. She was told not to drink water from ditches or dirty streams, and she did not, even when her throat was on fire. Others did, and became sick and died. When the weather got hot, many soldiers threw away their thicker jackets, but she kept hers even though she did not know where they were going. When they were cross-ing the high peaks, her extra layer saved her. Life and death were one breath, one flicker of thought apart. If she faltered it could be all over.

And how resourceful she was. Many died on the March from eat-ing poisonous plants when food was in short supply. Once she saw a bunch of berries but she was not sure if they were edible. She waited until a crow picked at them. "If the crows do not die, I will survive too," she told herself. Conscious that she was smaller than the others and could not always keep up with the troops, she made sure she learned how to tell directions so she would not be lost. She could do it in a for-est by seeing which side of the trees had got the sun—the bark was thicker. When she did lag behind and sleep, she would fix a twig in the ground to point the way to go when she woke up.

It was hard for me to match all this with the sweet old lady who sat talking with me. Very few could believe her story. When Wu first re-turned to Tongjiang in the 1960s, her family thought she was a ghost—thinking she was long dead they had even built a tomb for her. She had gone through untold pain and come through, a gentle, contented woman at peace with herself. Wu kept saying how tough *my* journey must be; it was as if the March had just been a detour for her. She represented to me an earlier generation of Chinese women. Centuries of subordination made them accept their lot with equanimity. If they rebelled, it can only have been because life had become completely intolerable. I may have thought her heroic; she was just grateful to have found in the March the way to her own liberation.

My last task in Tongjiang was to find the "Crazy Woman." I hired a car the next morning, and after an hour's drive, we came to a village and saw an old lady standing outside a house near the road which led into it. "That's her. She always stands there," the driver said. She was small, and thin as the stick she was holding. She had a woolen hat on even though it was quite warm, a blue jacket faded from the wash, and a patched apron. She held one hand up to shade her eyes, to follow our car. When we got out, she came up to us and asked who we were looking for. A big smile appeared on her face when the driver handed her my presents and told her we had come to see her. "Come on in, come on in," she said warmly, and led us into her house. It was almost empty. A TV sat on a small table in the corner; a few rattan stools stood here and there. She wiped them with her apron for us to sit on.

She had joined the Revolution as soon the Red Army came to their village. "It was for the poor, and we were dead poor." As a zealous member of the peasants' association, she confiscated five geese and a pig from a man at a market one day, thinking he was a rich peasant. He complained to the local Party committee, saying he was not rich and was just selling what he had because his father was sick. The complaint was upheld, and she was fined three silver dollars. "Where could we get the money? Not in this life," she sighed. Then they offered to cancel the fine if she helped them to meet the recruitment quota—ten men. She managed to persuade nine, including her two brothers, but was still one short. In desperation she asked her husband if he would go. "He was only 14. Our marriage was arranged by our parents, when I was 8 years old and he was 4. We had just got married ten years later. I'm not sure he understood what might happen. He thought it sounded exciting. After ten days, he left."

She waited for him for a couple of years, and then decided to look for him. She still could not get over having recruited him herself. She heard the Red Army had reached a place in northern China three months' travel away. She asked the way but people told her she would never find it; also it was in the Nationalist region so she might be caught. She had better wait and he would come back when the Revolution was won. Meanwhile, her mother-in-law wanted her to get married again, so that she could have another dowry, but she refused. She wanted to stay with the family so when her husband returned she would be there for him. She begged her brother-in-law to let her adopt one of his seven daughters and look after her. He happily obliged and today she still lives with the adopted daughter and her family.

In 1949, after the Revolution, she heard that the People's Liberation Army was marching nearby, so she went and stood on the riverbank where they were crossing and waited for three days and nights. She never saw him. Many times she went into town to ask the local government where he was, walking 30 kilometers there and back. She thought they knew but were afraid to tell her the truth. What did she say to them? I asked. "You know what men are like." She drew her stool up close, confiding in me. "They always need women, not one but many. I told them it would not matter if he had got married and had another family. I only wanted to have one more look at him, to know he was all right, and then I would be happy to let him go again."

In 1985, county officials came looking for her. She was working in her field and saw them coming. She thought they were bringing her good news, but they told her he had died. She fainted. When they revived her, she asked how they could be sure he was dead. Did they have any evidence? They said it was from a veteran they had just interviewed—her husband was killed in a battle to break out of the base, not far from Tongjiang. He did not even go on the Long March. She cried the whole day, and asked them again and again for details. Even then, she did not quite believe he was gone. Whenever people came to the village in cars, she would ask if they knew anything about her husband. She liked to stand outside her house, and look down the road, day in and day out, hoping he would miraculously turn up. "If I hadn't signed him up, he would be with me now," she murmured to herself, and then fell into a long silence.

I looked at her and I kept thinking of the women I had visited in the Glorious Old People's Home outside Ruijin. There were more than eighty people there, two-thirds of them women, many the widows of Marchers. The oldest was 110—she had arrived at the age of 64 in 1958 when the home was opened, and was still thriving. It was late morning when I arrived, and some of them were sitting outside, enjoying the sun. Beautiful even at this age, one wore a bright blue shirt and petite brown gauzy shoes complete with embroidery; one had a flower pinned to her hair; another had a beautiful hand-knitted sweater. Beauty was important to them, part of their bearing, and almost a necessity. Many of the people of Jiangxi were originally driven here from central China, therefore they called themselves *Hakka*, or "Guest People." Survival was their main concern. A woman was encouraged to have as many children as possible, even if they were not her husband's. The old custom was that when she had a birthday, she would invite all her lovers— the more there were, the prouder she and her husband were.

The old ladies had been animated, they talked, they laughed, they burst into tears. They all wanted to have their say at once, about the recruitment, about singing for the Red Army, about washing and making clothes for the soldiers, about life without their men . . . The 110-year-old kept saying how difficult it was to recruit, so she let her husband join. He never came back. She still remembered him with an aching heart. How much she missed him! He was good to her; she came to his family at the age of 7, and he did not beat her. After he left she waited for seven years, but her mother-in-law told her they did not want her anymore, and refused to give her anything to eat. So she married again, someone who gambled and beat her all the time.

She was still talking, but another woman broke in, 93 years old, tall and elegant. She was a member of the village propaganda team and offered to sing a song. The others stopped her, telling her to be patient and wait her turn. Patience, what a thing to say to someone of 93! She did not wait, and burst into a song about persuading a young man to join the Red Army if he really loved her. As soon as she began, all the other women joined in. Each of them remembered the song, every word of it. Their voices were hoarse, out of tune, out of breath, but in unison. The singing filled them with emotion, taking them back to their first feelings of love, their hopes for a happy future. They had remained widows, or remarried but were never so content. They lived in the memory of those fleeting moments. But then tears began to fall, sad tears that happiness was denied to them for the next seventy years. Still they sang.

When it was time for me to leave the "Crazy Woman," she came out and stood by the roadside with her stick for support. It was where she had stood saying good-bye to her husband seventy years before, and where she had been waiting ever since. Every visitor brought her a crumb of hope. All I had been able to give her was some fruit, instant noodles, honey, and powdered milk. It seemed pitifully little. I wished I had some comfort for her. As we drove away, I looked back at her lonely figure, and I suddenly thought of the Chinese legend about a fisherman's wife turning into a rock, after waiting a lifetime for her husband to come back from the sea. I thought it was just a fable, even laughable. Where could you find such a woman? Well, there she was, I had been talking to her: seventy years of love and seventy years of hope and despair. She was on a march that would only end with her life.

The 22-man Red Army Death Squad looked out over the Luding Bridge, 101 meters long, a single span of thirteen iron chains, each as thick as a blacksmith's arm. The wooden walkway was mostly gone. At the far end the Nationalists in the bridge-house stared over their sandbags, machine guns at the ready, waiting to send them to their deaths in the Dadu River which boiled and foamed below. The soldiers started crawling, each knee and boot on a chain, one hand grasping a side-chain, the other firing a rifle. The enemy guns sprayed them with bullets. One Red fighter and then another were hit and were swallowed by the rushing water. The rest kept coming forward. A third and fourth man fell, but still they came, firing without cease as the Nationalists' bullets zipped past and clanged off the chains. As they got nearer, the guards set the bridge-house and the few remaining planks on the bridge alight in a final desperate act. The commissar called out to the squad: "Comrades, don't forget the glorious task entrusted to you by the Party. Don't be afraid of death. Strive on courageously." The men stood up, ran the last yards into the flames, their eyebrows and their clothes on fire. The enemy fled in terror. The Red Army was saved.

This was the scene immortalized in one of the most successful propaganda films ever made by the Communist Party—*The Dadu River*—about the most celebrated of battles. The film symbolizes the Long March rather as *Battleship Potemkin* does the Russian Revolution. It has been engraved on my mind since I was a teenager. Before I set out on my journey, I consulted a military historian in Beijing, asking him which battles I should concentrate on. "Which one do you know best?" he asked. "The Luding Bridge," I said, hardly thinking. "You call that a battle? Just a couple of men fell into the river, and it was over in an hour. How can that be the biggest battle of the Long March?" I was stunned.

I thought I knew it so well. "Go and find out for yourself," he added, "and come back and tell me what you discovered."

When I stood at the bridge in late May 2004, seventy years after the event, it was just as I remembered it from the film, and just as spectacular—except that now the wooden walkway was back in place, and a few locals with umbrellas were strolling peacefully across above the torrent. They were obviously used to it. I took a few steps and quickly turned back. The whole bridge swayed alarmingly. If I went in the middle where the walkway is wider, I could not hold on to the side-chain. If I tried to walk at the side, there was only one narrow plank to tread on, and the raging water down below made me dizzy. What it was like for the soldiers when there were no planks at all, I could only imagine. How brave they must have been!

I felt better when I thought of Operator Zhong and Woman Wang. When Zhong crossed the bridge with the 1st Army, a lot of the planks had been put back, but he still had to go on all fours. "I was shivering like a jelly and could not stand up straight," he recalled with a shy smile. "I crawled like a snail, with my eyes half shut. I could not bear to see the water. I felt it could suck me in at any time. It must have taken me hours." But he was not the only one. "Lin Biao, the brilliant commander of the 1st Corps, had to be helped by three soldiers. They led him from the front, and held his arms on each side. He was just as hopeless as me." He giggled like a girl. Woman Wang, for the first time, was not her ebullient self. The Convalescent Unit had cases of medicine and the women roped them to poles, which they carried across their shoulders. "But when the bridge swayed, your body went one way, the boxes went the other. The boxes were heavier than we were, and we thought we would be pulled off balance and end up in the river, feeding the fish." She was almost reduced to tears when Mao passed by and asked his security guards to help with the task, while the propaganda team cheered them on:

> The Red Army took Luding Bridge
> Gunfire licked the heavens, iron chains rocked.
> Feet planted on iron chains undaunted,
> The women wrestled the medicine chests.[1]

I waited until a group of tourists arrived and then joined them. The swing was much less alarming with a lot of people walking across, and as I listened to the guide I almost stopped worrying. The bridge was built in 1705, exactly 300 years ago, after the last Imperial Dynasty had quashed a rebellion by the Tibetans with great difficulty. The Dadu River lies in the west of Sichuan Province and it separates the Chengdu Plain from the Tibetan region. There was no bridge over it for hundreds of miles, so it took too long to get the troops across. One was deemed necessary for the security of the empire. Blacksmiths were called in from all over the western counties, but they could not find enough iron ore—the thirteen chains were made of 12,164 links, weighing 21 tons, and each drum weighed another 20 tons. Legend has it that they searched for forty-nine days, and finally found the ore in a mountain far away. When it came to fixing the chains over the river, they could not lift them. Then a man with a long beard, and wearing a gown, floated up on the water and, with a swing of his horse-tail brush, the chains flew up by themselves. The old man then evaporated.

The local official sent a report to Emperor Kang Xi in 1706, together with a drawing of the complete bridge—perhaps without the story of the wizard. The emperor was so impressed he gave a name to the bridge: Lu Ding—Lu the local name for the Dadu River; Dìng, meaning "to pacify." He hoped the Luding Bridge would bring peace to this far-flung region and beyond. However, peace was a dream that took three centuries to come true; but trade flourished. The bridge became the main conduit for the region, with caravans streaming across it, carrying tea, salt, and silk all the way to Lhasa, and furs and medicine to Chengdu.

At the head of the bridge on the western bank stands a stone stele bearing the imposing characters of the emperor's inscription. Above it, hewn into the cliff, there is a temple where people offered incense and prayed for a safe journey. I climbed up to have a look. From the temple balcony, with the great sweep of the water on each side flowing down its wide gorge, I could see even more clearly how everything focused on this narrow bridge. The 1st Army had been marching in the region west of the Dadu River and now had to cross to the eastern side to meet up with the 4th Army. But, as the saying goes, if one man stands here, he can stop 10,000. Edgar Snow was quite categorical about it: "The crossing of the Dadu River was the most critical single incident of the Long March. Had the Red Army failed there, quite possibly it would have been exterminated."[2]

This indeed had happened to over 40,000 Taiping rebels in the mid-nineteenth century. They wanted to set up a Kingdom of Heavenly Peace, where people would worship Christ, the one and only God. But the God Worshippers, as they called themselves, failed to win the hearts of many Chinese. "When heaven is deaf to all judgment or feeling, how can I save the people with my bare hands?" lamented Prince Shi Dakai, the last Taiping leader. Here, on this very stretch of the Dadu River, the rebels were cornered by the pursuing Imperial Army. Most jumped in rather than surrender, while the wives, the generals, and the sons of the prince took their own lives. The prince himself was taken to Chengdu where he was sliced up piece by piece and bled to death. On dark nights along the Dadu, it was said, one could hear the wailing of the spirits of the Taiping warriors. They would wail until they were avenged.

But how did Mao's men avoid the same fate? Mao reckoned speed was the answer. The Taiping rebels were trapped because Prince Shi stopped for three days to celebrate the birth of his son while the Imperial Army was hot on his heels. Mao was confident that history would not repeat itself. He told the vanguard unit to cover 90 miles in just two days to take the bridge before Nationalist reinforcements appeared on the scene. "You must march at top speed and take every possible measure to accomplish this glorious mission. We wait to congratulate you on your victory."

In the film, the vanguard did not have time to eat or sleep; they marched day and night, climbing hills and wading rivers; they abandoned everything they carried except guns and ammunition. As they were hurrying on, they spotted a Nationalist battalion on the other bank of the river. They signaled to them by bugle using a Nationalist code, pretending they were allies. But the sighting of the Nationalists convinced them even more of the necessity for speed. After a slow start, they covered 70 miles in twenty-four hours and, as dawn broke on May 29, they arrived at the Luding Bridge. At four o'clock in the afternoon the attack began, and within an hour the bridge was taken.

Yet the more I looked at the bridge, the more puzzled I became. It was only three meters wide, so the Death Squad could only get along it in twos and threes. If there were heavy machine guns defending it, as I had seen in the film, how could any force, with no mortar fire or artillery in support, possibly get through and storm the bridge-house? And without the loss of a single man, as the head of the vanguard unit remembered, or with the loss of only four men as mentioned in the placard displayed on the bridge? Against a whole regiment? I found it hard to believe.

I asked the temple guard if anyone in the town of Luding was old enough to remember the Red Army's arrival seventy years ago. "You want Blacksmith Zhu," he said without hesitation. "He isn't that old, but his family has been looking after the bridge for generations. Their workshop used to be right next to the bridge-house. Now he lives a few houses down the river. Ask anyone and they will be able to direct you."

I found Mr. Zhu at his house. He was a tall, big-shouldered man, with a strong face marked by thick eyebrows and a determined jaw, and his hair standing straight up on his head. Everything about him conveyed a forceful nature. He no longer worked full-time. "Only when the bridge needs a major checkup every five years and a minor one every three years," he said. His life was less nerve-wracking than in the old days; his father and grandfather had to engrave their names on the chains, and if any fault was found, their heads would be on the block.

Zhu's father did not flee when the Red Army came—he did not want to abandon his workshop. He was asked to lend the doors of his house to replace the planks removed by the militiamen. Were all the planks gone as the film described? I asked. "Oh, no, only the stretch at our end." Then he added: "I don't know why they didn't remove all of them. It surely would have made it more difficult for the Red Army."

How about the battle itself? "The Red Army could not possibly have crossed it if a whole Nationalist regiment was guarding the bridge with machine guns. I can assure you of that. I know the bridge like the back of my hand," he said firmly.

So what really happened? "Only a squadron was at the other end. It was a rainy day. Their weapons were old and could only fire a few meters. They were no match for the Red Army. When they saw the soldiers coming, they panicked and fled—their officers had long abandoned them. There wasn't really much of a battle. Still, I take my hat off to the twenty-two soldiers who crawled on the chains. My father and I did it in the old days when we checked the bridge, but we were inside a basket. Those men were brave. They crossed very quickly."

What Zhu said was surprising. The film images were so overwhelming—could they really be wrong? This was supposed to be the most famous battle on the Long March, so if there was little fighting, as Zhu had told me, why was so much made of it? Zhu had no answer. Before I left, he had another shock for me. "Do you know that after the Red Army crossed, they cut through four of the chains? It took my father and his helpers months to repair it, and no one could use the bridge before they did." He said it matter-of-factly, but it was simply too outrageous to be mentioned in the film or the history books. No one had dared to do such a thing in the bridge's long history.

The idea came from Mao—perhaps the only person capable of it—as I found out later from the memoirs of He Changgong, the man who carried out Mao's instructions. He was the Commissar of the 9th Corps. At Luding, his men were the rear guard. After watching the bridge for a week, when all the troops had crossed, he received a telegram from the Military Commission to destroy it "to some extent" and slow down the pursuing Nationalist troops. He decided to leave the four chains that served as arm-rails intact, but of the nine in the middle he would cut through every alternate one. When he finally caught up with the main troop, he went to see Zhou Enlai. "He praised our good work, and ordered the cook to make me a special chicken noodle dish as a reward for my contribution."[3]

As to the other pieces in the Luding Bridge puzzle—why was the bridge so feebly defended, why were the planks not completely removed, and where was the regiment that was supposed to have guarded the bridge? These questions took me a little longer to solve. I went back to Chengdu, the provincial capital, after I finished this leg of my journey. There I combed the archives and also talked to local historians, including an expert who had spent years studying the Sichuan warlords and interviewing their surviving family members and staff. It seems that one of the warlords, Liu Wenhui, was a key figure.

Liu was quite a character, and a survivor. He once boasted an army of half a million men, and a reputation as the most generous man in Sichuan; his wealth came from his large opium crops. He was the overlord of Sichuan until his nephew challenged him with the help of Chiang Kaishek, after which he retreated to western Sichuan with barely 20,000 men. There he nursed his wounds, his poppy fields, and his hopes of regaining his dominance. When Zhu De and Liu Bocheng, his fellow Sichuanese, sent him money and a letter, asking for safe passage through his territory, including the Luding Bridge, he happily obliged, although Chiang had ordered him "on pain of a court martial" to hold fast at the Dadu River so that pursuing Nationalist troops could catch up. Why should he use his weakened men to fight the Communists? "Chiang gives my army no ammunition or food, how can we fight tough battles?" he grumbled.[4] He told his men to put up only halfhearted resistance, and to allow the Red Army through without much of a fight. It was not Chiang, as has been suggested, but Liu, who let the Red Army escape this time.

Liu kept his contact with the Communists—his wireless operator was sent by Zhou Enlai. In 1949 he mutinied, taking two other warlords with him over to the Communists. Chiang was incensed—his last order before he flew to Taiwan was to bomb Liu's residence in Chengdu, where enough treasure and gold were found to supply ten of Chiang's best divisions for two years. Liu was not too bothered. "As a Buddhist I do not think of such things, they are all external, and cannot last; only women worry about them."[5] In any case, he had over 100 houses in Chengdu and, more importantly, he had no cause for concern. Mao rewarded him for his "services": he was made Minister of Forestry, and then a minister in the Communist government.

Combing the local archives yielded another unexpected insight. The Sichuan Party historians went to Beijing in 1984 to interview General Li Jukui about the most important events of the Long March that happened in their territory. General Li commanded the division involved in the crossing earlier at Anshunchang, also guarded by Liu Wenhui's men. Here too, there was supposed to be a fierce battle before Luding, with a seventeen-man Red Army Death Squad braving enemy fire to capture two boats on the other side. Snow painted a vivid picture of the Dadu heroes. "The villagers of Anshunchang watched breathlessly. They would be wiped out! But wait. They saw the voyagers land almost beneath the guns of the enemy."[6] Fifty years on, Harrison Salisbury continued the drama. "The enemy opened fire. But the 1st Regiment had an expert gunner . . . He was a dead shot. He hit the target one hundred times out of a hundred. He had only four shells left for the mortar, but with four shells he put four enemy guns out of action."[7]

But the Sichuan Party historians' interview with General Li Jukui revealed an entirely different story. The gloss of the Dadu heroes vanished before my eyes. "The enemy was just a brigadier with a few soldiers . . . Liu Bocheng, the Chief of Staff, ordered a battalion into attack to get the two boats on the other bank . . . They stormed the position, and the enemy immediately took to their heels, and we got the boats without a fight." The Party historians pressed their point. Li reemphasized: "The crossing was without any problem." Then he added about the gunner. "Since we left Jiangxi, we had been throwing away the heavy equipment that we carried. We did not have cannons, or shells . . . Some descriptions of the event are excessive."[8]

Asked about taking the Luding Bridge—which was only necessary after the boats at Anshunchang proved too slow to ferry the entire army across—General Li said his division helped take the 2nd Division to take the bridge, and nothing more. Perhaps for him, nothing needed saying, but knowing how different his view was from the official version, he was at pains to say: "This matter was not as complicated as people made it out to be later. When you investigate historical facts, you should respect the truth." Then he told the Party historians: "How you present it is a different matter! Many of you have come to interview me but the versions are invariably exaggerated or too laced with propaganda."[9]

This interview was in 1984. The Party historians would have liked to make a big splash with the testimony of so important a man, but obviously it was unsuitable for the fiftieth anniversary of the Long March. It has remained buried in the local archives, and Li's cry for the truth to be heard still awaits a response.

I remembered the military historian's scornful reply to my Luding Bridge question: "Can you really call a battle lasting an hour with only a couple of casualties the most important battle of the March?" Now I understood what he meant. Just two days before Mao and his men crossed the Dadu River, the 4th Army had finished an engagement. They had been told by the Central Committee to leave their base in northern Sichuan and go to welcome the 1st Army. To distract the warlord and Nationalist troops, they threw in 30,000 men at Tumen Pass against an enemy of 160,000. They fought for almost a month, killed 10,000 on the other side, and suffered great losses themselves—but allowed the 1st Army to push ahead without much harassment. This was a real battle; yet for all the pages on the Luding Bridge and the Dadu heroes in the history books, there is not a single word about it. I only learned of it from a book, banned in China, published in Hong Kong.[10] Battle or no battle, in history Mao seems to have a monopoly of victories.

The battles over the Dadu River were not as we have been told, but it remains remarkable that the turbulent river which swallowed 40,000 Taiping rebels did not stop the advance of the Marchers. The collaboration between the Red Armies, including the 2nd Army which held back the pursuing Nationalists in Guizhou, played a crucial part in the Long March. And the Communists' manipulation of the conflicts between Chiang and the warlords worked its magic again, just as it had done in Guangdong, and would do in the near future. Credit where it is due.

Having crossed the Dadu River, the Red Army was now free of the pursuing Nationalist armies. They were entering a region of mountains and impassable grassland inhabited by Tibetans. Chiang thought that the forces of nature, the hostility of the Tibetans, and the lack of supplies would be enough to take care of most of them. Whoever survived would be met by his crack force at the other end. He was right in a way. Battles did not loom large in the memory of the veterans I talked to; it was nature's challenges they remembered most vividly. In the mountains and the swamps after Dadu, the Red Army suffered its largest casualties on the March. It was a miracle they survived at all.

Jiajin Mountain was the first challenge for them in this hostile landscape, just 40 miles from the river. The old county records say: "Jiajin Mountain is nicknamed Fairy Mountain. It is over 4,000 meters high, and snow is permanent over 2,400 meters. The Goddess of Cold sits comfortably on the peak, and no one dares to go near it." There is a local saying: "Jiajin Mountain, Jiajin Mountain, only three inches from the sky. Men take off their hats, horses take off their saddles." The Red Army had great difficulty in persuading the locals to be their guides. They said that would be the end of them. "If the Goddess of Cold is disturbed, we will all die. When you die up there, you will not even find the bodies—they will be snatched by the Goddess." But Mao chose to go. He could have taken his men round by the main roads, but they would have come up against Nationalist forces. A single ambush by the Nationalists could have wiped them out. When I walked the same way, I saw why. No one would follow them up the mountain paths, or could attack them on the way. Some might succumb to the rigors of the detour; but the strong would survive.

I met a cattle herder at the foot of the mountain, who offered to guide me to the top. Jiajin did not soar into the sky—it is not very steep at first, in fact the slope is quite gradual. We started among trees and streams. I thought it was easy, and hurried forward. The herder told me to slow down and save my breath—he was right. After a few hundred yards, the path began to climb and my legs started to feel heavy, like a weight I had to carry, not something propelling me on. I was breathing fast, and my mouth felt as if it was stuffed with cotton wool; my heart thudded as though it wanted to burst out of my chest. The herder picked a leaf from a tree: "Chew this, it will make you feel better." But it didn't, so he offered to pull me—barely a mile from the bottom!

"Are you sure you want to climb?" he asked with concern. "We can turn around. It will be hard further up." I told him that as long as he walked slowly, I would manage. I took one step at a time and stopped every few minutes. He was patient and used the waiting time to give me all sorts of tips about mountain climbing: you should always walk on a ridge in snow, not on the slope; you should never attempt a straight climb if you can go round the mountain. He also told me how his yaks sometimes got lost, how the Snow Goddess could suddenly change her face and cover everything with her white coat. Is there ever snow in the summer? I wanted to know. I could not see any, but in all the veterans' recollections they mentioned snow reaching their knees. "Not much nowadays; but in my grandfather's day it was much colder; you could get snow in June."

After six hours, I eventually reached the top and the pass. The view was spectacular, with a great panorama of mountains and beckoning distant valleys, making me forget all the strain. I even felt exhilaration and a sense of achievement, despite taking as long as the herder would to go up and down twice. There were flags, a sign saying that the Red Army was here, and a small temple to the Goddess of Compassion with a large banner reading "Safe Passage." The Red Army may not have believed in the Snow Goddess, but they suffered badly at nature's hands—they must have been relieved to reach this point. I had some idea now of what they went through. I did it on a fine day, dressed in a warm fleece and with proper boots. The herder carried my rucksack, with water, dried meat, and a few bars of chocolate, and we stopped whenever I was tired or out of breath. When the Marchers came up, they were already exhausted after nine months on the March; they were hungry and wearing just shirts and, if they were lucky, straw sandals. It was freezing at the top and the path was deep in snow, which most of them had never seen before. This and the altitude were a fierce shock to their bodies, and many succumbed.

Hygienist Chen was more aware of the risks than most. He had spent the previous day boiling barrel after barrel of water with chili and ginger, and he made sure each soldier in his unit had at least a few mouthfuls. "It wasn't much, but that was all the chili we could find. I think we exhausted all the chili within 20 miles of Jiajin Mountain," he said. He kept some chopped up in his pocket, just in case, and it turned out to be invaluable. When he saw somebody collapsing, he took out a tiny amount and told them to mix it with some snow and chew it slowly. "It warmed them up a bit; but it was more to take their minds off the difficulty." Everyone he gave it to managed to survive, but he had only so much. His eyes filled with tears. "It took so little to save them. But I had to watch them die before my eyes."

Woman Wang did whatever she was told and planned ahead as far as possible. But one thing she had not planned for: her period started. As she began to climb, the pain struck suddenly. She shuddered from it, and the cold. Blinded by the snow, all she could see was one white blur. The pain became so sharp that it made her double up. Blood ran down her legs and left a trail on the snow. Just when she thought she could not move another step, an officer with a horse walked past her and saw the red trail. She reached the top by hanging on to the tail of his horse. But she never had a period again.

Over half the women on the March lost their periods; some regained them later but many did not. "At least I was spared a lot of blood and pain," she said wryly, and then added, with her usual stoicism: "It was a small price to pay for the Revolution."

Soldier Huang thought the Goddess of Cold was going to take his life. He did not know he was so high up or that altitude would affect him so much. Huang felt drowsy and his legs did not seem to belong to him. "Death seemed so much easier than life, and so inviting," he said. He was tempted, and slumped down. He closed his eyes and felt as if a hand was beckoning him from afar with something delicious, and he was going, going . . . Suddenly he was shaken by a loud noise. When he opened his eyes, his commissar was slapping him hard on the face, left and right, and shouting, "Have I brought you all this way so you could die in this bloody place? Where not even a ghost will talk to you? Be a man!" Huang said it was not pain he felt—he was numb with cold. "It was the anger on his face, and the tenderness like a father toward a son, something I had never experienced. He stretched out his hands, pulled me up, and took my rifle—he already had three over his shoulders." When they reached the village at the foot of the mountain, his eyes were covered with a thick layer of frost. The commissar found some alcohol and spat it on them. He opened his eyes and felt an excruciating pain. He could never see properly for the rest of his life.

Not everyone thought Jiajin Mountain was such a challenge. Wu worked harder than most. She and her team fixed a shed halfway up in the deep snow. They made songs out of the instructions to spur the struggling men on: "Red Army soldiers, don't sit down. You are the greatest force on earth. The top is inches away. You can do it. Nothing can stop you." She had only a pair of black silk trousers confiscated from a landlord and no shoes, just cloth wrapped round her feet. Her cheeks were red from the wind, and her eyebrows white with the frost. "I must have looked like a clown, waving my arms to keep warm, and singing breathlessly," she recalled with a smile. "But to tell you the truth, the Jiajin was a dwarf compared with other mountains I crossed later. There was one much, much higher, and we had to stay overnight on it. Many were frozen to death. Some lost their ears from frostbite, others their toes. One man found three toes in the snow and shouted. 'Whose toes? Whose toes?' Everyone looked down. Fortunately, I still had mine."

No words could describe the joy that the 1st Army felt when they heard that after Jiajin Mountain they would be meeting up with the 4th Army, who had been waiting for them for some time. There was heavy mist as they came down on June 12, 1935. The leading men were trying to make out where the vanguard of the 4th Army was—they knew from cables that it should be in the vicinity. Suddenly they heard gunshots. They tried a bugle call, but the 4th Army men did not recognize it. Soon they could see each other through their binoculars—but many of the 1st Army, if they had uniforms at all, were wearing Nationalist ones. Finally, both sides unfurled their red flags, showing the hammer and sickle, and they knew they had found each other.

Huang remembered it vividly as a joyful moment. "We were all jumping up and down. I was so small, I could hardly see anyone's face. I hugged them round the waist, no one lifted me up. But one was very nice and put his big cap on me—I couldn't see a thing. It was quite a while before we calmed down." Once he got a proper look at the 4th Army soldiers, he was impressed. They did a march past, their heads held high, and making a thunderous noise, seeming to shake the ground. They were in full uniform, with smart belts and their trousers tucked into gaiters. "That was an army," he said. "We were just a rabble." A senior officer in his corps was equally impressed and noted in his diary: "Tonight we had a reunion gala with some men of the 4th Army. Everyone was so happy. They treated us cordially and with respect. And their morale and discipline are better than ours."[11] Eventually, Huang caught sight of Zhang Guotao, the supreme commander of the 4th Army. He was slightly shocked. "He didn't look like a Red Army commander; more like a landlord. He looked rich enough for fat to come out of his pores."

Woman Wu was as shocked as Huang had been impressed. "This was Mao's army? They looked more like beggars, wearing all kinds of clothes—some even had women's trousers and shoes on, with a red scarf over their head. Their faces were covered with dust, black except for their teeth. Their hands were black too, but cracked into raw flesh, and their hair was long and straggly. With their beards unshaved, they looked frightening." A couple of days later when they were all cleaned up, the 1st Army and the 4th Army had a big gala night in the Catholic church in Maogong. "We all sang a song specially written for the reunion, there was a play about Chiang's men finding only a worn sandal to take home after a fruitless chase. And a star of the 1st Army did a foreign dance she'd learned in Moscow. She was so elegant, twisting round free as a bird, we wouldn't let her stop. Wah! She was really hot stuff, she put our country hop in the shade."

When I came down from Jiajin Mountain I headed for Maogong, today's Xiaojin. The two armies must have been really happy to be here. It stands high over a bend of a river, on a rare broad plateau in the steep gorges which cover the region. It reminded me of an ancient citadel glimpsed among hills, mysterious, imposing, and inviting all at once. The streets are spacious and lined with quiet family shops, but this small town is dominated by the legacy of the Red Army. I first visited the handsome church, where the gala took place and where the Army made its headquarters. It is perfectly preserved with its foreign arched windows and crosses on the roof, as if transplanted from Rome, except that inside it is completely empty, with a huge picture of Mao where the altar should be. It looks like his portrait in Tiananmen Square, solid and confident-looking—not as he was at the time, taut, drawn, and preoccupied.

Outside the church is the town's small Red Square, almost dwarfed by the gigantic memorial of the meeting of the two armies. Against two huge granite columns there are two larger-than-life-size soldiers, standing on a platform, shaking hands and greeting each other enthusiastically. I sat on the steps and looked at them, the dark blue water below flowing gently by, as the mist gathered and the evening shade crept down from the rocky heights behind me. It was serene and mesmerizing—you could have no idea, just as the men of the two armies had no idea, of the terrible conflicts to come: a power struggle that put the Red Army in turmoil, amid accusations and mudslinging that led ultimately to tens of thousands of pointless deaths. The chasing and bombing by Chiang's troops and the fierce battles the Red Army engaged in were like surface wounds from which they would recover quickly. The challenges from nature inflicted large casualties, but those who survived were made even stronger physically and mentally. But the struggle within the Red Armies caused lasting harm; it casts its shadow even today.

Mao and Zhang's first meeting after the reunion did not go well. Braun, now relegated to the Red Army Academy as a mere instructor, was present, although only to lend an impression of Moscow's favor. He described Zhang as "a tall stately man of about forty who received us as a host would his guests. He behaved with great self-confidence, fully aware of his military superiority and administrative power."[12] Zhang wore a finely cut uniform of grey; Mao wore his old Long March tunic, threadbare and mended. In a bookshop in Xiaojin, I found a book with a photograph of the two of them standing side by side. They are the same height and of similar age, Mao the senior by four years. Mao has his hands on his hips, confident as ever, looking intense with searching eyes, but revealing nothing. Zhang, looking equally confident, appears opulent and lordly; almost smiling and with his hands behind his back, he is the picture of arrogance.

Zhang's confidence was justified. Few people in the Communist Party had better credentials than his. Born into a rich gentry family in 1897, Zhang received the best education of his generation. It was at Beijing University, the hotbed of all ideas and ideals, that he was attracted to Communism. Mao was there too for the same reasons, but as an assistant librarian who was very much ignored by the self-important students and lofty professors. An activist, Zhang became a founding member of the Communist Party and presided over its first meeting. That was when Zhang first met Mao, whom he did not hold in high esteem: "He was quite an active scholar, with a long gown and a lot of common sense, but limited knowledge of Marxism . . ." Zhang noted in his memoir. "Before and during the meeting, he did not come up with any specific suggestions."[13]

Zhang was not impressed this time either. He was shocked to see Mao so weak and gaunt, and his troop so small, hungry, and disorderly. On the Central Committee's instructions, the 4th Army had left their base in the Tongjiang area to meet the 1st Army and build a new base in Sichuan. Although the two armies had radio contact, neither knew much about the other. Zhang's propaganda teams had a slogan written on the walls and on trees: "Welcome 300,000 Central Red Army!" They were expecting far more men. When he met Zhou Enlai, the first question he asked was the size of the 1st Army. Zhou shrewdly replied: "Thirty thousand." Zhu De was more honest: "We used to be a giant. Now all the flesh is gone, leaving only a skeleton."[14] The skeleton was 10,000 men, reduced from 86,000 at the beginning, and 30,000 when Mao took over at Zunyi. Zhang had 70,000–80,000 soldiers, well fed, clothed, and rested.

As ambitious as Mao, Zhang felt his chance had come. If power came from the barrel of a gun, he had the most guns. He wanted power, a share of the leadership of the Party, and military positions for himself and his chosen men—they were currently all in Mao's camp. Mao's position was quite shaky: the 1st Army had lost two-thirds of its men under him since Zunyi; and the senior leaders were so unhappy with him, there was almost a mutiny, instigated by Lin Biao, his most trusted lieutenant. It was only by sheer brazenness and guile that he rode out the storm. But Mao was in no mind to give up what he had just regained with so much effort. There was a series of Politburo meetings to resolve the situation, as the two armies marched forward, stopped, and came back, while the haggling went on. What Zhang underestimated was Mao's acumen, shrewdness, and capacity to fight dirty. His arrogance and political inexperience also undid him.

Zhang could have made allies of the men who were dissatisfied with Mao. Bo Gu, the disgraced young Party Secretary, was the obvious one. But when he came to see Zhang, Zhang took an instant dislike to him. He thought Bo Gu was too keen to show his cleverness, too full of Moscow airs, accusing him of "warlordism" for using the traditional form of address. The accusation made Zhang angry. He gave the young man a severe warning: "If you intend to find fault with the 4th Army, it will be . . . very damaging."[15] As an old Chinese saying goes, "A prime minister can float a boat in his stomach." Zhang was just not a big enough man. He let himself be rubbed up the wrong way, and lost someone who could have been very useful to him.

He needed to win over the other Politburo members. Instead he angered them by launching a frontal attack on the Party and the Zunyi Resolution. He blamed the losses of the bases and the hardships of the Red Army not on military but on political mistakes, the very opposite of Mao's tactics at Zunyi. Whether he wanted to clarify what had gone wrong, or to show them in a bad light to strengthen his own position, he only managed to alienate them all.

As Mao knew only too well, if military errors were to blame, only a few men were implicated; if the entire political line was wrong, so were all the senior leaders. The greatest irony is that Zhang's analysis was correct—Mao later conceded as much. That very summer, Stalin made the same point at the 7th Congress of the Comintern, ordering the Chinese to give up the failed system of Soviet bases. The order was obeyed. Nevertheless, it was Mao who won the crucial allies, and Zhang who lost them. His bid for power was doomed.

They haggled for the best part of June and July. At stake were control of the army, of the Party, and of the membership of the Politburo. Zhang Wentian, Mao's man, offered to give up his post as Party Secretary to Zhang, but Mao rejected the idea. He made Zhang Guotao Commissar of the Red Army, the position held by Zhou Enlai, and allowed two of Zhang's chosen men into the Politburo. It was only later that others understood Mao's calculation: "If Zhang Guotao became Party Secretary and called Politburo meetings in such a capacity, and set up an alternative Central Committee, he would be legitimate."[16] While Zhang had become the effective head of the Red Army, the Party was still above him.

Nobody was happy with the compromise. The discontent and distrust continued, as was obvious when the army set off again—like a couple who decide to set up house together but use separate rooms. There was much debate about where they would now go—Zhang was for setting up a base west of the Yellow River near the Russians, Mao preferred east of the Yellow River in southern Shaanxi. Mao's idea won the day, but they would still go their parallel ways, like the two wheels of a cart. They formed up in two columns, each with units from the other's side, almost like hostages: on the right were Mao and the Politburo, and the bulk of the 1st Army, plus the Red Academy training contingent from the 4th Army, all now commanded by Xu Xiangqian, from the 4th Army; Zhang with almost all his much larger 4th Army, and two corps of the 1st Army, was on the left. Braun was not consulted, but as he pointed out, it did not make any sense. The two columns were separated by a vast swamp. The enemy was to the north and on the right, but the military headquarters was with Zhang's column and could not command the rest efficiently. If there was an attack, the left column could not come to the rescue.[17]

Only two days after they set off, Zhang received a cable from Mao, in the name of the Politburo, asking him to bring his men over to the right. Zhang was angry about changing course so soon. Also, he was now the supreme commander of the Red Army and he should give the orders! After another cable from Mao, this time in the form of a Politburo resolution, he reluctantly agreed. But heavy rain hampered his progress. Three days later, he cabled the right column saying he was turning back: "Swampland looks boundless. Impossible to go forward, seem to be waiting for our death. Cannot find guide. Sheer misery."

Perhaps the weather had something to do with it. But the fundamental conflict was all too obvious. And he made it clear that the fault was Mao's: "Now the whole strategy is affected . . . You forced us to move . . . and got us into this mess."[18]

It was a warm, bright day on September 9, almost cloudless. At the right column headquarters it looked like any other rest day. Some were busy with their domestic chores, others were out searching for grain, while the commissars gave motivational talks to the soldiers. Mao looked haggard and drawn after a sleepless night: he had sent Zhang two more cables, urging him to change his mind and come to join them, but Zhang would not budge this time. Now he had decided to stay in Sichuan where the new base would be, as had been agreed before the two armies met. He ordered Xu, his chosen man commanding the right column, to bring the troops back. Mao had to act. He decided on a drastic plan, and spent the whole day discussing it with Politburo members; he also sounded out Xu, but Xu pledged his loyalty to Zhang.

At two o'clock in the morning, Mao's plan went into action—to take his men and flee. He had no intention of going back—the conflict with Zhang would worsen and he might well lose it. He also knew that the swampland could not support both armies. Liu Ying recalled being woken up in the pitch dark: "'Get up! Get up! Set off at once!' We asked, 'What's happened? Where are we going?' 'No questions, just get a move on and go! . . . No noise, no torches . . . follow me!' We rushed for about 10 *li* and did not pause to catch our breath until after we crossed a mountain pass."[19] In the middle of the night, Braun was also told to go to the Red Academy camp and bring all the cadets out, but he did not know why. "He did what he was told. Their commissar was left behind, but there was no conflict. In the morning they joined the rest." It was a shock to him to find out that just the 1st Army was marching, not the entire right column. He was the only one who had managed to bring some 4th Army soldiers along.

Xu also got a terrible shock when he woke up and was told that Mao and his men had fled, taking with him the only map of Sichuan they had. The commissar of the academy rushed in to ask if there had been an order to take his men out. "The headquarters was as chaotic as a tangled ball of string," Xu recalled sadly in his memoirs. "I did not know what to think. I sat on the bed speechless for half an hour. Why? Why did they not tell us? I had not expected it at all. My heart was heavy, and my head numb . . . I was in such a bad mood, I threw myself on the bed, covered my head with a quilt, and did not speak a word."[20] Xu sent a senior officer of the 4th Army with a cavalry detachment to bring back the Red Academy men who had left with Mao. The air was tense: both sides had their hands on their pistols and swords out of their scabbards. But Mao said the men could leave: "You can't force a man and a woman to be husband and wife by roping them together. Let them go. They will join us eventually."[21]

This was the darkest moment in his entire life, Mao told Edgar Snow. "The Party was split. The future was uncertain. Who knows, there might even be an internal war!" He had lost a quarter of his weakened army to Zhang and now had barely 8,000 men left. Many of his senior commanders had received a generous gift of cooks, orderlies, and grooms from the 4th Army after the reunion and every one of them was taken back. They had to cook for themselves and mind their own horses. The split which happened barely three months after the reunion caused a huge stir among the soldiers. Officers were warned to keep an eye on their men to prevent desertion to the 4th Army. Mao was so concerned he even appeared in front of the troops—only the second time on the Long March. One of the officers remembered Mao watching them intensely, with a severe and sad expression. It was to assure them but also to gauge their mood. "To see if we were determined enough."[22]

When Zhang heard that Mao had left, he erupted with anger, shouting and shedding tears of frustration. "Only Mao is capable of playing this dirty trick. Power is the only thing he's cared about since the reunion," he said. "How can they betray the martyrs who gave everything for the Revolution?"[23] But Zhang did not have Mao's killer instinct. He ordered his own men to be brought back, but not Mao's. It was another act of indecision, one of his fatal weaknesses as a leader.

As soon as Mao got away, he denounced Zhang as an "opportunist," using military muscle to hurt the Party when it was at its weakest. But seventeen months later, Mao, secure in the caves of northern China, claimed that Zhang had sent a secret cable to Xu in the right column on September 9, which was intercepted by Mao's own man: "Break the resistance of the Central Committee, by force if necessary." This, Mao said, was what prompted him to take his drastic action. It was yet another piece of evidence of Zhang's criminal intent to split the Party and the Red Army.

But was there such a "secret telegram"? If so, it did not appear in any of the major historical documents of the day—not in the Party's denunciation of Zhang, nor its report of the decision to Moscow, nor its statement expelling Zhang from the Party. Every single telegram between the 1st and 4th Armies after their reunion has been preserved and is now kept in the Central Archives in Beijing—except for this one. There is even testimony from the chief of the 4th Army telegraph unit: he said categorically that any telegram the Army sent out would have gone through him, and he never saw it. "The telegrams we deciphered had to go straight to the person intended, and no one else. This was the rule, and also the principle of our job. The people from the 1st Army had no access whatever to our telegrams."[24] He was asked whether the telegram could be lost. "I was in charge, and I have never lost a telegram . . . The discipline of our unit was very, very strict. If the telegram had existed but had been 'intercepted' by others, Zhang would definitely have chopped our heads off!"[25] By now, almost all historians have agreed the "secret telegram" did not exist, although history books still carry Mao's claim.

All my life, along with most Chinese, I thought of Zhang Guotao as an evil man, nailed, as we say, on the pillar of history's shame. The power struggle ended with Mao the winner, Zhang the loser. As the Chinese say, there cannot be two suns in the sky. Compared with Mao, the sophisticated and ruthless politician, Zhang seems almost naïve. He was bound to fail—as did anyone who dared to challenge Mao.

Mao presiding at the opening of the First China Soviet Congress, Ruijin

The Xiang River

ABOVE: Orderly Liu
RIGHT: Hygienist Chen
BELOW: Luding Bridge

Mao's calligraphy over the Zunyi Museum entrance

The Red Army's road out of Zunyi

ABOVE: Propagandist Wu
RIGHT: Fighter Li
BELOW: Feng Yuxiang

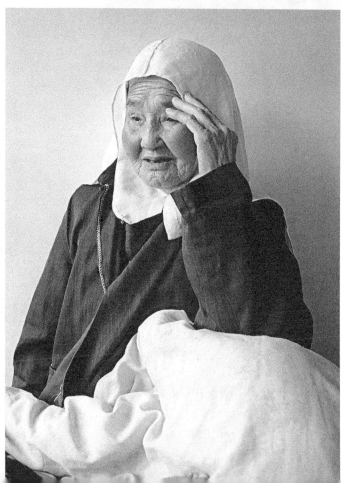

LEFT: Mao and Zhang Guotao in Shaanxi, 1937

BELOW: Sangluo

FROM LEFT TO RIGHT: Bo Gu, Zhou Enlai, Zhu De, Mao Zedong after arrival in Shaanxi in 1936

The Young Marshal, Zhang Xueliang (LEFT), with Chiang Kaishek (RIGHT) and Chiang's brother-in-law (BEHIND, CENTER)

The Red Army after they arrived in Shaanxi, 1936

ABOVE: Ma Fucai
RIGHT: Ma Haidiche
BELOW: Landscape with tombs where the
Western Legion fought and died

# 9 ★ IN TIBETAN LANDS

"On the plateau it was like another world. At first, it seemed peaceful, no planes pounding us, no Nationalists chasing us. But then it was just peculiar. No people, no houses, no roads—just grass, grass, grass up to the horizon, empty of everything except the occasional river snaking through the plain. Even the sky was different, so close, if you shot a bullet it would pierce it. Bright blue like porcelain, but it could change suddenly and in a moment it was dark with wind howling and sleet hitting your face. I asked our commissar where we were, had we left China? He laughed at me, then he stopped and said, 'Well, I've never seen anything like this. Wait till we see some people, then I can tell you for sure.' But I wondered why we had come here. It was so far from everything, would I ever be able to go back?"

Sangluo never did go back. He now lives in a village in Hongyuan County, deep in the grassland of western Sichuan, inhabited mainly by Tibetans. It took me seven hours on the road to reach him. There was a road; but otherwise after seventy years it was just as he described, except every now and then we saw a herd of yak with their Tibetan herdsman. It was late July, the best season in the grassland—also the time when the Red Army came through. The pasture has a strange beauty, this vast flat expanse, as if you are looking into the heart of infinity, and then huge carpets of meadow flowers, yellow, white, blue, vermilion, violet, purple, like announcements of heaven. Your eyes ache from the brilliant colors, and their fragrance makes you smile. The great empty land and its purity filled me with bliss, I wished it would go on and on. The only thing in the corner of my mind was—what if we break down? I asked the driver. He laughed. "We just wait till someone comes along." That could be a long time. The whole region has very few people—just one and a half per square kilometer. Above 12,000 feet, the grassland is 400 miles across.

At last, seemingly out of nowhere, we came to a settlement, a sizable cluster of pink, green, and yellow concrete houses like props transplanted from a film set. It was built by the government for the nomads, so they could have a school and a health center—this was the twenty-first century after all. I asked for Sangluo, and someone said he was "over there, in the middle row of houses near the pasture." I walked past a tall man in a crimson robe with a stick and a big round-brimmed felt hat. At the end of the houses, I asked again; the answer came in broken Chinese, "That's him." I was shocked. I had been expecting a Han Chinese—the people in the country government told me he had joined He Long's 2nd Army from Hunan at the age of 13, got wounded in the foot, and stayed on here.

When I went up to him, there stood in front of me a completely Tibetan-looking man, his wrinkled face the same dark red as his robe, his eyes opening in narrow slits from a lifetime of keeping out the sun, and his fingers all bent. His whole body was crooked with arthritis, the plague of the grassland nomads. With some difficulty, he kept turning the prayer wheel in his left hand. "Are you Sangluo?" I asked. He did not understand me but did recognize "Sangluo." My Tibetan was too patchy to talk to him; he had almost no Chinese. We just stood there. I had to go back to the village headman and ask him to help me. Over the next two days, I learned Sangluo's story. It was the strangest among all the veterans I met.

Sangluo remembered the day when he and his fellow Marchers entered the Tibetan area. The commissar told them the Tibetans were exploited by Chiang Kaishek's government—they had to go down on their knees every step for a mile just to pay their taxes. Some Han merchants also cheated them. "They are deeply suspicious of us. So do not call them barbarians." Sangluo recalled the commissar's words with a gentle smile. "We must respect their customs and not enter their monasteries without permission. We must do our propaganda work well to win them over."[1] The soldiers learned slogans such as "Tibetans

and Han enjoy equal rights" and "Tibetan and Han workers and peasants unite to sweep away the Nationalist warlords." The propaganda
teams made up songs quickly. Sangluo could still sing one:

> Tibetan brothers, arm yourselves quickly and come to your
>    senses.
> We seek our liberation, and you fight for your independence.
> Life for life, blood for blood.
> To safeguard you and the Red Army, let's wipe out the
>    Nationalists.

Did it actually say "independence"? I asked.

"That is how the song went. Maybe I remember it wrong," he said
uncertainly. When I checked the historical documents later, it was
there. The 4th Army, which spent the longest time in the region due to
Zhang Guotao's dispute with Mao, even helped the Tibetans set up an
independent Tibetan People's Republic, with its own army. Its constitution promised the equality and autonomy of all nationalities, and independence for the Tibetans . . . The Tibetan people will rule their
own land. That year, 1936, was declared as "year zero" for the Tibetan
People's Republic. Of course, this would all become ammunition in
the later attack on Zhang, even though he was clearly doing it to help
the beleaguered Red Army. The Tibetan People's Republic had this
clause in its constitution: ". . . it must sign an eternal treaty of friend-
ship with the Red Army; unconditionally help the Red Army get grain,
fodder, and wool; arrange for guides, translators, and other laborers for
the front; find homes for and look after the wounded."[2] The Tibetans
did their best to fulfill these promises, but as soon as the Red Army left,
their chiefs and the Nationalists ganged up on those involved in the Republic, killing most of them, and their families. For all its lofty ideals,
the Independent Tibetan Republic was nothing more than an expedi-
ent for Zhang Guotao.

While the Red Army tried to win over the Tibetans on the plateau,
the Nationalists found a significant ally in Tibet itself in their fight
against the Communists. The Panchen Lama, together with the Dalai

Lama, is the most powerful man in Tibet—he is god in the eyes of Tibetans. He told his faithful with no ambiguity:

> Wherever the Communist bandits go, the first thing they do is to burn the temples and monasteries, destroy the Buddhist statues, kill the lamas, and silence the sound of prayers . . . No wonder everyone hates them. They are a big threat for us Buddhists . . . Arm yourselves, help the Nationalist troops, and prepare to defend our people against the evil enemy of our religion. Don't believe in their sweet propaganda! They will burn your house and destroy your family. I am telling you out of a kind intention to save you and the world.[3]

Chiang also appointed Nuona, a senior lama, as his Propagating and Pacifying Envoy. He traveled from monastery to monastery, reinforcing the Panchen Lama's message: "The sky is everlasting, the clouds will disperse. We are the sky, the Communist bandits are clouds. We will drive them away." He offered the lamas rifles and ammunition and told them to fortify their monasteries—the people should either seek shelter in them or hide in the mountains and bury all their belongings. Those who did not bury or hide their grain would have it confiscated. People who led the way, interpreted for, or sold food to the Red Army would be executed. And anyone who refused to fight against the Communists would be tried as a traitor.

"You tell me who the Tibetans would listen to," Sangluo said. "And that was before rumors flew around, like 'The Red Army feeds on humans.' 'Mao especially likes children. He drills seven holes in their bodies and sucks out all the blood.' 'The Han women's tits are so long they throw them over their shoulders while they march.' They all fled to the mountains with their animals and grain. The old and the sick were carried. It was just as we do when we move the herds from summer to winter pasture. No wonder we didn't see a single soul." Braun's account in his memoirs confirms Sangluo's story. "If we encountered few people south of Maogong, to the north we saw no one . . . Towns and farms were abandoned, food stored or carried away, animals were driven off. There was nothing to be bought or confiscated from the landowners."[4]

For the Red Army, the biggest battle was for food. Soldier Huang and the 1st Corps of the 1st Army were the vanguard, so they found plenty of unripe barley in the fields. He thought harvesting them was like a battle, except it was harder than fighting the Nationalists. "It was an all-out assault. There were soldiers everywhere. Each battalion targeted a village and attacked it with military precision. The trouble was that we had no tools. All we had to cut the barley with was our bayonets or else we pulled it up with our bare hands. While we were doing that, the Tibetans sniped at us from a long way off. They were good shots, and many soldiers died."

After a long day's harvesting amidst the snipers' bullets, Huang would sit down to roast the barley and take off the husks. He found it harder than he had imagined. It would have been easier to grind it with stones, but the grain was so tender, the stones would have reduced it to nothing. He had to use his hands, or wrap the barley in his clothes and knead it. Within a few hours, his hands were covered with blisters and blood from the sharp ends of the barley. Still, he had to carry on until he finished one kilo—his quota for the day. Early next morning the work would start again. It went on for almost a month as they had to go further afield, until they gathered enough supplies to last them through the grassland. But all that effort to collect the barley did not do them any good at first. They had never eaten it before and could not digest it. "What went in at one end came out the other," Huang laughed bitterly. "My diarrhea was so bad, I could hardly stand up. Someone said horse pee could cure it, so there was a long queue every morning in front of the few horses that belonged to the senior officers. But the horses were so mean, I waited several days for my turn. Whether it was the horse pee or something else, I wasn't sure, but I recovered, although many died at that time."

Catching livestock proved to be even more of a challenge. It was crucial for the food battle—a yak weighed 500 kilos and could feed 300 people for several days. The Tibetans had taken them to the mountains, so the troops went in pursuit. That was when many were killed—

ambushed, hit by snipers in the forests, or crushed by huge boulders they rolled down narrow ravines. The soldiers had to make war for a few animals. Mao told Snow that one sheep cost one life.

Occasionally luck did come their way. Huang recalled with joy till this day the biggest flock of yak he had ever seen. "Ten thousand? I can't tell you for sure. The flock was like clouds in the sky. There was a small army guarding them—they must have belonged to the richest man in the area." A brigade attacked the stragglers, while Huang watched with bated breath. "Our soldiers got a couple of hundred, and everyone was so happy. Suddenly the herdsman whistled and the yak started galloping away. The soldiers opened fire frantically, killing a dozen more, but frightening most away. And they ran so fast, we could not catch them." Huang sighed. "It would have been enough to feed the entire army for a while. Those barbarians are so cruel! It was not as if we were robbing them. We had money to give them, silver dollars!" Why did he think the Tibetans did not want to sell to them? I asked. He stopped, thought for a few minutes, and said, "You know, apart from those herdsmen, I did not see a single Tibetan the whole time. We could not find a guide. Those barbarians did not understand us. How could they trade with us?"

In the end, the efforts of Huang and his comrades in the 1st Corps paid off. In Heishui County they reaped 3.7 million kilos of grain, of which they consumed 3 million while the troops were stationed there, and took away the rest. In the village of Jawa alone, they confiscated 100,000 kilos of barley. They also killed 30,000 animals—the meat for food and the skins for clothes.

For the Tibetans, it was also a battle for survival. In 1935, the area that the Red Army passed through had a population of 220,000, with just about enough grain and cattle to feed themselves with a small reserve.[5] They only had one harvest a year, and the rest of the time they were totally dependent on what they kept in store. Mao's 1st, Zhang Guotao's 4th, and He Long's 2nd Armies had over 100,000 men altogether at this time, equaling nearly half the local population; on the main route of the March, they outnumbered the locals by four to one. In total, the three armies spent sixteen months there. If they took what they needed, what could the locals live on? They were going to defend what they had with their lives.

First, they gave their warnings. A commissar in Huang's division remembered: "The Tibetans sometimes came down at night from their hiding places in the mountains, and shouted outside our camp: 'Red Bandits, when are you leaving? If you stay any longer and finish our grain, we will starve!'[6] But when they found the Red Army was not going away, they went for the kill." The diary of Chen Bojun, Commissar of the 5th Corps of the 1st Army, gives a vivid picture of the daily clashes with the Tibetans. An entry in his diary for August 1935 reads:

> The Tibetans were firing at us across the river. So we stopped . . . Continued after dark so we could not be seen . . . After another five km, they began to fire again. Rifle fire and shot poured over us, amidst huge noises from horns. They completely blocked us. We climbed up the mountain and went around behind them . . . Although we came through safely, we were worried there would be more ambushes.[7]

Sangluo also remembered the skirmishes with the Tibetans. "We could hear their tribal horns calling them to battle from the cliffs and mountains: Mraa-aw! Mraa-a-aw! Mraa-a-a-a-aw! More battles than we ever had with the Nationalists. The Tibetans would not fight properly. They attacked us at the rear. Once they isolated a few men, they pounced on them like vultures on corpses. We lost many soldiers that way." Sangluo was shot in the foot during one surprise attack. He fell. His comrades were all running for their lives. "I shouted, 'Help! Help! Don't abandon me!' I could hear the hooves of the Tibetans' horses clattering on the mountain path. In no time they would be trampling on me." But suddenly his platoon commander ran back with another soldier. They pulled him by one arm, but kept looking back, holding their rifles with a finger on the trigger. "I was worried we couldn't go fast enough, but I lost so much blood, I fainted. I have no idea how I was saved."

The fate of those caught could be horrendous. Propagandist Wu remembers walking into the most appalling scene of her life. She and a propaganda team had gone to a village to sing for the soldiers. They were very happy with their rapturous reception. On the way back, they were still singing just in front of the same bridge they had crossed in the morning, but now it was covered with blood. Suddenly one of the women shrieked, "Look! Look! Over there!" Wu looked where the woman was pointing. From the trees by the river hung the naked bodies of four soldiers; their skin had been peeled, their stomachs were cut open, the woman's breasts were missing, and the three men's genitals were stuffed in their mouths. "How could they be so cruel? They butchered our comrades worse than dogs. We didn't call them barbarians for no reason."

The Red Army knew the Tibetan region was not a place to linger. After they had gathered all the supplies they could find, they wanted to get out fast, but they needed guides to lead them out of the hostile land, especially the miles and miles of treacherous swamp at the end. It was hard to tell it from grass, but the boggy water was deep enough to swallow a horse. I asked Sangluo how the pasture was where we were. "To me it is just a carpet of flowers." He laughed. "Even now, if you don't know the way, it is very dangerous. You can easily drown in it. The cows know, and they don't go near the bad parts. I know where they are—I'd make a good guide! If they'd had someone like me then, I would have saved lots of lives."

But none was easily available. The vanguard spent days searching for one. Liu Zhong, a commissar in the 1st Corps, was told to try his luck. He took a battalion, some feigning an attack on a Tibetan village from the front, while others struck from behind. They caught three men: a Tibetan who knew the way but did not speak Chinese, a Muslim trader who spoke Tibetan but did not know the way, and a Han merchant from Sichuan who had traveled the route often but spoke little Tibetan, and was very reluctant to help. After their capture, Liu was called into headquarters and told: "Look after them well, and get us out of here. This is your number one priority." The three were given a horse each, a wool blanket, and as much butter, roasted barley flour, meat, and salt as they needed. "They were the best fed men on the March," he wrote grudgingly.[8]

He quickly realized just how precious they were. "Sometimes even they did not know where to turn. I held the compass and they talked among themselves to find their landmarks—sometimes it was a strange-shaped stone, sometimes a bleached yak's skull, or a special curve in a river. Often they argued among themselves for a long time before they finally confirmed the path ahead."[9] The trio led the 1st Corps out of the grassland in the shortest time, seven days, and on the safest paths. Tong Xiaopeng, who was with the 1st Corps headquarters, kept a detailed diary throughout the March; these were his entries for those seven days:

AUGUST 23: Have heard we are going to enter the grassland for a long while. Today we started. Everyone was very keen to taste what it was like . . .

AUGUST 24: Entered the grassland. Gradually the forest was gone, and the land opened up . . . had it not been for the guides, we would not have had a clue which way to go. The worst was the rain . . . We saw forest again, and we broke camp.

AUGUST 25: Pure grassland, not a stick to be found . . . Everyone had a cold meal.

AUGUST 26: A big road, and dry! A vast plain and I can see in one glance the tens of thousands of soldiers who are marching . . . Crossed river five or six times, and was nearly swept away. Quite a shock.

AUGUST 27: Saw over one hundred houses with cow pies pasted on the outside. We were very happy . . .

AUGUST 28: Arrived today . . . Can't believe we crossed it so easily . . . [10]

Despite crossing so quickly the 1st Corps still lost 15 percent of their number, 400 men in all. The deaths were mainly due to the extreme weather. Huang never forgot his first night on the grassland. It had rained the whole day and the grass and the ground were sodden. They built a tent with tree branches and oilcloths, and two dozen men squeezed into it. "It was so packed, you couldn't get a needle in." Late at night, they could hear four men outside begging to come in, but they just could not help them. The next morning, they found them frozen up against the tent, as if they had been trying to draw some warmth from the men inside.

After spending two days with Sangluo and his yak, I began to see why the weather was such a killer. When I met him outside his house in the afternoon, the sun was so ferocious that I almost melted. Half an hour later, as I returned with the village headman to interpret for me, dark clouds had gathered from nowhere and whipped up a ferocious storm, lifting me up like a clump of yak wool. We went inside and thunder and sleet followed, with hail as big as sheep's eyes pounding on Sangluo's windows. At five o'clock, everything was wrapped in thick fog—from Sangluo's sitting room, I could not even see the fence beyond his window. Fifteen degrees below zero at night ruined my chance of roughing it in a yurt, so I slept in his house, or tried to—with all my clothes on, a duvet, and a woolen blanket, I shivered uncontrollably. At dawn, the world was one white sheet of snow. The sun made several feeble attempts to break through, and when it finally succeeded, it looked more like the moon on a cloudy night, turning everything a sickly grey. By lunchtime we were back to blue skies, the yak munching away while the women milked them, the children collecting cow pies, and the dogs lolling about and watching. A young man in the village who spoke good Chinese sat with Sangluo and myself on the grass and listened to more of his stories: he told me the names of the wildflowers and grasses which he and his comrades had been able to eat.

The wild grasses and plants could be lifesavers. They were quite plentiful—dandelion greens, nettles, bitter lotus, insect grass, snake plum, mushroom, wild peach, prune, garlic, onion, celery, and spinach. "Of course, some were not their real names," Propagandist Wu recalled. "We did not know what they were or whether they were edible, and many were poisoned. Had we found a Tibetan guide, many more would have lived. The nomads didn't have any vegetables but they were healthy. Whatever their secrets were, those barbarians didn't want to share them with us." Because of her weakened stomach she could not digest the grass at all, and for days Wu was totally constipated. Like many men and women, she had to kneel on the ground and get a friend to loosen her stool with their fingers. "The things we went through, you can't imagine."

Crossing the grassland last, the 2nd Army had the worst of it. As Sangluo remembered, "The vanguard had the beans, the later troops had the leaves, the rear guard had the stalks, those who followed had nothing, even the roots were eaten." Most of the monasteries had been emptied and so their only hope was to dig for the buried stores that had escaped the last two armies—in the mountains, under trees, in the stables, under the altars, inside Buddhist statues even. "It was as if they went through everything with a toothcomb—even the lice had gone," Sangluo joked. They spent a week looking for supplies after they joined up with the 4th Army in early July 1936, and set off a week after them. What they found was barely enough for three days for each soldier— and they were in the grassland for a month.

It was a rule that the troops had to stick to the path trodden by the previous armies. At first, Hygenist Chen did not understand why they could not leave the path, but soon he saw with his own eyes. People who strayed fell into the swamps, and often drowned before their comrades could rescue them. Their bloated bodies drifted in the water, giving off a nauseating smell. Chen wished he could march with his eyes shut. "I couldn't bear to see them, especially with the sun on them. They were crawling with maggots. Often you had to step on the bodies because you didn't know whether the ground was safe. So you trod on their stomachs and they squelched as your foot went in." He told the men in his battalion to wash their feet every night if possible, otherwise they would be infected. But staying on the trodden path, all Chen and his comrades could find to eat were grass roots.

Fortunately for Chen and many in the 2nd Army, the treacherous water came to their rescue—the water flowed into rivers which had plenty of fish. The Tibetans did not eat them because they disposed of bodies in the water. The trouble was they found it difficult to catch the fish. Without hooks or nets, they used their needles or even their bayonets. What they caught was pitiful. He Long, their Commander-in-Chief, showed what they could have done with the right gear: he had a fishing rod, and using it only for a few minutes a day he never wanted for fish all the way. Yet Chen found eating the fish almost harder than fighting a battle. "I know it is the most nutritious food. But at the time, after what I had seen, I had so much difficulty swallowing it, as if a fish bone was stuck in my throat." But hunger won through.

Another, if unlikely, source of protein was animal hides and leather; the story is repeated in all the accounts of the Long March. Sangluo told me how it was done. At first, they ate the animal hides left by the previous troops. They put them on the fire and roasted them. "It wasn't bad—like crackling. It still had some taste of meat." When that was gone, they used belts, rifle straps, and leather bags. But they had no flavor and were really tough, so they had to boil them as well and chewed the pieces. He said frying them in butter helped, but there was not much of that around. "You know how desperate we were. We even ate the horses' reins. Not a single horse in our regiment had any reins left. We had to make ropes for them with grass or from dead men's clothes."

Horses were eaten too. Woman Wang acquired a horse after the union of the 1st and 4th Armies. With the special protection it gave its officers, the 1st Army had ended up with more officers than soldiers. They reassigned some to the 4th Army, which in return gave over 3,000 men to replenish its depleted ranks. Wang was appointed head of the Women's Department in the 4th Army. She cherished the hours she spent on the horse, when her tired legs and body had rare moments of rest. As Bo Gu's wife said, perhaps only half jokingly: "On the March, I prefer a donkey or a horse to an Old Male!" But most of the time, her horse carried the sick, the weak, and their burdens, with an extra person holding on to the horse's tail. It saved so many lives, including her own when she fell into a bog but hung on to the reins. On the fifth day into the grassland, Wang's privilege had to go too. She was in the rear, collecting those who were too weak to keep up with the rest of the army. She saw little point in trying to help them unless they had some nourishment—and the only thing she could think of was her horse. The flesh, the blood, the innards, the bones, and the hide—every part of the horse was eaten, and kept any number of Marchers alive. Wang could not bring herself to eat it. Instead, she cut off a lock from the horse's mane, which she kept in a piece of red silk. She has it still.

The grassland could be crossed in six or seven days, but the 4th and the 2nd Armies spent much longer—they had to cross it diagonally from the southwest corner, while Mao's army did it from the southeast corner. Their despondency was almost palpable. "Can we ever get out of here? Why did we come here in the first place?" the soldiers questioned their commissars. "You told me it was good to join the Red Army. It's all lies. We are starving." Some even shot themselves.[11] For most men and women, the biggest wish was to get out of the grassland alive and find other human beings, even if they were the enemy. As one man explained, "None of us had ever had the experience of living in a world where we saw no people, heard no people, talked to no people . . . We were alone, as though we were the last men on Earth."[12]

Wu and her team tried to cheer the soldiers up with songs, even though they were almost too weak to sing. "We could do without food for a day, but not without songs," she recalled. She had fond memories of the singing sessions around the flickering flames of the camp fire at the end of a day's marching. She offered her favorite, "The Shepherd Boy," and more folk tunes from different parts of the country; in the end, everyone joined in for "The Internationale":

> This is the final struggle.
> Unite and fight for another day.
> The Internationale *will come true!*

As this final stanza soared into the black starry night, she felt released and hopeful. The pain, hunger, and despair were forgotten for the moment, and their resolve to carry on was restored. "Without singing, we would never have reached the end," Wu insisted.

At last they saw a blur of low hills on the horizon, and here and there smoke rising. Then there were stones on the path, and more smoke, and the next afternoon some trees far off and houses in amongst them. They tramped on like men in a desert who had seen an oasis. Finally, they saw the end of the grassland and found bushes hanging with red and golden berries. Wu said, "I can't tell you what it was like when we saw those first stones. The soldiers told those behind them, and the message went down the line. It meant we were out of the wet and onto solid ground! We picked up the stones and kissed them. We touched the earth, we bowed to the road, we embraced each other. We broke into songs, dances, and tears." An officer expressed in his diary the relief felt by all the Red Army:

> Everyone was unusually excited, and could not wait to get out.
> We set off soon after breakfast. The area ahead was a plain,
> like a different world. Ten miles down in a valley, we saw
> houses and fields of wheat, cows, sheep, chickens, and dogs—
> and, above all, people, of whom we had hardly seen a trace in
> the last three months. They were waiting for us on the road-
> side, smiling. We were so happy that we jumped up and down.
> When we think of the past three months in the Tibetan area,
> we had been living a life not fit for humans.[13]

Crossing the grassland was the worst part of the Long March, the most painful, with the greatest losses. There are no overall figures, but the accounts of individual units reveal a tragic story. The 1st Corps hospital staff numbered 1,200 when they left Jiangxi, but had only 200 left when they were out of the grassland.[14] The supply unit started with over 100 men and ended with only a dozen; of the whole company of guards, only 5 survived. Of the combat units, 400 men froze to death.[15] The 4th Army must have suffered even more—they were in the Tibetan area the longest, though we only have some illustrative figures. Wu's 57-strong propaganda team was reduced to 11 by the end. The Struggle Theater lost three-quarters of its people. And even Zhu De's body-guard, which started with 17 men, finished with only 7. The 2nd Army had already lost over 7,000 before they even reached the grassland. But even that was exceeded by the losses crossing it.

There were more casualties to come in one last awful moment. Wu saw it happen. When they got out of the grassland and found fields full of corn, they pounced on them, but the corn was not ripe yet. They wolfed it down, but in a few minutes some of them collapsed, holding their stomachs. "Their whole bodies shook, and they screamed and hurled themselves on the ground. The officer knew what was going to happen and fired into the air to stop them from eating, but nobody listened. He had to fire again and again. The fields were full of groaning men, squirming this way and that. There was nothing they could do. Their stomachs could not digest the sudden intake after starving for so long. The pain on their faces was even worse than those who died of hunger." Later, their bodies were shown to the troops who came after them. Wu only dared to eat normally after three days.

So many died—and there were also the sick and wounded, and the youngsters such as Sangluo who were left behind in the Tibetan area because they were thought unlikely to make it. The largest number of these was in Luhuo County in western Sichuan on the southwest corner of the grassland. It was where the 4th Army was based for six months before the 2nd Army joined them; it was also where they had suffered the heaviest casualties in the Tibetan area. I decided to go there, hoping I might learn something about the fate of the Tibetans too.

Luhuo town is clean and spacious, in a broad valley surrounded by mountains on three sides; the calmly flowing Xian River curls round it. It was a welcome sight after my eleven hours on the bus, traveling west from Kangding—the regional capital—by a steep mountain road. It is also rare among these mountains to find such an expanse of cropland, large yellow fields of mustard, green broad beans, pink blossoms of the fodder plants, and silver barley swaying under the rain. This is a fortunate community where nature provides for every need; I could see why the 4th Army chose to wait here.

I walked along the main street. There were numerous teahouses where everyone, young and old, sat and chatted, and milk-sellers on

street corners were doing a brisk trade. I was surprised to see a basketball match in progress. While I walked with some difficulty—we were
over 10,000 feet up—the Tibetans were running about like young yak.
Since this was a contest for teams from six counties, there were so many
people in town I had a job finding a hotel room. I tried to imagine what
it was like when the 4th Army brought its headquarters, Political Department, Propaganda Team, and Transport Unit to the much smaller
old town up on the hill and stayed there, together with the rest of the
40,000 men scattered throughout the valley. The county had 14,000
people, but had to support an army three times its population, plus
those of the 2nd Army. Local historians estimated that they provided
4 million kilos of barley, wheat, and beans, and 400,000 kilos of roasted
barley flour. That was over 300 kilos per person—more than the annual
crop output for the people who lived there. In addition, the army took
34,000 sheep and yak, tens of thousands of kilos of salt and butter, and
over half a million kilos of dried yak pats and other fuel.[16]

Luhuo was dominated by the Shouling Monastery, which was
perched on the hill overlooking the town. It was rebuilt here after the
old one, a mile away, was destroyed during the Cultural Revolution.
That was the scene of one of the toughest battles the 4th Army fought.
The 1,000 monks only had 140 rifles, but for twenty-eight days they put
up a fierce defense against a whole Red Army division. They refused to
negotiate and killed three messengers. At night hundreds of them galloped into the 4th Army camps on horseback, killing dozens of men
with knives and spears. When the soldiers tried to force their way in,
digging tunnels underneath the walls and using ladders to climb over
them, they were met with stones, homemade explosives, and swords.
The commander of the division was sacked, and another division was
called in. It feigned a withdrawal, the monks relaxed their vigil, and the
monastery was finally taken.

When the soldiers rushed into the monastery, they could not believe what they saw: room after room was filled with grain, dried meat,
wool, butter, salt, and sweets—the reserve supplies of the monastery
and the people from four surrounding districts. Those, and what the
4th Army took from the rest of Luhuo, kept them going for months—

and through the grassland. Over 1,000 soldiers were wounded or killed taking the monastery; the monastery lost 130 monks. It was a heavy price for the 4th Army.

I climbed up to the monastery and found there was still building work going on. A large statue of the Buddha covered in gold had just been installed. A few workmen were painting devils and scenes from hell in garish colors on the doors near the main shrine hall. Inside, the morning studies were in progress, but I found a few old people leaning against the wall enjoying the morning sun after their daily ritual circuit around the temple. Nima, perhaps the oldest of the group, wore a long silver plait down to her waist like many Tibetan women, but she was very alert, and her weathered face had an appealing warmth.

I asked her about the summer of 1935 and 1936 when the Red Armies came through the area. "I don't know how we got through after they were gone," she said. "Normally, in a bad year we could borrow from the headman or the monastery and pay them back after the harvest. But all their stores were taken too. Soon enough we had to start killing the cattle. We hate to do that, they are our lifeline—we drink the milk and eat the butter, and sell it as well to buy salt and tea and clothes—but we had to. The only other things left were in the mountains. We searched for mushrooms, nuts, and other wild plants. It was difficult when everyone was looking for them. We even ate tree bark. My father had to shoot snow hens and other birds. That was the worst thing of all. We do not hunt—killing is bad. If you take a life, it can lead to rebirth as an animal or a devil in the next life. But it was that or starve. Many did starve."

The Red Army mostly kept their discipline and left money or IOUs in the fields they harvested or for the animals they took away. Only a few years ago, the *Sichuan Daily* reported that a nomad had found a wooden plank in his field. It read: "The Red Army took 100 kilos of barley from your fields. You can take this plank to any Red Army unit or Soviet government to redeem it as silver or tea." I told Nima the story. She said quietly, "They left money in our storage place too. But what was the use of money when there was no food to buy? We couldn't eat the silver dollars." An old man who had been standing nearby and listening, chipped in: "The Red Army said they came to liberate us, but it was they who needed liberating, from hunger, from starvation, from destruction."

There is no doubt the Tibetans suffered at the hands of the Red Army. Mao spoke of what happened when he told Edgar Snow: "It was our only foreign debt. One day, we must return to the Tibetans what we had to take from them . . ."[17] Deng Xiaoping also apologized: "When the Red Army marched north, they really made the Tibetans suffer. It finished everything they had. They were badly done by. But we had no choice if we were going to preserve the Red Army. We must compensate them."[18] I had been shocked and saddened by Bosshardt's account of the hostage taking and the other means the Army resorted to in order to sustain itself. It must have been desperately bad here—it was the only time Mao acknowledged any of the Red Army's depredations, out of all the places and people they took from, all the confiscations and ransom. Events here seem to have penetrated his normally steely conscience—perhaps because they were taking from the very poor, ten months from their next harvest.

While I was talking to Nima, a huge throng of monks came through the courtyard in their crimson robes and matching felt boots. Their morning study was over; they were smiling, talkative, noisy, friendly, and curious, competing for me to take their photograph and inviting me to have tea with them. It was hard to imagine that the monks in this monastery, who could not bear to kill an ant, inflicted such heavy blows on the 4th Army. But when their survival was at stake, they did what they had to do.

Seeing the monks, I thought of the one who saved Sangluo. When the 2nd Army and 4th Army left Luhuo, he was ordered to stay behind because of the injury to his foot. "Look after yourself and keep your revolutionary zeal. We'll be back in seven or eight years, maximum ten years," the commissar told dozens of them. Sangluo cried his eyes out, begging to be taken along: "I've walked thousands of miles, I promise I can keep up." The commissar told him to get some sleep and he would have news in the morning. But when he woke up, the troops were gone. Over 1,100 of the sick and the wounded, and some nurses, were left behind.

"I screamed, as if I had lost my parents," Sangluo recalled, his voice choking. The army had left him nothing: no food, no medicine, and no rifle. He dried his tears, and told the others he was going to chase after the troops. "They were my family. How could I live without them?" He followed their footprints, but after five hours he collapsed with pain. When he woke up, he found himself in the arms of a monk. "I was so frightened I struggled to free myself. Suppose he was from the monastery that we attacked! He would kill me," Sangluo recalled with some embarrassment. "But he put his hand on my head, telling me in a very gentle voice not to worry. He was going home. Would I come with him?"

The monk took Sangluo to his village and asked his mother to look after him. After a few months, he returned to the monastery—only then did Sangluo learn why the monk had come home: his monastery had been sacked by the Red Army and the abbot told him to hide until they were gone. At first, Sangluo felt uneasy, but gradually his concern left him. He was treated like a member of the family, and he helped to tend the yaks and learned Tibetan. He was the only Chinese in the whole area. He never had a chance to speak Chinese, and soon forgot it. The only words he could still remember were "home village," "Mao," and "He Long," but he did not really feel at home until he went on a pilgrimage to Lhasa as a monk's helper six years later. "It took three years on the road, there and back, longer than the Long March. It was hard, prostrating every step of the way, but the kindness of the monk who took me in and the people we met convinced me. When we finally reached Lhasa, they told me that from now on I would lead a good life, free of suffering. What more could you ask?"

Sangluo said he was lucky to be alive. Of the 1,100 sick, wounded, and the young left in Luhuo County, only a small number survived: a few became monks, but most died of hunger or were killed by the locals. Even today, the older people in Luhuo like Nima still remember the deaths of four women soldiers. In deep winter, they were made to run through the street naked, with crowds jeering at them. On a bridge over the Mian River, they ran into a monk. He stopped them, took off his robe, tearing it into pieces so the women could cover themselves. But they did not understand, thinking he was going to tie them up and rape them as a group of Tibetans had just done. They held each other's hands and jumped into the river together, shouting "Oh, mother!"

After ten years as a herder, Sangluo married a Tibetan woman whose family he had worked for. "She said I was a good man, and defers to me in all matters, big and small," Sangluo said with a smile. "But I am the lucky one to have married her. Tibetan women are the best in the world. They are so hardworking and so loving." They have two sons and one daughter, and a herd of 100 yak. "It used to be 30, then 60; it just kept growing," he said proudly, pointing to the yak beyond his window. "You know the Tibetans are very honest. If a yak goes missing, someone will bring it back. If it is pregnant, they will return it with the baby."

Sangluo put more dried yak pats in the stove to keep me warm, and a blanket over his legs. Arthritis is the only thing that causes him pain, otherwise he is content. Did he regret coming on the March? I asked. He thought for a minute. "Perhaps, if I had finished it, life would have been different, just as the pilgrimage to Lhasa changed everything." Then he fell into a long silence. Maybe he was in contemplation; his prayer wheel was running faster and faster, and his eyes were fixed on the flames in the stove.

Since he was the only Han Chinese in the village, then and now, I wondered if the Tibetans treated him differently. "You know, I only stopped being the village accountant a few years ago. I held the post for over thirty years. They put their hard-earned money and trust in me. That was the highest honor." When I asked Sangluo whether he thought he was a Han Chinese or Tibetan, he turned his prayer wheel, looked me in the eyes, and said, "Does it matter?"

After the green desert of the grassland came a grey one. For mile after mile, Soldier Huang trudged along steep-sided ravines and over strange wind-sculpted hills, with no trees, just unremitting caked-up dust. "It was as bald as a monk's head," Huang said with a laugh. The dust was loess, blown down from Mongolia and Siberia; here and there he saw some caves hewn out of it—and that was where people lived. When there was an occasional river and they stopped to drink, the water was brackish and bitter, but there were men with donkeys carrying buckets and women with jars who said they came 15 miles to fetch it. The few fields with crops of corn and sorghum were dried up for lack of water.

They had been marching for three weeks through the Yellow Plateau. It was the most dismal landscape he had ever seen, and he wondered whether it was the end of the earth. "Even the sky was grey as lead, and looked as though it was about to burst into tears," Huang recalled. But then came the news: they were nearing the border town of Wuqi in the Shaanxi Soviet base. "We were told it was the Ruijin of the North, and everything was available, all the food we could want. And we didn't have to walk any further. The end of the March! At last! Everyone cheered up."

It was a cold day this far north, on October 19, 1935. They marched in single file, tidied themselves up as best they could, and tried to sing songs and shout slogans—although they could hardly open their mouths; the keen wind was whipping dust all over them. At dusk they entered Wuqi—and Huang's jaws dropped. A single street barely 100 meters long closed in by low hills on either side, with a few dilapidated houses and some dirty-looking cave dwellings. Was this it? For a fleeting moment, he hoped it was a mistake and they would march on. Then he saw the familiar characters on the wall of a cave: "Long Live the Communist Party!" The few people who dared to venture outdoors stared at them, equally bewildered. "They must have asked themselves, 'Is this really the Red Army?' We looked like gangs of workmen in rags. They also spoke a dialect we could not understand at all. So we just watched each other in silence."

There were nowhere near enough caves for them to sleep in. The men lay down on the open hillsides, shivering in what was left of their flimsy clothes in the cold autumn night. Huang looked up at the black sky and wondered dejectedly why they had come. All the soldiers grumbled. They should have been joyful—after all, they were out of the grassland, safe from Tibetans and Chiang's troops, and had been told there would be no more marching—but he couldn't understand why they had walked for a year and suffered so much, just to end up in this wretched village. He longed for home. His own village was so much better, with trees, fertile fields, and rivers that gave them everything they wanted. "Anywhere in the South would have been better than that bloody dump," he said. As usual, food was his uppermost concern. He could not see how they were going to survive here.

Braun had his reservations too. He was struck by the desolation of the new Soviet, barely a third of the size of the Jiangxi base.

> From ancient times, this has been the poorest and the most backward area in China . . . Not only do the locals have little to eat and wear, they do not have enough water to drink . . . The area is often at the mercy of drought and floods. The Nationalist press gloatingly predicted that the Red Army could never survive. There was nothing with which to clothe or feed it and hardly any men to replenish its ranks. "The march from Sichuan to northwestern China was a march into death," it reported.[1]

But Braun's opinions no longer carried any weight. He would have been equally concerned with the dwindling force of the 1st Army, now only 4,000 strong out of the original 86,000. A Nationalist report showed that in one county alone, over 1,000 Red Army men gave themselves up after they emerged from the Tibetan grassland in mid-September. Most of them stayed on locally; some found their way back home. They simply did not want to walk another step into the unknown, and crept away at the first opportunity.

What brought Mao's army to northern Shaanxi has always been presented as almost an accident. The first town they had come to in Gansu after the grassland was Hadapu, a bustling trading place and a center for collecting and distributing herbal plants. Many traditional medical houses from the rest of the country had their agents here and kept in touch with news from home. The soldiers remembered Hadapu well. Each was given a silver dollar to spend—enough to buy five chickens—and they ate their first full meal in months. One of the orderlies bought some steamed buns wrapped in a newspaper for his commanders—and the paper reported the Red menace in Shaanxi Province. For Mao, this was a revelation. They had no idea that local Communists were already so strong in the area. At last they had somewhere to go!

I took a look at the July and August issues of the newspapers available in Hadapu at the time. There was indeed plenty of news about the Red Bandits in northern Shaanxi. *Dagong Daily* ran this piece on July 23, 1935:

> The Communist bandits are running rampant in Shaanxi. Of the twenty-three counties, every single one has been affected. Eight are run by them, with another ten partially controlled by them. They are powerful enough to expand their influence without the use of force.

But the true story of how Mao came to know about them is less dramatic. The director of the Red Army Museum at Hadapu told me that in the 1st Army there was a young man called Jia Tuofu. He was from Shaanxi and had been sent to Shanghai in early 1934 by the Shaanxi Communist Party to report their work. But the Party headquarters had moved to Ruijin, where he eventually made his way and joined the March. When he saw the Party still undecided where to go in Hadapu, he told Mao about the base in his home province. Up to then, Mao only had the idea of heading in a general northerly direction to be near the Soviet Union. To find a place where they could settle instead of starting from scratch to establish a base was an enormous relief. Mao was overjoyed: "Such a big base. Let's go." As far as he was concerned, the March was over—at least that was what he would claim, and use for his propaganda purposes. The real facts, as so often, were somewhat different.

Mao and the 1st Army set up their headquarters in Baoan, two days' walk from Wuqi. Today it is called Zhidan after the local hero Liu Zhidan, who created the Shaanxi Soviet and made Baoan the Red capital in the north. As I headed there, I had plenty of time to reflect on Huang's memory of the scenery during the long hours by train and bus from Xian. I think I might have preferred it in his day. Carved into the grey and brown hills are endless terraces for crops to feed the growing population. There is still not much water around. The plants looked pathetic, the spindly stalks of the maize the thickness of my thumb with a single tiny ear at the top: average yields in the region are 500 kilos an acre at best, a fraction of what you can get in most of China. The thought of all the work in the terracing and the tending of the crops for so little reward made me sad. Zhidan County is still one of the poorest in China, with a peasant earning about $180 a year. Only relief from the state keeps them going.

The government has plans for them—but then it always had. Tired of the depressing scenery, I looked at the propaganda slogans painted on the walls and houses in every village. Although television has come to most households in the country, the method of getting a message across used by the Red Army is still very popular in rural China. The characters are huge, sometimes just one to a house, and in garish colors: violent reds, pinks, greens, and blues. Because they are so hard to remove, some of them are decades old: "Long live the dictatorship of the proletariat!" "Glory to the parents who have girls!" "Welcome economic reform!" The most recent one you see over and over again: "Create beautiful green mountains and clear rivers in northern China." If only.

Unlike Huang, I got a warm welcome in Zhidan. People were

pleased to see me—and I soon realized why. Jobs were so hard to come by that the taxi drivers practically fought for the privilege of taking me two kilometers for 30 pence. The town's thoroughfare was neat and tidy, lined with new buildings and not-so-fancy shops, schools, and factories, many of which were named after their local hero, Liu Zhidan. The dust everywhere reminded me I was on the Yellow Plateau. Still, it was a far cry from what awaited the Red Army in 1935. There is a vivid description of Zhidan by a senior officer in Huang's corps:

> This was a truly poverty-stricken spot . . . The people were poor and the wolves were hungry . . . They often sneaked into the town at night searching for food. Each of us put a mug or washbasin against the door, and a stick next to our bed. When the wolves knocked down the mug, we would spring out of bed and chase them away.[2]

I checked myself into the newly opened three-star Zhidan Hotel. I was filthy after my dusty journey, and made a beeline for the shower. The water came out in a thick brown trickle. At first I thought I might have struck oil in the shower-room. When water is scarce, we say it is as expensive as oil. In Zhidan County and the rest of northern Shaanxi, they definitely have plenty of that. It was first mentioned in the first century AD in the Annals of Han. The local county record lists it as good for "lamps and curing scars," although people also made ink from the soot when it burned. The Americans exploited it in the 1920s before the Red Army threw them out. Now oil has become the lifeline of the county.

I waited for the brown water to clear, but it just stopped. When I called reception, I was told I could only have a shower after eight in the evening. Even that was a luxury, I discovered—many of the peasants here still had only one wash a year, on the eve of the Chinese New Year. I could understand why local women have yet to abandon the custom of choosing their husbands by whether they lived close to a water source. It made sense, otherwise they would spend their life carrying water. But maybe they will not have to do it much longer. Zhidan County has invested in four rain-inducing missiles and an antiaircraft gun to turn clouds into rain. I wondered whether this battle with nature could really be won. Certainly Mao and his men almost did not succeed here.

The problems began as soon as the Red Army settled down. The winter was bitterly cold, with temperatures often dropping to minus 10°C at night. Lin Biao sent an urgent cable to Mao from the front, where the Nationalist troops were pushing toward the Shaanxi base: "We are short of 2,000 winter uniforms for the soldiers. Over 1,000 men were sent to the hospital because of illnesses caused by the cold."[3] But none were available. Lin Biao was at his wits' end. At the age of 31, he was one of the most talented commanders in the Red Army, and rarely lost a battle, earning himself the nickname of "the Invincible General." He simply could not see any way out. He was so despondent he asked Mao to relieve him of his duties. But Mao was never one to give up easily. He proposed to strike east across the Yellow River to take food and money from the richer neighboring province of Shanxi. His other goal was to find an opening to the Soviet Union via Mongolia, but most of the top military men were against the plan. The Red Army was still very tired and weak; they might not be able to cross the river. "Suppose we cross it," one cabled to Mao, "and Chiang's troops increase their pressure on the base? We must guarantee that we can come back." "I cannot guarantee you anything," Mao retorted.[4] He decided to lead the attack in person. He was on his way to the front in late February 1936 when the first snow of the year engulfed them. The soldiers were shivering and one might have thought Mao would be tense and daunted by what lay ahead. Instead, he showed his optimism and expansiveness of spirit by writing one of his most brilliant poems:

*The Yellow River's swift current*
*Is stilled from end to end.*
*The mountains dance like silver snakes*
*And the hills charge like wax-hued elephants,*
*Vying with heaven in stature.*
*On a fine day, the land,*
*Clad in white, adorned in red,*
*Grows more enchanting.*

He went on to reflect how the land was so rich in beauty it had made countless heroes bow in homage. He cited some of the most remarkable emperors in Chinese history, but they were nothing, even Genghis Khan:

> *That proud son of Heaven,*
> *Genghis Khan,*
> *Knew only shooting eagles, bow outstretched.*
> *All are past and gone!*
> *For truly great men,*
> *Look to this age alone.*

No doubt he was referring to the Red Army. Or just himself?

After two months Mao returned from east of the Yellow River a disappointed man. He had collected 30,000 silver dollars—only enough to keep the army and its 6,000 new recruits going for a few months. He had failed to open up a channel for Soviet aid via Outer Mongolia—the Japanese presence in northern China was too strong and blocked any possible route. On the way back, Liu Zhidan, Mao's host in the Shaanxi Red base, was shot in the chest and died.

There was much unexplained about Liu's death. But I never found out more. I went to his cemetery, halfway up the hill on the edge of the town. It is an oasis of evergreen pines amid the yellow loess, with a rare pond in the middle. The handsome traditional arch stands out in this tiny place, almost fitting for an imperial tomb. Built in 1940 and rebuilt many times since, it shows the respect and affection in which the locals hold their hero, and also the continuing sense of loss for his death at the young age of 33.

Educated at the Whampoa Academy under Chiang, Liu turned to Communism to help the poor. He robbed the rich, including his wealthy clansmen, and killed corrupt officials to redistribute what they had stolen. The mere mention of his name was a promise to the poor, and enough to send the powerful fleeing. But just a few months before Mao's arrival in Shaanxi, a purge of Liu and his men started, ostensibly on the orders of the Central Committee. Who gave the order? No one seems to know even today. The Central Committee was mostly with

Mao on the March. Liu was imprisoned and hundreds of his followers were executed. Then Mao came on the scene as the rescuer, taking over Liu's men and his base. Liu was shot in the chest six months after that. Mao later said, "I met Comrade Liu Zhidan only once. He was a good Communist. His heroic death was an accident." But was it? Liu's two most trusted lieutenants had also died mysteriously in quick succession; the founding leaders of the Shaanxi Red base were gone.

Although Liu's cemetery was grand, in the official history of the Communist Party the real importance of the place was not due to him. It was because Mao and the other senior Party leaders spent six months here. The caves where they lived a few hundred yards down from the cemetery were hewn into the hill; they were quite spacious and airy in the October sun. There was a row of them, with their patterned wooden doors newly painted, the paper over them replaced by glass, and not a grain of dust on the tables or the *kangs*—beds made of mud. They were anything but ordinary caves. For a moment, I thought I had walked into a film set—the caves were brightly lit. A television crew were filming an old peasant; he was rigid as a corpse in his brand-new outfit and a snow-white towel wrapped around his head, something peasants here wear all year round. He was talking in a trembling voice of how as a child he used to see Mao taking his stroll and how friendly the great leader was.

The crew was making a television series to celebrate the seventieth anniversary of the Long March. I was curious to see how they would do it and what else they were filming in Zhidan County. I waited for the interview to finish before I approached the director. He was warm and friendly, with a mischievous smile on his not-so-youthful face. In China, his crew on such an important series would normally receive all the help they needed from the local governments. He could access materials I could not see, and if he had an idea, ten people would be there to help him realize it. I had gone to the local pensioners' office in the morning, inquiring about Long March veterans in the county, and was told they were all dead. Perhaps he would have some other avenues for me to follow. Besides, I would like to chat with him and the crew and see how they tackled the issues on the Long March.

"You see that old man?" The director pointed to the peasant, who was clearly more at ease now that he had taken off his new jacket and snow-white towel. "He complained to us about the Red Army cutting down their precious trees for firewood in the cold winter, making Zhidan even more uninhabitable. It is an interesting point—I often wonder how the Red Army survived here. But it won't make it into the final film. Although it is true, and it did happen seventy years ago, it reflects badly on the Red Army, especially now when people are more conscious of the environment."

I asked him about the mystery of Liu Zhidan's death.

"You must have been to his cemetery. We filmed it yesterday. Officially it was Mao who saved Liu Zhidan and the Shaanxi Red base from the purge. In fact, they saved Mao and the Red Army. The local Party historian told us in private he did not believe Liu's death was accidental. He may have a point."

"You know the song 'East Is Red'?" he continued. Of course, the song was more famous than the national anthem when I was growing up. I sang or heard it every day for over a decade—in praise of the Great Leader Chairman Mao.

*East is red*
*The sun is rising.*
*China has Mao Zedong.*
*He seeks happiness for the people.*
*He is our savior.*

"That was a Shaanxi folk song originally, dedicated to Liu Zhidan. You can see how much the locals loved Zhidan—they compared him to the sun. After his death, Mao's name appeared."

Shaanxi folk songs are known throughout China. The locals call them "Sad Tunes" or "Wandering Under the Sky." They pierce your heart, as if the singers are putting into them all the strength saved from their mothers' wombs, as if they want to shake off the monotony and barrenness of the Yellow Plateau, as if it is the only way they can convey the despair of living in such a hostile land. They are free-spirited, reminding me of a shepherd and his flocks roaming the yellow earth, his songs echoing in the deep valley and endless loess. They have the power of the uninitiated, the raw, the deeply rooted. I never knew that "East Is Red" was not written for Mao.

"I only learned that during my interviews. But the story won't make it into the film either."

So he could not mention the purge, the maybe-not-so-accidental death of Liu Zhidan, the origin of "East Is Red," the desertions, the power struggle, the battle for food, and, of course, the real reasons for the Long March.

"Absolutely not," he nodded emphatically. "I want to break the boundaries. I want to make something new and exciting, especially about an event so daring, so heroic, and so tragic. But as you know, television is the voice of the Party. On such an important event we have to follow the line it lays down."

And what was the line?

"You know it as well as I do—that speech Mao gave when they got to Shaanxi," he said, and went back to work, interviewing another peasant. I thought about what he had said. Of course I knew the speech. Mao made it, defiant as ever, in December 1934, when the Red Army had barely recovered from their exhaustion; he used the phrase "the Long March" for the first time:

> For twelve months we were under daily reconnaissance and bombing from the skies by scores of planes, while on land we were encircled and pursued, obstructed and intercepted by a huge force of several hundred thousand men, and we encountered untold difficulties and dangers on the way; yet by using our two legs we swept across a distance of more than 25,000 *li* through the length and breadth of eleven provinces. Let us ask, has history every known a long march to equal ours? No, never. The Long March is a declaration. It has proclaimed to the world that the Red Army is an army of heroes . . . The Long March is propaganda. It has announced to some 200 million people in eleven provinces that the road

of the Red Army is their only road to liberation . . . The Long
March is a machine for sowing. It has sown many seeds which
will sprout, leaf, blossom, and bear fruit, and will yield a harvest in the future. In a word, the Long March has ended with
victory for us and defeat for the enemy.[5]

The tone was set, but Mao wanted a vivid, flesh-and-blood Long March,
one that illustrated his verdict. He told the Political Department to collect stories from the rank and file about their experiences on the March.
Ding Ling, a famous young Chinese writer who had made her way to
Shaanxi, was given the job of editing them. She found that

> articles poured in from North to South, from East to West,
> from hundreds or thousands of *li* away, even from the edge of
> the desert. They are written on waxed paper, rough paper, red
> and green pamphlets, smudged, crumpled, and covered with
> dust. Piece after piece of awe-inspiring battles, crossing the Wu
> River at night, taking the Dadu River, occupying Zunyi the
> second time — all the stories have all come across so vividly. A
> giant volume of over 300,000 words has been prepared, and
> will appear soon before the eagerly waiting audience.[6]

They selected 100 stories which conformed to Mao's instructions, and
the book came out in 1938. What we know about the Long March today, seventy years later, largely comes from these accounts. The events,
the battles, the themes, the victories, the historical significance, its impact on the world, the heroism, the invincibility, the wisdom of Mao —
these are the standard texts in the history books which I and most
Chinese studied.

The stories were powerful, but many soldiers were illiterate and
printed materials were not easy to access. So Mao asked for a special
song to be composed about the Long March, as they had done all the
way on the March. The *Tune of the Long March* had thirteen parts,
each covering a month and what the 1st Army did, and the last stanza
summed up the March. Every soldier could sing it; every soldier began

to see the Long March as portrayed in the song; for many, the song began to color their own memories. All the veterans I talked to could sing it, and sometimes burst into it in the midst of our conversations. Once I asked Propagandist Wu what she did in the summer; she paused, and then started singing: "July comes and we enter the Northwest. The river flowing and barley growing, what do we suffer for? To fight the Japanese and save China." Then she launched into August: "August saw us march further, fear no cold in the snow-land, the impassable grassland. We are the invincible Red Army."

Mao's foresight was quite extraordinary. To think of turning the Long March, which was essentially a retreat, into a glorious victory, was itself a stroke of genius. To be able to make it the founding legend of Communist China showed a political acumen, a gift for propaganda, and an optimism and self-assurance that few possess.

Mao's flair for propaganda did not come out of the blue. He showed an interest in it very early on in his life. He told a close friend that he was drawn to two professions—teaching and journalism. When he was at Beijing University, he attended lectures by famous journalists, and after he went back to his hometown he edited magazines to propagate new ideas. During the first collaboration between the Communists and the Nationalists, he was the acting head of the Nationalist Propaganda Ministry—he was so successful that he made himself irreplaceable after just two months. In December 1929, he laid down the rules for propaganda in the Red Army and the Communist Party after rows with other commanders on how the Red Army should be run. He told the soldiers that they were not just any army, but an army with a political purpose. They did not fight battles for the sake of battles. They must communicate with the people, organize them, arm them, and help them set up their own governments for their goals. Without these activities, their battles would have no meaning, and the Red Army would lose its *raison d'être*. He even gave detailed instructions on how many there should be in a propaganda team, who would make ideal members, and what they should do.

On the Long March, the Red Army did exactly as Mao instructed. Critical to his designs was the *Red Star* newspaper. It is next to unbelievable that through all the rigors of the March the one thing they never abandoned was the printing equipment, initially a lithograph press that needed a dozen men to carry, and later a wax-paper printer. Over the course of the March, there were twenty-eight issues of *Red Star*, four pages with 30,000 words to each. The editor was Deng Xiaoping, who at the age of 30 was a deft hand at propaganda. *Red Star* put across the orders of the Party and praised the heroism of the soldiers; it also gave practical advice on how to deal with shoe shortages, disease, and clashes with ethnic peoples. At the same time, it did not shy away from problems: slack discipline, inadequacy of personal hygiene, overzealous confiscation, and desertion. Deng wrote in an editorial on November 11, 1934:

> In the last few days' march, we did badly with our discipline . . . Crapping everywhere, leaving straw bedding about, taking things from people without permission—this happens frequently . . . People do not listen to our sweet talk; they observe our actions. An army without discipline will not win their sympathy and support, no matter how much propaganda we do.[7]

He also had plenty to say about the Red Army's propaganda.

> Writing slogans and painting on walls have always been the strength of the Red Army. But many units have neglected this tradition on the march. They fail to obliterate reactionary slogans completely. They only erase a few words or cover them up with paint. But where are our own slogans? This is an extremely important task that should not be forgotten.[8]

I found the frankness and honesty of *Red Star* refreshing. The work of an open mind came across and I doubted whether some of Deng's editorials and articles in *Red Star* would have been published today. A few years ago, a small Chinese publisher brought out *Herald of History: The Sacred Promises of Half a Century Ago*. It is a collection of editorials and articles from *Xinghua Daily* and *Liberation Daily*, the two main

Communist newspapers of the 1930s and 1940s. Many of the pieces were penned by Mao, Zhou Enlai, and other Party leaders demanding freedom of speech and information. The book was later banned. It is sad that the demands of the Party leaders of the time seem too much for today. This was the Party's youth, and realism has overtaken it.

If *Red Star* set the tone, at the grass roots there was a propaganda team in every unit, often ten to twenty people. They were divided into three groups: speech and agitation, performance, and putting up posters. Propagandist Wu never forgot what she was told after she was selected for the performance group: "We are the soldiers of the workers and peasants. Propaganda is our weapon. Fight for the Soviet, expose the dark old society, praise the new, sing for our Revolution, and create a heroic history." Cheerful and noisy as a magpie, which the Chinese call the Happy Bird, Wu sang the whole way on the March. But it could not be just any folk songs. She asked me if I knew the song "Jasmine Fragrance Everywhere in August." I did: it was a song I learned in primary school; its joyful tune and words were as festive to my young mind as the Chinese New Year. Wu and I started singing together:

*Jasmine fragrance is everywhere in August;*
*red flags are fluttering.*
*Banners and lanterns are going up, and up,*
*to welcome a glorious and luminous new world.*

When we stopped, Wu launched into it again, but with very different lyrics.

*The little carp with a beautiful red jaw,*
*she has swum upstream from down below.*
*How many steel nets and sluice-gates she has to navigate!*
*All for the pleasure of seeing you, my kind brother.*

I was speechless. I never knew that the famous Red Army song was actually a love song. "Because the tune was so well known, people learned the new song quickly, and also the message in it," Wu said with a big smile. "We made them happy and we made them learn."

For plays, the propaganda team had to try harder. They were all specially written short pieces on landlords exploiting the poor, Chiang Kaishek betraying the country, wives persuading their husbands to join the Red Army, or Nationalist troops chasing them in vain and collecting nothing but a worn sandal. But there were tricks too, Wu told me with her voice lowered, as if it was still a secret. As soon as they reached a village or town, they made a point of finding out the names of the rich and powerful. Then she put on her rudimentary makeup—lard for foundation, charcoal to draw her eyebrows and eye shadow, red paper soaked in water as rouge, and clothes confiscated from the landlords as costumes. The curtain was a sheet and burning pine branches their lights. But the result was astonishing. "They could not believe we knew so much about their pain and sufferings. They were stunned we could do a play about them so quickly." Wu laughed heartily. "Little did they know we performed it so many times, with only a change of the name of the landlord or warlord in each new place!"

Wu also helped the poster team whenever she could. She thought they had the toughest job. They had a minimum quota of 50 posters every day, and sometimes as many as 200. Whenever the Red Army came to somewhere new, the poster team had to cover it with posters and slogans—"Workers and peasants, rise up to kill the landlords' pigs and grab their grain for your new year!" "Support the Red Army!" "Down with Chiang Kaishek!" "Only Communism can save China!" In Zunyi, the propaganda team wrote 18,400 slogans in two days, turning the town into a world of color.[9] Even the Nationalists were overwhelmed. One bureaucrat reported to his superior: "The Red Bandits pay particular attention to propaganda work. There were so many slogans that they covered every street and every lane, every window and every wall, occupying every inch of available space. No wonder people follow them like water flows downstream."[10]

When the poster team ran out of ink, they scraped the bottoms of woks or swept soot from chimneys. If they had no paper, they used the backs of landlords' account books, paper offerings for the dead, Buddhist scriptures, even split bamboo which they floated down the river to reach people miles downstream. It was hard to post slogans in winter. The glue froze as soon as it was on the wall, so they invented a new method: raw eggs do not freeze so easily, so they would crack an egg and mix it in water, then brush it a few times. The poster stuck to it and you could not take it down. For soldiers who were constantly hungry, the eggs were so inviting. But nobody stole them.

The propaganda on the Long March was a major feat. What better way to pacify frightened locals, explain Communist ideas, and win people's confidence? And who would not love some entertainment and color in their life, especially the peasants? They toiled on the land all year round; their only relief came during the Chinese New Year, when the whole village might pool money together and invite an itinerant opera troupe for a week or two. They were more than willing subjects for any propaganda when it was packaged attractively. The "entertainment" was particularly enjoyable when it followed a struggle meeting, after which the poor received a tool, a shirt, or a few kilos of rice from the stores of the rich; or on a market day, when the Red Army killed some of the landlords' pigs and stewed them in a huge pot in the middle of the market square. Wu would ask people to help themselves to the meat, saying if they joined the Red Army they could eat like this for the rest of their lives. Many young men signed up on the spot, without even bothering to go home and tell their parents.

Over the centuries our rulers always tried to keep the masses ignorant; if they knew too much, they would rise up. The Communists tried to change all that: rising up was just what they wanted. It was propaganda together with literary education that would make it happen. The efforts they made really were extraordinary. There were classes not just for soldiers, but for children and women; mass literary campaigns and drama campaigns. The Jiangxi Soviet eventually boasted over 3,000 primary schools and 66,000 evening schools. This increase in literacy probably explained the large circulation of newspapers and magazines: *Red China* reached 40,000, *Youth Truth* 28,000, *Struggle* 17,000, *Red Star* 17,000.[11] They did not stop teaching on the March either. Huang remembered: "We never stopped. You won't believe it, but I was memorizing new characters every week on the March, especially on the days of rest." Of course, Huang learned not just words, but also Communist ideas, making him aware why he could not accept the status quo.

The Communists' trump card, though, was to make the Long March an anti-Japanese crusade. Before its pullout from Jiangxi, the Communist Party dispatched the Anti-Japanese Vanguard Column, declaring that

> the Red Army cannot sit here and watch the Chinese nation fall under Japanese Imperialism; it cannot allow the Nationalist traitors to pawn the whole of China; it cannot tolerate the wholesale butchery and rape of the Chinese people by the Japanese Imperialists . . . The Anti-Japanese Vanguard Column is willing to work with everyone and all the armed forces in the country to fight against the Japanese.[12]

The column of 6,000 men carried more than 1,600,000 copies of this declaration and other pamphlets, and marched into the Nationalist-controlled heartland. They were promptly wiped out by Chiang's troops; their commander, Fang Zhimin, was captured, put in a cage, paraded around the countryside on a cart, and then executed. To the day they died, Fang and his men thought they were fighting the Japanese, totally unaware of their true role—to deflect Chiang's troops and give the Red Army a chance to escape. All the veterans I talked to also believed they were marching north to the anti-Japanese front. "Why else did we abandon our fertile base in the South and go to that desolate place? Because that was where Japanese imperialism was," Wu said confidently. Then she sang one of the anti-Japanese songs which she taught the soldiers and the people:

> We give you land and forests;
> Our struggle is for you.
> Don't forget your hatred of Japan—
> March with us to fight the Japanese.

Huang still remembered the two huge paintings outside a county government office in Guizhou. One depicted Chiang taking the hand of the Japanese and leading them to the Great Wall; in the other, Chiang chopped the map of China into several pieces and offered a piece to a Japanese officer who was aggressively waving a sword. The caption splashed over the painting read: "Chiang betrayed the motherland." "We hated Chiang even more after we saw those cartoons. We were marching north to fight the Japanese. Chiang Kaishek did not lift a finger against them. Instead, he spent all his money and gunpowder destroying us. What a bastard!"

The anti-Japanese propaganda turned a dispirited retreat of the Red Army into a lofty march of salvation for the whole nation. It gave the soldiers a purpose without which the army could easily have disintegrated and, crucially, it gained them public sympathy and support. Wherever they went, anti-Japanese propaganda heralded the way. "This skilful propaganda manoeuvre must be noted as a piece of brilliant political strategy. It was to a large extent responsible for the successful conclusion of the heroic trek," Edgar Snow wrote prophetically. "In one sense, this mass migration was the biggest armed propaganda tour in history . . . I'm not sure that it may not prove to have been the most permanent service of the Reds . . ."[13]

Little did Snow know when he wrote those words that he himself was to perform a permanent service for the Communists. A young man from Kansas City with great curiosity about the world, he had sailed to Shanghai in 1928, the year after Chiang's purge of the Communists, searching for what he called the "glamour of the orient." He was 26, idealistic and impressionable, writing for the *Herald* in London and the *Sun* in New York. It was not long before he became outraged by the poverty he saw in China. After he visited a famine area in northern China in 1929, he wrote:

> Have you ever seen a man—a good honest man who has
> worked hard . . . when he has had no food for more than a
> month? It is a most agonizing sight. His dying flesh hangs from
> him in wrinkled folds; you can clearly see every bone in his
> body; his eyes stare out unseeing . . . If he has been lucky he
> has long ago sold his wife and daughters. He has sold almost
> everything he owns—the timbers of his house itself and most

of his clothes. Sometimes he has, indeed, even sold the last
rag of decency, and he sways there in the scorching sun, his
testicles dangling from him like withered olive seeds—the
last grim jest to remind you that this was once a man![14]

By 1931 he just said: "I have seen so much pain and suffering that it has
entered my own blood." Japan's aggression and Chiang's incapacity to
take things in hand appalled Snow. He thought Chiang's government
was the epitome of corruption, impotence, and oppression. All the officials cared about was putting money in their own pockets and keeping a lid on the people. China needed change, but Chiang was not the
man to bring it about. Could the Communists be the solution? Because of Nationalist censorship, there was little information about
them. Chiang controlled the media and made life difficult for journalists such as Snow. He had been in China for seven years, but had been
unable to answer the most basic of questions. Who were these Reds?
What were they like? Did they carry homemade bombs in their brief-
cases? What motivated them? What had kept them going for nine years
against overwhelming force? What were their lives like? How strong
were they? It infuriated him that ". . . for some time not a single non-
Communist observer could answer those questions with confidence,
accuracy, or facts based on personal investigations."

Snow's journey into the Shaanxi Red base was no accident. I had
always thought the initiative came from him, but this is not quite so.
He tried to go there but was only able to when Mao and the Communist Party decided they needed him. They wanted to put pressure on
the Nationalists by using a sympathetic reporter to write up the Communists' anti-Japanese stance and give them a positive image. A trust-
worthy but non-Communist Western journalist, with access to Western
and Chinese media, would make the world listen. Mao wrote to Song
Qingling, the widow of Sun Yatsen, and—ironically—Chiang's sister-
in-law, asking her to find him a sympathetic journalist. She had read
Snow's coverage of China in the press, liked it, and become friendly
with him. So she proposed Snow.

Mao left nothing to chance, and dictated detailed instructions for handling Snow's visit: "Security, secrecy, warmth and red carpet."[15] He asked for the best cave in Baoan to be given to Snow, named the Foreign Ministry Guest House. I was directed there by the guide from the Mao Residence Museum. The door was locked but even from outside it looked quite big, prosperous, and modern, with tiles turning the cave into a twentieth-century dwelling. After Mao left Baoan, his cave and those of the other leaders which I had just seen were abandoned to the goats. Later they were used to hold criminals, until the Red Guards came here in 1966 and "enlightened" the locals—they denounced the county government and asked them to turn the caves into a shrine to remember the Great Leader. But they were not sure about Snow, a foreigner, and an American at that—all foreigners were imperialists in their eyes. Besides, peasants were still living in the cave he used, so they let it be.

Standing in front of the cave, I tried to imagine what Snow must have felt when he set foot on Red soil, excited, anxious, uncertain. What he did not expect was to be greeted by banners, a military band, and all the top echelon of Red leaders there except for Mao. "It was the first time I had been greeted by the entire cabinet of a government, the first time a whole city had turned out to welcome me; the effect produced on me was highly emotional."[16] Luxuries such as coffee, milk, and cigarettes which were hard to come by were made available; soldiers were trained to look after their foreign dignitary: they had to be welcoming, thorough, and meticulous. A special messenger was arranged to deliver his letters to his wife in Beijing, and a special translator was ordered from there. Zhou Enlai proposed a ninety-day schedule, to go to the front, talk to senior leaders and ordinary people, but the questions that Snow would ask had to be submitted in advance, and the Politburo carefully coordinated their answers.

He had his first interview with Mao soon after his arrival, and it lasted until 2 a.m. Snow's impression of Mao was accurate. Mao looked

> gaunt, rather Lincolnesque . . . [he] seemed a very interesting and complex man. He had the simplicity and naturalness of

the Chinese peasant with a lively sense of humour and a love
of rustic laughter . . . Something about him suggests a power
of ruthless decision when he deems it necessary . . . [I felt] a
certain force of destiny in Mao . . . It is nothing quick or
flashy, but a kind of solid elemental vitality. You feel that
whatever extraordinary there is in this man grows out of
the uncanny degree to which he synthesizes and expresses
the urgent demands of millions of Chinese, and especially
the peasantry . . . If these demands and the movement which
is pressing them forward are the dynamics which can regener-
ate China, then in this deeply historical sense Mao Zedong
may possibly become a very great man.[17]

Snow also wanted to question Mao about his life. Mao was reluctant:
what did that have to do with the Revolution? Snow explained that people had so many prejudices about the Communists, a personal touch
would go a long way to convince Western readers. So Mao agreed.
Over several nights in his two-roomed cave, Mao gave the first and only
interview about his early years. At first, Mao's secretary served as Snow's
interpreter. Snow's interview notes, based on his oral translation of
Mao's replies, were translated back into Chinese, and then read and
corrected by Mao. Later Mao also took the added precaution of check-
ing everything Snow wrote, amending and rewriting parts of it. Zhou
Enlai and many others did the same. Snow was not entirely happy with
this; on July 26, 1937, he wrote to his wife, who was then with the Red
Army in Shaanxi, "Don't send me any more notes about people reneg-
ing on their stories to me . . . As it is, with so many things cut out it be-
gins to read like Childe Harold."[18]
    Mao and Zhou Enlai opened all the doors for Snow; they also
made sure he had a memorable time in the Red base. His life was not
luxurious, but it was privileged. He spent his time riding, and playing
tennis and cards, even starting a high-stakes gambling school. Millet
was his staple food—boiled millet, fried millet, baked millet—with occasional pork or mutton *shashlik*. For a change, he made a huge effort
to gather the ingredients for a chocolate cake—lard was substituted for

butter. It ended up as a sticky mess but still got eaten. "I lived a holiday life," he said.

Snow was truly impressed by his experience with the Communists. It was not just Mao but the other Red leaders, Zhou Enlai, Peng Dehuai, Bo Gu, Zhang Wentian, and many others. They were men and women mostly of his own age; young, optimistic, determined, and passionate, and he forged a genuine bond with them. He was also impressed by the soldiers he met on a four-month trip to the front, who kept marching, playing games, and singing, with plays put on every night. "You would not have supposed that these people were aware of their impending 'annihilation,'" he wrote of the increasing threats by Chiang to the Shaanxi Red base. Compared with the Nationalists they came as a breath of fresh air. He was as comfortable as if "I were with some of my own countrymen . . . I had found hope for the nation in that small band of survivors of the Long March and formed a favourable impression of them and their policies . . . I admired their courage, their selflessness, their single-minded determination to save China under their leadership and the outstanding ability, the practical political sense, and personal honesty of their high commanders."[19]

His feelings for the Red Army and the Communists come through clearly in the pages of *Red Star over China*. The appeal of the characters, their selflessness, fortitude, indomitable spirit, and sense of destiny, their supreme confidence in a final victory, were so vidid, so infectious. I remember when I first read Snow, I felt passionately moved. He was a good journalist, stylish, colorful, direct. More importantly, he cared deeply about what he wrote. I was carried away by his ardor, his commitment, and his sense of mission. If I knew nothing about the reality of the March, I would buy his whole story today, as millions have done in the past.

Snow knew he had a coup. But the success of *Red Star over China* still took him by surprise. In the United States, *New Republic* said: "To Edgar Snow goes the credit for what is perhaps the greatest single feat performed by a journalist in our century."[20] Another reaction was, "How can fiction hope to compete for intelligent reader interest with books that are so closely tied up with the most important happenings of the day?"[21] No wonder an American general said the only power the Chinese Communist forces had was what American newspapermen tell Americans about them.[22] In the United Kingdom, the book sold 100,000 copies in its first weeks.

The book changed Western opinion of Mao and the Communists. Its very title voiced the author's underlying conviction that the Communists were ordained to occupy a central place in the war against Japan and after it. As Snow's biographer rightly said, "It holds a unique place as a journalistic *tour de force*, and as an integral factor in the history it recorded. It was no less than a political instrument that brought the Chinese Revolution and its makers to life in the minds of readers around the world."[23] It was also a mark of Mao's acuity and extraordinary farsightedness, turning what was a retreat into a victory, and making of it a powerful symbol of Communist success that has lasted till the present day.

Its publication in Chinese with Snow's active cooperation also helped to shape Chinese people's views of the Communists and the Red Army. They finally began to understand who these Reds were, what they were like, and what motivated them. Many young radicals in the Nationalist-controlled areas joined the Communists in Shaanxi as a direct result of reading Snow. Mao's third wife, Jiang Qing, a film star in Shanghai, was one of them. It was the beginning of the Chinese Communist Party's renaissance. Mao was deeply grateful to Snow and gave him the highest praise a Chinese could. He said *Red Star over China* had a merit no less than that of the Great Yu, the mythical emperor who was supposed to have brought China's floods under control and saved the people.[24] A genius of propaganda, Mao knew the importance of the pen, but even he did not expect Snow's pen could be so powerful—it profoundly influenced the fate of the Red Army, the Communist Party, and Mao himself.

# 11 ★ THE END OF THE MARCH

We rushed to greet each other, throwing our packs and rifles on the ground. We laughed; we jumped up and down; we burst into dance; I was ecstatic. I grabbed a soldier from the 1st Army and started crying. We surged toward Huining like a flood breaking through a dam." Woman Wang was recalling the special day of October 10, 1936. "The gate to the ancient town was covered with bright posters and flags, like a bridegroom's chamber on his wedding day. There were firecrackers and drums banging away." As many soldiers as could be crammed in were gathered in the square outside the Confucian Temple. Big gas fires were burning near the podium, dispelling dusk and the crisp cold air. The soldiers were still wearing their thin clothes from the South, torn and dirty, and their hats had lost their peaks, but nobody minded: the friendly atmosphere, the union of the 1st, 2nd, and 4th Armies for the first time, was so heartwarming. They felt even better when they heard the speeches.

Zhu De, the Commander-in-Chief of the Red Army, read out the telegram from the Central Committee and the Military Council to the three armies. "The union of the three main Red Armies and their entrance into the anti-Japanese front line will be crucial . . . We will fight to safeguard northwest China, north China, and the whole of China." The declaration of the 4th Army was equally rousing: "We are coming together. By all accounts, this is a most remarkable victory . . . Comrades, let's march shoulder to shoulder. The traitors to our nation and the Japanese imperialists are already shivering in anticipation of our great reunion. Victory is right in front of us."[1]

Wang sat in the crowd, almost overwhelmed with relief. She could hardly believe she had come through so many bombardments, so many battles, so much hunger, sickness, and death, and now she was back with her old comrades from the 1st Army. But many were no longer there; the 4th Army she was now attached to had lost half its original numbers. Mao, who was in Shaanxi, said of the union: "Huining, Peace Town, the Red Armies' union heralds peace for China." Ever since, October 10, 1936, has been celebrated as the end of the Long March. The exhibition in the old Confucian Temple, now the Reunion Museum, ends on this high note: "The Reunion declares the total failure of Chiang's pursuit and encirclement of the Red Armies, and marks a turning point of victory in the Communist Revolution."

I was hoping to have my reunion with a fellow Long March traveler in Huining. We first met in Ruijin in front of Mao's residence when his soldier's uniform soaked with sweat, his heavy rucksack, and the determined expression on his face caught my eye. I found out he was also retracing the Long March. "Quite a few people have done it— a Long March veteran, descendants of the veterans, journalists, foreigners, even a peasant. No soldier has done it. I feel ashamed—the Long March was a soldiers' march! So I decided to be the first soldier to retrace it. I also plan to cover it in the shortest time," he told me. He only had six weeks' leave, hence his hurry.

I wished him luck. We exchanged numbers and promised to keep in touch about our progress whenever possible. Before we said goodbye, he told me I should be proud of myself: "You are the first Chinese woman to retrace the Long March." I was not sure of his claim, but he said, "Yes, you're the first. No other Chinese women have done it." I must say it had never occurred to me to be the first. It was not a race. I wanted to find out what the soldiers went through, the obstacles they faced, how they surmounted them, and what they thought of their experiences. What was important to me was how we should look at the March and appreciate this extraordinary human odyssey. I had no sense of pride in my achievement: although my journey was tough and it certainly had its moments, it was nothing compared with the experience of the original Marchers, who went through untold privations and danger. I did not tramp every inch of the way, carrying huge burdens over mountains and swamps—as even he was doing.

I received calls from him now and then, telling me what impressed him most—the cold night that caught him by surprise—and coatless—the exhaustion from such an impossible pace, the poverty along the way, the beautifully preserved towns and villages, the locals' lack of interest in the past, the sense of awe he felt crossing the steep mountains and the expanses of grassland, his wonderment at how Mao had miraculously led the Red Army through the numerous challenges of nature and man, and his admiration for the Red Army soldiers who had done the seemingly impossible. I remember asking him once whether he could have finished the Long March under the conditions of the old days. "Never," he said firmly. "We soldiers are spoiled today. We don't have the faith that motivated the Long Marchers either. We would ask ourselves why we were doing it. We cannot endure that kind of hardship either and would certainly desert. Even if we stayed the course, Chiang Kaishek would have discovered our plans and finished us off because nowadays we cannot keep a secret."

"But you are doing it," I reminded him.

"Barely," he said modestly.

His toughness, determination, and honesty took me back to the Long Marchers. If all the soldiers were like him, the Marchers' blood would not have been shed for nothing; their spirit would have survived; the Chinese army would be invincible. I would have loved to tell him that, here in Huining or wherever we met. But I was too slow for him and we did not meet.

My regret was minor, but Wang's shattered her life forever. In Huining, she heard that her husband was still alive but was with Mao in Shaanxi. She cried with the good news and wished she had wings to carry her to his side. She had last seen him fourteen months before, when the 1st and the 4th Armies split. For all those months she had tried not to give way to her emotions, while so many comrades were dying all around her. Now she went to see Zhang Guotao. "I told him we had won. It was time for me to resume the studies I had not finished in Ruijin. I asked for permission to go to the Red Army University in Shaanxi."

Zhang Guotao, who was an amiable leader in Wang's eyes, told her not to bother him with such trivial matters. She was hurt but not shocked. As a senior cadre in the 4th Army she knew that the reunion had brought both joy and concern for Zhang, perhaps more the latter. After the split with Mao and the 1st Army a year ago, Zhang set up a temporary Central Committee, which denounced Mao, Zhou Enlai, and other senior Party leaders for destroying the unity of the Red Army, for losing hope in the Communist Revolution, and for running away toward the Soviet border. He decided to strike south toward the Chengdu Plain where he hoped to secure a base. His plan failed because the warlords, with the help of the bulk of Chiang's pursuing troops, defended their territories vigorously. He then looked toward western Sichuan which was largely inhabited by Tibetans, but the extreme shortage of food and supplies in the Tibetan area put a halt to Zhang's ambitions.

Meanwhile, Mao was doing everything he could to make Zhang cancel his alternative Central Committee and come up north. As Zhang Wentian, the Party Secretary, later admitted: "We induced him step by step and drew him out of his den . . . We sent him so many cables, and finally he agreed."[2] A key character in this intrigue was Lin Yuying, who had just been sent back from Moscow by the Comintern to reestablish contact with the Chinese Communist Party; it had been all but lost for two years. Lin was not authorized by the Comintern to be anything other than a messenger, but Mao persuaded him to make Zhang Guotao an offer as though it had the Comintern's blessing: the 4th Army under Zhang would be the Central Committee's "Southwestern Bureau," while Mao's 1st Army would be the "Northwestern Bureau." They would have equal status; the final decision on who should eventually assume the leadership would rest with the Comintern.

After Lin had served his purpose, and in case he might be tempted to reveal the truth, he was sent into Nationalist territory. Not much more was ever heard of him again. But his mediation worked and Zhang agreed to come north. As he said, "All decisions by the Comintern were regarded as divine, and must be obeyed." He knew very well that the Chinese Communist Party was not independent but a vassal of Moscow. At the same time, Zhang was worried about the heavy losses the 4th Army had suffered—40,000 men and women died in battle or as a result of shortages of food and medicine. He had little option.

While Zhang was preparing to join him, Mao sent him a cable, confirming what he had suspected all along: "The ditches [in the Shaanxi base] are deep and without trees; the soil is eroded, with few people. Transport is difficult, not suitable for the movement of a large army . . . The crops here are very poor; grain and pulses are all in short supply. A large army cannot survive here for long."[3] Zhang must have been pleased to hear that. Mao and the others had been proved wrong! Shaanxi was no better than western Sichuan as a base. Both of them had been misguided, so Mao could not possibly be too tough on him. Had he known the full detail of how Mao and his men survived from hand to mouth in the last twelve months, he would have been even surer of himself.

Zhang had little idea that the man who saved Mao and the Red Army in Shaanxi was the Young Marshal, Zhang Xueliang, who had driven his 4th Army out of its base in the Dabie Mountains in central China. The Young Marshal was one of the most colorful warlords and controversial figures in twentieth-century China. After losing his homeland to the Japanese in September 1931, he and his 100,000 men were to do Chiang's bidding, first fighting against Zhang's 4th Army, and then dealing with Mao's troops in Shaanxi. He did not want to fight the Communists. His campaigns against the 4th Army, although successful, cost him dearly. His troops had had a few skirmishes with Mao's beleaguered army soon after its arrival in Shaanxi, and lost an entire division. What might the Reds do with enough men and resources, after they had fully recovered from their grueling march? Besides, their calls to fight against the Japanese appealed to him. He would rather Chiang stopped fighting the Communists and helped him repel the Japanese and reclaim his homeland. He had been waiting for almost five years—Chiang insisted on finishing off the Communists before taking on the Japanese. Perhaps the day might never come, just like the Yellow River would never reverse its flow. He had to think again.

The grand Zhang Residence in Jiangguo Road, Xian, was the headquarters of the Young Marshal, where he was supposed to command the final elimination of the Red Army in the Northwest. I made a special trip there, even though the Long March did not come near Xian. But what happened in Zhang's residence changed the fate of the Communists and the course of modern China. Deep in an old lane was a compound with three buildings in rococo style, ornate, flamboyant, and busy, not unlike its owner. At 36, the Young Marshal was known for his love of fun, gambling, and adventure; his residence was an open-house party. He, his wife, his concubine, and his son lived in the west building, his staff in the next one, while his guests were housed in the east building. The note in the exhibition hall mentioned that Zhou Enlai graced the residence later but it did not say a word, nor did most people know, about the Communist agent who lived there and kept daily radio contact with Mao and the Communists, in the very house of the commander-in-chief of the campaign to eliminate the Communist bandits.

For the Young Marshal, the only people strong enough to help fight the Japanese were the Russians. He would have loved the Russians to help him reclaim his lost territory, and perhaps to support him as the new leader of China. He approached them, but they did not trust him; they strung him along so that he would help Mao and his army. Mao, however, welcomed the Young Marshal's idea. The Communists appointed a liaison officer who worked closely with him. The Young Marshal flew to northern Shaanxi in his private plane for secret meetings with Zhou Enlai, and at one point even offered to join the Communist Party. They came up with a plan for an alternative government based in the Northwest, with the Young Marshal as the head and the Soviet Union as their backer. A top envoy was sent to Moscow to report it—the Young Marshal personally flew to Lanzhou and made himself responsible for the envoy's journey.

But the plan was rejected by Stalin. He did not feel the playboy warlord had it in him to hold China together. Stalin's bet was still on Chiang, the only man he felt could unite China, and Mao should be talking to Chiang. A disintegrating China would only help the Japanese and drag Moscow into a conflict with Japan which Stalin was desperate to avoid—at the time the threat from Hitler was quite enough for Stalin to deal with. The Young Marshal, unaware of Moscow's attitude, went on with the scheme which he thought would realize his ambition and save the Communists.

He ordered his men to keep a safe distance from the Red Army, making sure that all his troops' movements and Chiang's military plans were cabled to the Communists. At the same time they had to appear to be fighting, although they would return to one another the same day any men that they caught. There were clashes because the Young Marshal's officers were not kept aware of their master's scheme. A Red Army commander cabled the Young Marshal one day, "We had some fighting. I'm returning all your men we've caught to the division. But we are keeping their rifles and ammunition. I hope you do not mind."[4] Much more seriously, in the confusion of miscommunication, one of the Young Marshal's officers let Chiang's troops into the Shaanxi Red base, and they captured the Communist headquarters outside Baoan. The senior leaders only escaped with difficulty.

The Young Marshal was now practically keeping the Red Army alive with the supplies he received from Chiang. Whether it was rifles or bullets, winter clothes, radio equipment, medicine, money, or his private planes, the Communists only had to ask, and he would satisfy them. Sometimes truckloads of treats such as cigarettes, cocoa, and condensed milk turned up in Zhidan County, much to the delight of the nicotine-starved Mao and other senior leaders, and in particular to Deng Xiaoping, who owed his recovery from typhoid to the condensed milk. The 10,000 winter outfits supplied by the Young Marshal saved the Red Army from freezing in their first winter in the North. But the most critical contribution was cash. In 1936 alone, he lent—or gave them, because he did not expect it to be returned—over 700,000 *fabi*, the Nationalist currency. It was a colossal sum, considering that in 1937 the Communists' total expenses were 560,000. Zhou Enlai wrote to him with profound gratitude: "Clearly you treat us like your own family, without any distinction. We are like brothers. We cannot thank you enough."[5] But at the same time he did not breathe a word about Stalin's rejection of the Young Marshal.

Meanwhile, Mao continued to try to persuade Moscow to back his alliance with the Young Marshal. He requested urgent aid. Apart from solving the immediate problem of survival, it would also show the Young Marshal that Moscow was serious and could throw its weight behind the alliance. In early September 1936, Stalin approved a shipment of arms to the Red Army Soviet. Mao's wish list included monthly aid of $3 million, together with planes, heavy artillery, shells, rifles, machine guns, antiaircraft guns, and pontoons, and Soviet personnel to fly the planes and operate the artillery. The Russians sent confirmation in October: the aid would be very substantial even if not everything Mao had asked for. The delivery would be near Ningxia, the province in Outer Mongolia closest to western China.

Mao and Zhang Guotao agreed to fight for Ningxia: the combined Red Armies would cross the Yellow River, take Ningxia, and receive the Soviet aid. Zhang was happy with the arrangement: once he had the supplies in his hands, he would be in a much stronger position. The 4th Army, by far the largest of the three armies, would spearhead the operation, and it created the Women's Vanguard Regiment to enlist the locals' support. Woman Wang was summoned by Chen Changhao, the Political Commissar of the 4th Army, a few days after the union. "After careful consideration, the Party has decided that you are to command the Women's Vanguard Regiment. It is a crucial job and it is a great honor for you. Work hard. Work well. Don't let the Party down." Wang suddenly understood why she was not allowed to go to see her husband.

She was in turmoil. All her training, all her discipline, all her sacrifices, everything she had suffered for, pointed in one direction: taking on this new challenge. But her heart pointed the other way. She had only spent two nights with her husband. She was young, only 23, she just craved time with him, to have his company, to be in his arms. But the Party came first, and at once she set about motivating her soldiers. She, like everyone in the 4th Army, realized the battle would be tough. They had been marching and fighting ceaselessly for a year, without adequate food and supplies. Now they had hardly rested for a week before they were off to the front. And it would be a crucial battle, a battle they could not afford to lose.

"Get close to our Russian big brother, receive Soviet help, and herald in a new phase of the Revolution—this is the last battle. It is an honor to sacrifice our lives for the final victory." The solemn pledges poured out of the 1,300 women. Wang supposed she could bear the separation from her husband for another few months. In fact, she would not set eyes on him for fifty-five years.

Under cover of darkness the Ningxia battle began on October 24, 1936. A dozen boats ferried the headquarters, the 30th Corps, and the Women's Regiment across the Yellow River. The 9th Corps was supposed to follow, but it was ordered by Mao to wait. The 31st Corps went across, only to be called back. Mao moved the troops back and forth constantly. And he kept the bulk of the Red Army—the 1st and 2nd Armies and two crack corps of the 4th—south of the river, when the decisive battle was to take place north of it. Xu Xiangqian, the Commander-in-Chief of the 4th Army, and Chen Changhao, its Commissar, were confused by Mao's commands and pleaded with him to send the entire 4th Army across the river quickly: "Otherwise it will jeopardize the overall plan for the Ningxia battle. We will be hard pressed to clear the route, provide cover, and fight at the same time."[6] But he did not understand Mao's real reason: protecting his own 1st Army and exposing the 4th Army to the brunt of the enemy's attack. Two weeks later, amidst constant bombing and attacks from the Nationalists, the Ningxia battle had to be abandoned. But the headquarters and three corps of the 4th Army, which had already crossed the river, were not informed of the change of plan; they headed west to go on fighting. They were now the Western Legion. As a totally insufficient force, they were doomed.

In desperation, Mao wrote in person to senior Nationalist generals or influential figures who could put pressure on Chiang to fight the Japanese instead. One such letter read:

> We have been fighting each other since the Jinggang Mountains for a dozen years. We should have a rest. We sincerely want to work with you to fight against the Japanese. This is the voice of the whole nation. You are patriotic and I'm sure you feel the same . . . If we can communicate with each other, you would reduce the losses to your troops, and preserve your strength to fight against the Japanese.[7]

Mao was even ready to send Zhou Enlai to Nanjing to negotiate: they were willing to be incorporated into Chiang's army if Chiang stopped attacking them and provided a base and supplies for them. By now Chiang was in no mood for compromise; he made his conditions so tough that the Communists could not possibly agree. He thought the Red Army was under his thumb, and he was now ready for the final push. "What conditions do they have for negotiation?" he said.[8]

The Red Army was forced to ask the Young Marshal for another 100,000 silver dollars. Moscow promised $350,000, and was prepared to send more, but it would be another few months before the money reached Shaanxi. Other drastic measures were also called for. The 4th Army women who had reached Shaanxi were told they were no longer needed since a big battle with the Japanese was now looming. They knew it was a lie, but in any case they did not want to go. How could they be treated like that after all they had gone through? "Landlords treat their hired labor better," they shouted angrily. Some hit the officers with their fists. The men were ordered to rope them up and restrain them. Then they were let go, given two dollars each, and set on the road. But they refused to go, tagging along behind for days when the army marched off. In the end, they were allowed back into the main column.[9]

Mao sent a cable to Moscow in late October: "It looks as though the Red Army will have to turn back to Sichuan or Hubei if we are to survive . . . We are in a dire situation. We haven't got a penny left. We cannot print money. Zhang Xueliang has no more money to lend us."[10] Nor could the Young Marshal appear to be helping them. Chiang had long suspected his secret dealings with the Communists. He had flown to Xian to command the final battle against them, as he had done during the last campaign in Jiangxi—he even made a plan to replace Zhang's army in Shaanxi with his own forces. This put the Young Marshal in an impossible position. He could no longer protect and provide for the Communists as before. He either had to fight them or join them.

Nobody had any idea how to get out of the situation, not even Mao. He had thought the Shaanxi base would support his army, but it could not. One of his staff remembered going into his office and finding a notepad with two phrases on it repeated over and over: Long Live the Communist Party! Long Live Communism! "It was clear that he was extremely anxious."[11] He should have been. His plan had totally failed. On November 13, 1936, the Politburo decided that the rest of the Red Army should go east into Hebei, or south into Henan and Hubei, where the 4th Army had come from, to find a base. They would be retreating for another year before returning to the Northwest.[12] The Long March was to continue. Moscow and the Young Marshal were informed of the decision.

On December 12, 1936, before dawn had broken, shots rang out near the hot-spring villa outside Xian where Chiang Kaishek was staying. Moments later, Chiang, in his nightshirt and without his false teeth, jumped through the window and over the garden wall. With his two servants and a dozen bodyguards, he tried to run into the hills above the hot spring. But he had hurt his back and knee escaping, and could not get very far. He found a crevice in a rock and hid there. The 120-strong raiding force surrounded him. He came out with his hands up, standing on the snow-covered ground barefoot, blue in the face, shivering in the cold. They carried him away. He had been kidnapped by the Young Marshal's men. This was the famous "Xian Incident."

When the news of Chiang's capture was confirmed, the Young Marshal was relieved. Things had gone as he had planned and Chiang was in his hands. Now he could rescue the Red Army as well as realize his own ambitions. When Mao told him that the Red Army was to leave Shaanxi and continue its Long March, he was as worried as the Communists. He still thought Russian support would arrive, and the Communists would fight with him against the Japanese. He had done a great service to the Red Army by kidnapping Chiang; Moscow would be pleased and would have no choice but to support him. It was a high-risk strategy typical of the man. "My philosophy is to gamble. I might lose once or twice, but as long as the game goes on, the time will come when I get all my stakes back."[13]

He cabled the Communists to come to Xian immediately and discuss what to do with Chiang—and life after Chiang. When the wireless operator handed Mao the cable in his cave, Mao could not believe what he was reading. In his wildest dreams he had not expected that the Young Marshal would take such a drastic step. Then he exploded with laughter. The other senior leaders, who crowded into Mao's cave, were equally jubilant. Zhu De's first response was: "What is there to talk about? Let's kill the bastard first." All of them thought that was a good idea.[14]

But Stalin was outraged when he received the news from Mao. Instead of endorsing it, he had a stern cable sent to the Communists, which began with this warning: "The Young Marshal's motive, whatever it was, can objectively only damage the anti-Japanese united front and help Japan's aggression against China." He told them to "take a decisive stand in favour of a peaceful resolution." *Pravda* denounced the coup as helping the Japanese imperialists and accused the Young Marshal of throwing China into chaos in the name of resisting Japan. Under pressure from Moscow, in their first public reaction to the Xian Incident, the Communists made no mention of their early promise that they would support the Young Marshal as the new head of the government. Even the normally ruthless Mao felt they were letting him down. "When Zhang clearly needs our open support, we can only give him a few hushed promises."[15]

For the Young Marshal the responses from Stalin and the Communists came like a thunderbolt—they had led him to believe they would support his scheme. He knew that this time he had lost his bet, and everything he had staked on it. The government in Nanjing threatened to bomb Xian, and the Nationalist troops were moving in on the city. War loomed, coming closer each day. The whole country, instead of backing him, was denouncing him for harming national unity in a time of Japanese aggression. Far from being a hero, he was now a villain. When Zhou Enlai flew to Xian in his private plane and conveyed Moscow's orders to him, omitting the harsh words in the Moscow cable and their early promises to support him, the Young Marshal felt as if he were the one kidnapped, with no way out.

Whatever the Young Marshal might have felt, the show had to go on. In the Zhang Residence, he and the principal actors—General Yang Hucheng, the local warlord, Chiang's brother-in-law, Song Ziwen, and Zhou Enlai—gathered to resolve the crisis. For fourteen days they bargained hard on the conditions for the release of Chiang, while he remained under house arrest in another compound nearby. On Christmas Day 1936, all sides reached an agreement: removal of the Nationalist troops from the Northwest so that it would be left to the Young Marshal and the Red Army; reshuffling of the Nanjing government to give more weight to the anti-Japanese faction; releasing of political prisoners; an end to the Nationalist campaigns against the Red Army; legitimization of the Communist Party; national mobilization against the Japanese; and rapprochement with Russia, America, and Britain.

The Communists clearly came out as the biggest winners. They got everything they wanted and conceded nothing. Their only regret was that the agreement was oral and not written, because Chiang wanted to save face—he did not want to appear to be caving in to the Young Marshal and the Communists. But the Xian Incident brought an end to the continuous retreat by the Red Army. Chiang put a stop to his ten-year anti-Communist crusade. The Communist Party and the Red Army were saved at the eleventh hour, and their fortunes changed for good. They were no longer "bandits," but were legitimate, with their own independent army and secure base in the Northwest, receiving regular supplies of arms and funds from Chiang. In this sense, the Xian Incident marked the true end of the Long March. Perhaps it was not too far-fetched to claim, as Chiang Kaishek's biographer has done, that "had the Xian Incident not occurred, Mao might well not have survived to become Chiang's successor as ruler of China."[16]

Chiang also came out well—as a national hero who was ready to die for his country and people. He let it be known that he had written his will and given it to his wife, but few knew of his secret agreement with the Young Marshal and the Communists. When he returned to Nanjing, spontaneous crowds lined the streets to hail him. Fireworks crackled all night long. Chiang went back on most of the agreement, but he kept to the part most crucial to the Communists: he stopped fighting them, and made them his allies in confronting the Japanese. Six months later, on July 7, 1937, Japan formally declared war on China.

The Young Marshal accompanied Chiang back to Nanjing—he

did not heed Zhou Enlai's warning that Chiang might never let him back. In fact, he was to remain Chiang's prisoner for more than half a century, and his 100,000-strong army was absorbed into the Nationalist forces. Like everyone, I had always been curious about why he walked to his own doom. Did he really not know what awaited him after all that had happened? It was something he never talked about for the rest of his life. Still, I made a special trip to Taiwan in the Young Marshal's last year there. Through the kind introduction of a journalist friend, I was invited to his house in a quiet part of Taibei. The house was very simple and there were no guards in sight. When I rang the bell, a man came to the door. He addressed me in a strong accent that suggested he was from the Young Marshal's hometown in northeastern China—he must have followed his master for many years. The Young Marshal was sitting in the lounge, with Madame Zhao Yidi next to him, his companion of over seventy years.

This was the man I had grown up revering as a hero, the man who saved the Red Army and the Communist Party, a man who changed the course of modern Chinese history, a man Zhou Enlai said was "of eternal merit," although I knew that in Taiwan he was regarded as a sinner for betraying Chiang Kaishek. I had always remembered him as a handsome and dashing young uniformed general, with confidence and arrogance written all over his face; a man of destiny. I could hardly believe he was the same person. It was not just that he had aged. He talked about the events in the 1930s as if he were telling me a story, a familiar story which had nothing to do with him. When I questioned him on the sensitive issues of the Xian Incident, he listened attentively and then said: "Some matters can never be explained properly; others are better left unsaid." When I finally asked what he really felt about the Communists, he said very politely, "Please have more tea." I got the message and did not persevere. His silence on the subject, and the fact that he never came back to the mainland, said enough.

We talked for three hours, with Madame Zhao Yidi sitting demurely at his side, not speaking except to prompt him with a date or a name, or to ask the servant to bring us tea. She was the beauty he took as a 15-year-old concubine and who became his enduring love. Her affection, devotion, and care for the Young Marshal gave him the strength to live. He also achieved a kind of tranquillity by becoming a Christian. He died in 2001 at the age of 100, maintaining to the very end that he had kidnapped Chiang out of "pure motives."

Back in the Zhang Residence in Xian, when I came to the end of the exhibition on the life of the Young Marshal, I found this summary of the man:

> History will remember for eternity: he is a true patriot; a man who devoted himself to the country's independence and the nation's liberation; a man who gauged the will of the people and marched with the tide of the time; a true Chinese, even though he had his weaknesses.

This is the Young Marshal both he and the Communists wanted the world to know, and remember.

## 12 ★ THE LEGION OF DEATH

Operator Zhong of the Western Legion was huddled over his wireless receiver listening to the faint code tapping out an extraordinary message. It seemed to say that Chiang had been kidnapped. Zhong assumed he had made a mistake. He was in the town of Yongchang in a mud hut riddled with shell holes, and bombs were falling all around him. The troops belonging to the Mas, the Muslim warlords Ma Bufang and Ma Buqing, had been trying to take it for weeks. Zhong managed to check the message three times and it was clearly right. He wrote it out and dashed from the house; as he did so, a bomb scored a direct hit and the house was turned to rubble. He shook off the debris, wiped the blood from his face, and ran to the command post. A big smile appeared on the worried face of his commander. In no time the Red Army soldiers were cheering throughout the town, much to the surprise of the besieging Muslim troops. What was there to celebrate when they were about to be defeated? Then the Red Army loudspeakers started blaring out: "Hold your fire! Your Generalissimo Chiang Kaishek has been captured."

"We were jubilant. For two months we had been fighting the two Mas in freezing weather, and with hardly any food or bullets. So many of our comrades died. We were not sure how long we could hold on. I could not imagine it would be much longer because we would die of cold and hunger if nothing else. Now we could get out of that damned place and go home," Zhong recalled. But their troubles were far from over.

In fact, catastrophe was at hand. Two months later, the Western Legion, which had been dispatched across the Yellow River to get aid from Russia, was completely wiped out by the Mas. All but 400 of the

20,800 men and women were either killed or captured, yet this tragic story has been virtually left out of Long March history, except for a brief denunciation. The reason was simple—Mao had concluded that the failure of the Western Legion was the result of carrying out Zhang Guotao's escape policy. "[Zhang] was fearful of Chiang's reaction force. He was fearful of the Japanese imperialists," Mao declared. "Without the approval of the Central Committee, he took his troops across the Yellow River and tried to find a secure place in the Northwest, where he would be the king, and bargain with the Central Committee for power. This wrong policy was bound to fail."[1] Once Mao had given this verdict, the subject was no longer a matter for discussion.

For the next fifty years anyone who questioned this would have been challenging Mao—an unthinkable crime. The few memoirs that referred to it were suppressed; veterans of the Legion were treated as traitors; scholars who dared to ask questions were warned by the Party and followed by police. But, as we say, you cannot wrap up a fire with paper. At last, the truth is now beginning to emerge. Oral histories of the veterans which caused storms after their publication were the first to break the logjam. In 2002, the new *History of the Communist Party* carried a brief revised entry, saying the Western Legion was not carrying out Zhang Guotao's scheme, as Mao had claimed, but was fully under the command of the Central Committee. Just before I embarked on the journey, two volumes of telegrams between the Western Legion and the Central Committee were published. The full story is yet to be written, but at least the Western Legion is finally ceasing to be taboo.

I was now on the last leg of my journey, on the train from Xian to Gansu Province, western China. This was where the Western Legion met its end. In the November chill, the earth itself seemed to be in hibernation, cold and hard. Occasionally, there was a village of 50–100 households of mud-built houses, surrounded by carefully cultivated fields, dry as chalk. The meager harvest of barley and wheat was already gathered in, airing on the winnowing grounds or on rooftops. Poplar trees were shedding their golden leaves, picked up by eager sheep and goats which otherwise roamed the unrewarding ground or wandered into the Gobi.

My first port of call was the Gansu provincial archive in the capital, Lanzhou. It was in a handsome modern building, and the service proved to be really efficient. I filled in the form requesting all the files on the Western Legion and they were on my table within ten minutes. There were telegrams from the Western Legion headquarters, weekly bulletins by the Muslim army on the battles they fought, their victories and casualties, confessions by former Muslim officers, old county government reports on the Red Bandits in their territories, Nationalist newspaper clippings, photos of dismembered bodies and mass graves of the Western Legion soldiers, and surveys of the survivors in the province. All of these confirmed the Legion's desperate situation.

The statements by former Muslim officers—who were natural targets in all political campaigns since 1949—made up a large proportion of the archive material. They were clearly extracted under interrogation, especially when they began with quotes from Mao: "Confession leads to leniency; stubbornness will result in severe punishment," or "Our every sentence and every action must suit the interests of the people." The files were thick, the confessions monotonous, as though they had agreed to say the same things. After a while, I was reading them but no longer taking anything in. Just when I had decided to skip them, I came across something that brought me up with a jolt. In a series of statements by Ma Gelin, the former Commander of the Special Task Force of the Mas, I found a file on Woman Wang—how she slept with him and worked with him to manage the 130 women prisoners.

I could hardly believe it; the first Long March veteran I had interviewed, and here in a distant provincial archive, buried in piles of paper, was information that could have affected her life. Could it be true? It was not likely that the officer was making it up—that he had raped a senior Red Army officer, a crime that could increase his penalty significantly. As I read the confessions one by one, I found other references to Wang with similar accusations. I was shocked because the Woman Wang I had come to know was so firm in her beliefs, so total in her devotion, so strong in character, she was a rarity even among the veterans. If she did it, the only question was why.

In the same confession, Ma Gelin also mentioned another woman prisoner, Li Wenying, who was tortured for refusing to give in to the Mas' men. A truly brave woman. Could this Li Wenying be the same woman I had read about in a Chinese newspaper? I had even brought the paper with me.

After two very fruitful days in the archive, I went to the pensioners' office for information about the surviving Long March veterans in Gansu. It was also in a modern building, a brand-new high-rise, and the young man there was just as impressive: open, modern, and most helpful. Yes, there were still nearly 100 Long March veterans in the province who received pensions from the state, more than anywhere else in the country. Many of them lived in the Linxia area, where the two Mas and their followers came from, and where a large number of captured men and women of the Legion were given to Muslim officers and their families as servants, wives, and concubines. I was very grateful for the information. I ventured to ask if there was a woman called Li Wenying in his register. "Oh, she lives in Wuwei County," he replied, and then looked up. "But if I were you, I would go to Linxia. You are more likely to find veterans who can still remember things. After all, the Long March was seventy years ago."

I took his advice and boarded a bus from Lanzhou to Linxia that afternoon. The countryside was barren and bleak, with few trees. Shepherds and their goats were roaming in the fields which had just yielded their meager autumn corn harvest. As we approached Linxia, the human scenery began to change. Men in white caps, women in blue and black headscarves, and the young and the very old women in white ones. And there was mosque after mosque, sometimes two or three in a village, some in traditional Chinese temple style, others in Arab style, mostly brand new and standing among old mud-brick houses. According to the guidebook I was reading, Linxia has over 1,700 mosques—more than the number of schools—earning it the nickname of "China's Little Mecca." The ancestors of the local Muslims were Persian and Arab traders from the Silk Road going back to the seventh century. When Genghis Khan's army conquered central Asia, it brought back large numbers of Muslim prisoners and settled them in northwestern China, with many ending up here. Today, Linxia is a Muslim Autonomous Area, one of only two in the country, with a third of its 1.8 million people Muslims. When we arrived at Linxia City, it was time for *Dhuhr*, noonday prayers. The streets were empty. The calls of the muezzins echoed over the city. On the way to the local government pensioners' office, I passed three giant mosques, with hundreds of worshippers overflowing onto the pavements outside — they were all full.

I was lucky to find anybody in the pensioners' office at all, although the man was clearly not keen to help. Why did I want to interview these people? What was my real motive? Did I not know it was very sensitive, talking to the Muslims? Perhaps he thought I was a journalist looking to expose trouble, such as drugs and organized crime, low school attendance, or resentment of Muslims toward Han Chinese — and vice versa. I explained again and again that I had no other motive than talking to the veterans of the Long March. The man was relentless. "What do they know? They cannot even read and write. Some claim they even met Mao and other senior leaders. I think they are losing their marbles," he said looking down his nose. I just sat there. In the end he drew my attention to the local paper on his desk. It had a full-page article on one Long March veteran in the area. "The paper is doing a series on all the veterans. I have quite a few, but not all of them. Why don't you take them? It will save you the trouble of finding them yourself." I took a look at the articles and left, feeling like prostrating to him, as we do to express our profoundest gratitude. I never found so many veterans at one go, in one place, all alive and with so much background material prepared for me. A treasure from heaven.

The veterans in the series, a dozen so far, were spread all over the area. They had come to Linxia after the defeat of the Western Legion and had never left. Some were in poor health and their stories were patchy, but a few recalled their experiences so vividly that I could not wait to hear them in person. I tracked them down from the information given in the articles.

Ma Haidiche was 93. She lived in a market town outside Linxia City with her adopted grandson, his wife, and their children. Like all Muslim women in Linxia, she wore a headscarf. She was sitting on a stool in the courtyard, bent forward, her eyes watering. She looked up but her stare was blank. When her granddaughter-in-law said I wanted to talk to her about the Western Legion, she straightened; her eyes lit up, and she invited me into the room in a voice surprisingly loud for someone so frail. "She is like another being when anyone talks to her about the Western Legion. But not many are interested in that old stuff," the young woman said.

"You came all the way from Beijing to talk to me? Ah, we've been through so much. Where should I start?" While she was talking, she struggled up to get apples, oranges, watermelon seeds, and sweets for me. "Eat, eat, eat. You must eat plenty," she urged.

"I tell you I am so afraid of hunger, I have to eat five times a day," she said. For the Long Marchers who were mostly in their teens at the time, hunger was harder to bear than cold, disease, or even death. It was her job to find supplies on the Long March—she was a company commander in the supply department of the 4th Army. It must have been an impossible job, I said. "The grassland was tough, but at least we had grass to eat and snow for water. Compared with what we suffered later, the early part of the March was easy." She paused to hand me an apple she had peeled for me.

"I don't know why we came to this region," she went on. "It is so poor. Even in the 1950s many people starved to death. It's only in the last few years that life has got better, with food in our bowls and a little money in our pockets. How could the locals have fed tens of thousands of extra mouths? Look at this place. It used to be as empty as the moon. There wasn't even grass to eat. No rich men to confiscate from, no food, no clothes, no shelter, no ammunition, and no base. Nothing! But on the way here, our propaganda team was singing 'North Gansu is a good place. Crops are plenty and supplies ample. We can defeat the Mas any time, any time.'"

I asked her to tell me some other songs she could remember from the propaganda team before she set foot in Gansu. She paused for a second: "'The Mas' bandits are far removed from their nest. Their line is long and ammunition short; their men are tired, their horses are thin, their faith is wavering. Prayers morning and night won't save their lives.'" Then she added ruefully, "I would say we were like that, not the Mas' men."

In desperation, they grabbed anything they could find. She could never forget the expression on an old woman's face when she and a comrade tried to snatch a sack of corn flour from her, probably the only food in her house. She held on to it fiercely, begging them to leave it for her four children. Her comrade shot the woman. She said the locals had a saying, "Three days without food turns a good man into a thief." "It turned us into murderers," she added almost inaudibly. That evening, the sack of flour was divided among the soldiers of her company, a few spoonfuls each with a mouthful of water. She could not eat. She was haunted by the old woman — they killed her so they could live, but for how long?

Not only food was scarce; water was equally in short supply. Her whole company had only one barrel a day. Their lips cracked; their mouths were full of blisters; their tongues were so dry they had difficulty speaking. Without water, the corn or roasted barley flour was like sawdust, impossible to swallow. Every time she finished a meal, she had tears in her eyes, blood in her mouth, but still an empty stomach. Things got so bad that in late January 1937, each soldier received two ounces of horse meat and half a bowl of muddy water as a special treat for the Chinese New Year — some even drank horses' pee.

Ammunition was as scarce as food. The soldiers had five bullets for a battle; then it was reduced to three. "We used to go to the villages and give people opium in exchange for copper or brass to make bullets. But how many brass door handles could you get? Without bullets our rifles were just sticks," she sighed deeply.

Could they not get rifles from their enemy as they used to do? I asked.

"You are right. We used to arm ourselves with what we captured from Chiang. That is why we called him our 'Head of Supplies,'" she said with a smile, the only one for the whole afternoon. "But things were different here. The Mas' troops were grinding us down. They were well fed with mutton and warmly dressed in lambskin coats. They were strong and they were on four feet — they all had horses. We were on our two feet, with little to eat and just one shirt. We marched for a night while they were sleeping soundly. And then they caught up in no time. It was easy, the land is so flat. We hardly had time to rest, let alone build defenses, before they pounded us with their cannons. When we got ready for a counterattack, they galloped away like a swirl of dust. We could only watch and curse. We never got near them. How could we get anything from them?"

At the end of our talk, I produced the article about her from the local paper. She was not as interested as I expected. She looked at it hesitantly, and then addressed me as if I was her family: "My daughter, I want to ask you a question, but I'm not sure if it is proper." When she talked about her life of seventy years ago, she spoke rapidly, but now she was very unsure. When the journalists from the local paper came to talk to her, she mentioned her pension problem. Long March veterans like her should receive a pension of $80 a month. She never received that much, at most $14 a month, mostly $6 or even less. For the past three months she had not received a penny. "Did I say something that made them unhappy or something wrong?" she asked me. "It was like what I told you today. It was what happened. I never lie. Allah tells us not to lie. You are from Beijing. Couldn't you tell them I am telling the truth? If I have said anything I shouldn't have said, I'll correct myself."

I felt so sad, I just managed not to cry. There was little I could do — I met many veterans like her. Some provinces were so short of money, government employees did not get their own salaries for months. Pensions were often diverted to something else. I tried to comfort her, telling her things were getting better and she did not have to worry about what she said; the government cared about the Long March veterans, and she would get her money before long. I was embarrassed by my feebleness, and practically fled. When I turned to look back, my tears came. For all her sacrifices for the Revolution, she asked very little in return, and she was denied even that.

Feng Yuxiang received her pension, but barely a dollar out of the $80 she was due. She was also a member of the Women's Regiment. At 85, she still worked on the land. When I arrived at her house at the back of the village, she was unloading a cartful of cornstalks, the autumn wind whipping up her white head-cover. Whether it was the cold or the work, her cheeks were as red as apples. "Come in, come in. It's freezing. Don't stand in the cold," she said, without giving me time to say who I was. She put down her work, washed her hands, and rushed me inside the house. It was almost as cold inside. The house was new and empty and the roof was not on properly; there were gaps here and there, and the thatched straw flapped in the wind.

"Come on. Take off your shoes and get onto the *kang*. It will keep you warm," she told me and then disappeared. I climbed onto the *kang*, which could be heated in the winter with coal or wood from the kitchen. And sure enough, I felt warmth underneath me in no time. When Feng returned, she had a smile on her face, and a teapot and cup in her hand. "Have some tea. Then you will feel really warm. You aren't used to the cold out here." She handed me the cup of tea and joined me on the *kang*, pulling a duvet over our legs and tucking the edges in carefully.

What must it have been like for Feng and her comrades with only the scanty uniforms they had worn since they left Sichuan? This was exactly the month they arrived, November 1935, and it was a particularly cold winter—the locals remembered seeing birds falling from the sky with their wings frozen. I asked Feng about it. "It was hell. Nothing on the Long March, even on top of the Jiajin Mountains, could compare with what we went through here in the Hexi Corridor. We weren't prepared for it," she said, grabbing a corner of the duvet. "The ground was like rock and we couldn't dig trenches. Our hands were so numb we could hardly pull our triggers. That was why so many of us were killed, more than in any other battle I had fought on the March. We often marched at night to escape the enemy; the temperature could be as low as minus 30°, and the wind was like knives. I had one of my periods at the worst time. The blood on my trousers froze, and my trousers went stiff and cut my legs while I was trying to keep up." Talking of that fatal winter of 1936 made Feng shudder. She pulled the duvet up to her chest, as if she was back out in the open. "The state we were in, even without the battles the cold and hunger would have finished us."

The revenge by the Mas' men was unique. When they finally took Yongchang after two weeks' siege and heavy bombardment, they found over 2,000 wounded Western Legion soldiers abandoned in houses.

The Mas' men did not torture them or kill them. They simply took away all their clothes, and left them there tied up and naked. The next morning, they were all dead. I saw photos of their frozen bodies in houses and fields, their fists tight, their bodies curled up, some clutching together trying desperately to keep warm.

We talked until the sun began to set. I had to return to Linxia by the last bus. When I opened the door the cold wind gushed in and I shivered. I buttoned up my jacket. Feng said, "You aren't wearing enough. I'll find you a coat." I told her the jacket was made of special material that would keep me warm in the snow. She touched it with her hand carefully, and sighed. "If we had a coat like this seventy years ago, the Mas' men would not have been able to do us much harm." As I was standing on the edge of the village waiting for the bus, Feng's story lingered in my mind. I was still mortally cold, even with my Gortex jacket and two layers of sweaters. The cold in the Northwest was unlike anything I had experienced in China. It seeped through my bones and chilled me to the core. Perhaps it was not just the weather, but the sufferings of the veterans in this unforgiving land.

But Ma Fucai's home warmed me up a little. After four hours' drive through country lanes and nonexistent roads, I found myself standing in front of a small gate painted with green pines and white cranes—both symbols of longevity. An old man with a beard and a white cap was shelling corn ears on a washboard. I could tell he was the Long Marcher I was looking for—he looked just like the photo in the local paper. I handed the paper to him as an introduction, and a broad smile appeared on his face. He called out his wife, and then shouted something. A young woman's voice answered and then she appeared with two children through a gap in the wall that separated his house from the next one. "That is my second son's wife and my two granddaughters," he explained. In no time, the quiet courtyard was filled with a dozen men, women, and children, all part of Ma's big family. The men disappeared, and the women passed the newspaper from one to another, each adding their witty comments and laughing.

Ma returned an hour later from the mosque, and apologized for keeping me waiting. During Ramadan he prayed five times a day. I knew from the article he was a Han Chinese from Sichuan, who had joined the Red Army at 15, and was a messenger in the wireless unit of the 4th Army. How long had he been a Muslim, and such a pious one? I asked.

"Long time! Almost seventy years," he replied. After his capture, he was brought to this village. "They changed my surname from Wang to Ma, and gave me a new name, Fucai, 'Luck and Fortune.' Everyone here has the same surname. Then I followed my master and became a Muslim. He was executed after the liberation because they said he was an evil man for exploiting the Red Army and the poor. But by then I really believed in Allah."

I asked him why he had joined the Red Army. "For a bowl of rice, for a roof over my head, for a patch of land, for the poor to be treated the same as the rich—that was what we were told when I signed up." He paused to tell his wife to bring more water for our tea. Then he continued, "You know, Mao's *Little Red Book* is not that different from the Koran. Both tell us to do good and no evil, help the poor, and make the world a better place. It is a pity that you can't buy the *Little Red Book* so easily anymore, otherwise I would ask my sons to read it."

Why did he think the Mas were so cruel to the Red Army then?

Ma Fucai did not hesitate. "You can see the land is too poor to support many people. For their own survival, they had to get rid of us. That was why their soldiers were so brave, as if they were on drugs. They were unlike any of the warlord troops we fought before and we could not get any recruits."

For Ma Fucai, the other important reason why the Mas hated the Western Legion was the animosity between the Han Chinese and the Muslims. He only found out about that after he settled here. The Northwest had the largest concentration of Muslims in China. In 1862, the ones in Gansu and Shaanxi rebelled against the last Imperial Dynasty, the Qing. It took the Imperial Army fifteen years to put them down. To claim their reward from the emperor, the Imperial Army needed the heads of their enemies; but there were too many to carry. In the end, they cut off their ears and took them back to the capital strung together. Gansu Province had 2 million Muslims at the time, and half of them were killed. That was not the end. Wherever the uprisings had taken place, villages were burned, fields were laid waste, and people were exiled to the remotest places where they were kept like prisoners. "You can imagine, the hatred was like a volcano, it was alive and ready to erupt any time," Ma said. "It was not just the land; it was their faith the Mas were protecting."

Before I left, Ma took me to his mosque. It was small but exquisite, especially the deep-green traditional Chinese tiles that made up its flying rooftops. Perched on a high point, it had a panoramic view of the whole village, including two other mosques belonging to different denominations. "They may be bigger, but ours has the best view," Ma said proudly. He wanted it to be bigger still. He told me each family contributed 30 kilos of grain and free labor to building the mosque. "That was all we could afford at the time. In the future, we will have the money for the biggest one—not just in the village but in the whole district—but I doubt I will live long enough to see the day." There was no sadness on Ma's face or in his voice. He said he was getting old and the time was coming for him to go. "Life is too short. There are so many things the Koran requires of us. I won't be able to do them all." His biggest regret was that he was poor and could not contribute more to the mosque or help the deprived families in the village.

Did he regret joining the Red Army?

"Never," he said without the slightest hesitation. "My family was very poor. If I hadn't joined the Red Army, I might well have died of hunger anyway. But I never expected to suffer so much." Then he slowed down and said: "There are so many good people in the world, so heaven must be very crowded. I pray that if there is no room in heaven, Allah will at least not let me suffer again as I did with the Western Legion."

We have a saying: to succeed in anything, one needs the help of heaven, earth, and men. Heaven is weather or timing, earth the physical conditions, men the sympathy and support of people. From the stories of these three veterans, I formed a clear impression of why the Western Legion could not succeed here. The question was why Mao ordered them to fight it out when neither heaven, earth, nor men was on their side.

From Linxia, I headed for western Gansu, the main battleground for the Western Legion. My first destination was Wuwei, one of the headquarters of the Mas and the home of Li Wenying, who was confirmed to be alive by the man in the provincial pensioners' office. The newspaper article did not give an address but it said she lived in the old town near a church. I had no difficulty in finding it, a modest brick building in Western style, dating from the turn of the last century. I asked the bicycle repairman around the corner if he had heard of her. "Oh, old Li, she can't stay still for one minute. She went out very early in the morning and I haven't seen her since. Come at supper time, and have a look round the town first."

I took his advice. I had been through here once, but without stopping. The town has a long history going back at least 2,000 years. In the glory days of the Silk Road, Wuwei was renowned for its large number of foreign residents, its hybrid music drawn from various countries, and its exotic goods. The good taste of the inhabitants of Wuwei is still in evidence. The beautifully preserved Confucian temple, the pristine Buddhist monastery, the brand-new square, and the spacious avenues—money alone cannot explain them; it is local pride in their long past.

At 5 p.m. I returned to the bicycle repairman. No, he had not seen old Li. Could she have returned without his noticing? "You mean she has wings and flew past me? Impossible. This lane is so narrow. Nobody can pass here without my seeing them," he said. If it was urgent, I could go to her flat and leave a note on her door. I knew I was in the right place when I saw the couplets on the door: "The Red Army fears not the trials of the Long March; ten thousand crags and torrents do not trouble it." There was another slogan above the door frame: "Follow the Party," and light came through the glass pane at the top. I knocked.

The door opened and two old ladies appeared before me: one short and boisterous in the front, the other tall and quiet at the back. No doubt Li was the loud one. She had a heavy quilted jacket on, which made her look more bulky. She was all smiles like a flower; her small eyes and the deep lines on her face were just like her picture. Was she really 87?

I showed her the article in the newspaper. She was genuinely surprised to see herself in print. "It's me. That's me," she pointed out her picture to her quiet companion. Then she started giggling like a little girl: "How ugly I am! Look at my messy hair. I am like a madwoman."

"What do you mean, you are like a madwoman? You are mad," her companion said gently, and then got up to make tea.

"You wretched old thing, I'll sack you," Li shouted after her. Then she turned toward me. "She comes here in the evening to keep me company." She had been to see the plot of land she had paid for in a cemetery outside town. "I don't know why heaven allows me to live for so long when so many of my comrades died so young." She began crying, but then she wiped the tears from her face, and stopped. "Silly me, why am I boring you with this stuff? You haven't come all this way to listen to my grumbling."

I said I wanted to hear all her stories. "You'll have to spend three days and nights with me then. Even that won't be enough. You don't have the time. My suffering is so long. It has no end." I knew I had come upon someone willing to reveal all. Many of the veterans I interviewed didn't really want to talk about their life. Why was I interested in them when their own grandchildren could not be bothered? It often took me hours just hanging around with them before their stories emerged. Fighter Li was different. She could not help talking about her past, but I had to wait till the next day. "It is too late now. I'll tell you in the morning. Otherwise you will have nightmares."

I did as I was told—even in those few minutes I had got the impression of a thoughtful and strong-minded woman, and I thought it better not to contradict her. But I could not help asking the question that had been burning inside me: Did she know Wang Quanyuan? "Of course, she was our commander," Li said almost before I finished my sentence. "Is she still alive?"

I nodded.

"You know, last time we met was twenty years ago. Chinese Central Television made a program about the Women's Regiment to mark the fiftieth anniversary of the Long March. They brought a dozen of us together. When she came up to me, I almost burst out, 'You aren't dead yet, you witch?' But I bit my tongue and said instead: 'How are you?' I can never forgive her. It is a long story. I'll tell you another time."

Back in my hotel room, I was too keyed up to sleep. I checked my watch every hour. Finally day broke—it had been a long night. I got dressed quickly and walked toward the church. To my surprise, I found Li chatting with the bicycle repairman in the crisp cold of the early morning. "She has been waiting for you for almost an hour," the man told me. "She kept asking if you had gone by without my noticing."

"You're a bad scout, aren't you?" Li interrupted him. "I came back by taxi yesterday, and you did not even know. You told her I wasn't at home. You should stick to repairing bicycles." Li laughed heartily. Then she picked up her bag, tightened her scarf, and put her arm around me. "You're not wearing enough. I'm taking you to Yongchang County today where we fought one of the toughest battles." I showed her all the layers under my jacket, and off we went.

We took a taxi. We were in what was called the Hexi Corridor, which links the hinterland of northern China with the Taklamakan Desert to the west. Throughout my journey on the March, I never saw anywhere as barren. The grey Gobi Desert stretched for miles, with no trees, no plants, no sign of life, nothing to see, just the snow on the distant Tianshan Mountains to the north and the undulating Qilian Mountains to the south. Only very occasionally was there a village. Even I could see why the Western Legion could not possibly have survived here—it was just a corridor, a passage, not a place to stay.

Mao also knew the Hexi Corridor was unviable. When the 1st Army was in the grassland and debating where to go, Gansu came up as an option, but Mao was strongly against it. He told the Politburo as early as August 1935 that the area was barren and hostile, totally unsuitable for a base. "The weather is too cold and supplies are rare. Ethnically there are very few Han Chinese and most are Muslims, so we cannot possibly recruit there. If we venture into their territory, they will rebel against us."[2] It puzzled me why Mao insisted on their staying.

It was a long ride, and I had plenty of time to find out about Li. Like Wang, Li was born into a very poor family, who had sold her as a child bride when she was 7. She was never given a square meal by her in-laws. Twice she tried to kill herself; twice she was saved—once because she did not know how to knot the rope and fell from the tree; the second time she threw herself into a pond but was saved by a passing farmer. One day at a market, she saw soldiers in uniform talking to people. One of them was standing on a bench and making a speech. She thought it was a man, but when she got closer she could hear it was a woman's voice. Was she really a woman? How could a woman speak in public? How could women leave home? What army would take a woman? Li asked. "The Red Army!" the woman replied. She put Li's hand on her earlobe and Li could feel the little hole where the earrings used to be. "Now you know for sure I'm a woman. The Red Army welcomes anyone. Come and join us, my little sister. You'll never be hungry again!" Li signed up on the spot. First she was with the supply unit of the 4th Army, making clothes and tents; then she joined the propaganda team. When the Women's Regiment was created, she was chosen as one of the 1,300 woman fighters.

Li was looking out of the window, her face hard and her expression pensive. Suddenly we saw two rows of brick houses by the roadside—restaurants, motels, hair salons, and truck repair shops. It was a welcome change from the rare clusters of mud houses isolated in the monotonous Gobi. I even felt quite excited, like a traveler reaching an oasis after days in the desert. But then it occurred to me why Li had stopped talking. This was where the Western Legion had tried to set up a base. She asked the taxi driver to pull up in front of a temple. "Come on. We are in Sishi Li Village. This was the headquarters during the battle!"

"Anybody here?" Li called as soon as we entered the courtyard.

An old man stepped out of the caretaker's hut in the corner. "Nice to see you again, my old sister," he smiled.

"Do you have the keys? This young lady is from Beijing and I want her to see the temple." The caretaker nodded and we followed him up a steep flight of stairs. A small crowd appeared from nowhere and tagged along.

It was a very small temple, with the main shrine holding a statue of the Heavenly Emperor, flanked by two gods of fortune. The offering on the giant altar table was slender, only a plate of apples and three sticks of incense. "How many times have I told you not to burn incense here," Li said, poking her finger at the old man. "This is our revolutionary heritage. What would happen if a fire broke out?"

"You're absolutely right, my old sister," he murmured. "But people have been praying here for hundreds of years. I cannot stop them from coming. Besides, we need donations for the upkeep of this very important site. The government does not give us a penny."

"Money, money. All you think about is money. We died for you and you cannot even look after this place properly. Look, there is not a single sign here about the history of the Western Legion." Li was almost shouting at the poor man.

"The monument outside explains it all," he ventured gingerly.

Li's outburst was embarrassing for me, but not shocking. She wanted the souls and the spirits of her dead comrades to be worshipped, not gods and goddesses. Communism had no room for gods. Had she not sung the Communist anthem often enough to know that? "There is never a savior. It is entirely up to us humans to create happiness in the world." What was God compared with the heroic men and women of the Western Legion? But for a long time after 1949 she had been shunned like a leper; the Western Legion was as forbidden as religion. It had only been in the last fifteen years that she and her comrades could hold their heads high again. Her frustration, anger, and outbursts had little to do with the old man. It was the injustices they had suffered that demanded an outlet.

I felt a bit sorry for the caretaker. I interrupted Li, asking her how the temple was used in the battle. "Here," she pointed to the statue by the side. "At night the commander curled up on the floor; during the day he used the altar as his desk. A whole division camped here and in the village."

Li said Sishi Li Village was quite different in those days. It was just three big compounds protected by a thick outer wall. The villagers lived in the enclosures for fear of bandits. "They might have been safe havens for the villagers, but they were graveyards for us," she said. "Once inside, we were trapped. We could do little but sit there, waiting for the bombs to drop. We had nowhere to hide. What we were defending, nobody was sure. Where could we retreat if the enemy pushed through? It was a death trap, yet we were asked to dig in here. We were stuck like animals in a cage, ready catches for the Mas."

A general who was a senior commander in the Western Legion was also indignant about the way they fought. "Don't mention the bloody mud compounds. My lungs would explode. If you are fighting a battle, you need a place where you can defend or attack, push on or retreat. Those compounds were hopeless. If you put a battalion in there, it wouldn't be able to defend it. If you put a regiment in there, it was not big enough to hold it . . . What's the point of defending a lone compound or town here and there? How could such a base be any use to us? . . . Motherfuckers. I fought all the way from Hubei, Hunan, Sichuan, but I got fucked up in that damned place."[3]

After only three days, the division holding the village ran out of ammunition and food. The defenses of two of the three small compounds were broken through, and many of the soldiers were killed; the rest fought their way back to Yongchang, 40 miles to the west. The caretaker said he could not recognize his village when he returned with his family from hiding in the mountains. "You wouldn't believe it was a village. The roofs of the houses were all gone; bodies piled up everywhere, some against the walls, others on top of each other, with bullet holes all over them. They must have been used as cover during the attacks. The Mas' men had taken away their dead; what was left was the Red Army, well over 500 of them. Wild dogs were gorging themselves. Their mouths and noses dripped blood; their eyes were bright red. They were so full they could hardly run. They didn't want to run—I bet they never had so much to eat in their lives." When his father and the villagers were told to dig a ditch and bury the soldiers, they had to wrestle the bodies away from the dogs.

Xu Xiangqian, the Commander-in-Chief of the Western Legion, and its Commissar Chen Changhao did not understand what was going on either. Suddenly they were told to forget about Soviet aid; instead, they had to build a base in Yongchang, which was clearly impossible. The Western Legion had intercepted telegrams between the two Mas, which made it clear that if they only passed through the Mas' territory, they would not be attacked; if they stopped to set up a base, they would be wiped out. The Mas said they would "rather sacrifice 10,000 men than lose one inch of land." Their army was six times the size of the Western Legion. The Military Council was told this, yet Mao asked Xu to build a base in the heart of the Mas' territory. Years later, Xu understood Mao's purpose—Chiang's troops would be diverted, relieving pressure on the Red Army in Shaanxi so they could escape and continue the Long March. But he was only ordered to do it, not told why.

After the Xian Incident, Mao told the Western Legion to come back east so as to put more pressure on Chiang. In the midst of their preparations to move off, Mao sent another order: go west and get the Soviet supplies. Days later he countermanded his instruction and told them to stop and set up another base—the negotiation with Chiang was still not clear and they should not rush west. But this order too only remained in force for ten days before Mao called them back; he wanted the Communists to occupy more territory and strengthen their hand in negotiations with Chiang. When the negotiations had eased, Mao reverted to his earlier command: the Western Legion should stay where it was and fight a guerrilla war.

These erratic stop-go-stay orders were lethal for the Western Legion. Whenever they stopped, they were attacked. After Yongchang came Gaotai, where the 5th Corps was completely wiped out, all 3,000 men, and the head of its commander-in-chief was cut off and displayed on a pole hanging from the gate. The neighboring Linze was also taken by the Mas' troops after three days' fierce fighting. The next was Nijiaying, a cluster of forty-two compounds, where another 4,000 men were lost in a week. The Western Legion was running out of ammunition, food, and medicine. Survival was as tough a challenge as the waves of attacks from the Mas. Yet when Xu Xiangqian and Chen Changhao cabled Mao, informing him of their desperate situation and asking for support and clear instructions, Mao told them that they were fighting the wrong way: "I feel that you are not concentrating your troops. In my opinion, you should put all your 18,000 men within 20 kilometers. Push on or retreat as one. When you decide to fight a battle, you must put all your men into it. After two or three such campaigns, all problems will be solved."[4]

Xu and Chen expected that Zhang Guotao could persuade Mao. They were wrong. As the Chinese say, Zhang was a clay Buddha who could not save himself. He had lost the command of the 4th Army and Mao had got him under his control. Zhang cabled Xu and Chen, telling them that "the Military Council's instruction to the Western Legion has always been correct . . . They are mistaken if they regard the Central Committee's line as wrong, or have doubts about the leadership."[5]

Xu and Chen had to make up their own minds now. In the end, they decided to stick to the original plan and move west to be near the Soviet border. Mao sent them a stern reproof in the name of the Central Committee and the Military Council:

> We think the danger you find yourself in is partly due to the
> difficulty of logistics and supplies, but mainly due to lack of
> confidence. The commanders of the Western Legion have
> lost any belief in themselves to defeat the enemy and finish
> their task; instead they put their hope entirely on outside
> support . . . Judging from your strength and the enemy's, you
> should certainly win. The Central Committee sincerely hopes
> that you will reflect thoroughly on your losses, learn your
> lessons, confess your mistakes past and present, and carry out
> all our instructions in the Bolshevik spirit of self-criticism.[6]

In the history of the Communist Party and the Red Army, military errors could be corrected, but political denunciation was lethal. It was like a death sentence. Chen Changhao, the Commissar and erstwhile right-hand man of Zhang Guotao, knew the weight of Mao's criticism only too well. Even if he had made mistakes in the past when he was with Zhang Guotao, what had it got to do with now? Twenty thousand men and women had been fighting with their lives to save the Party and the Red Army. Now they wanted to break out to survive. Why were they denied such an opportunity? He could not understand, but he knew the Western Legion was doomed even before the last battle was fought.

He ordered his men back to Nijiaying, as instructed by Mao. The bodies of their dead from the last battle were everywhere, the locals gone, the houses full of shell holes, walls fallen, wells filled up with mud, trees cut for firewood. It was more like a cemetery, waiting for their deaths. And here they battled with 70,000 of the Mas' men for forty days. When the Central Committee decided to send help, it was too late. Anyway, the help was called off after only five days: the Western Legion had been written off.

Xu and Chen were not informed that the mission to rescue them had been canceled, just as they were never told that the Ningxia battle had been abandoned, and that the Red Army was going to continue the Long March to find a base elsewhere. Xu said in his memoirs that he only learned these facts in the 1980s, fifty years later.[7] Nobody could fight a war that way. He and Chen were completely in the dark.

Seventy years on, historians are equally in the dark about why two-fifths of the Red Army were left to perish. Perhaps Mao really was in a quandary, but perhaps he wanted the Western Legion out of the way; otherwise Zhang Guotao would be in too strong a position in the final power struggle. It is conceivable, but there is no hard evidence. We do know that nobody could examine the events for half a century. The truth is that terrible mistakes were made; 20,000 proud men and women who had survived the Long March up till then paid the ultimate price in suffering and death.

There was one last battle. Xu and Chen finally decided to ignore Mao's orders and escape to the mountains to save whatever was left of the army. Fighter Li could remember every detail of it; so could Wang. It took place in Liyuankou, a narrow pass into the Qilian Mountains. Wang pleaded with Xu Xiangqian: she wanted the Women's Regiment to serve as the rear guard, covering the retreat. Xu was against it—he knew what the 800 women would suffer if they were caught. "I told him if we lose, we would just run away. It was easier for women." They were each given five bullets and two grenades.

"Hardly had we taken position than the Mas' men galloped up in waves. We saw the clouds of dust they raised, so huge the sun went dark. We could hardly see the men but heard them shouting. Then they came over. We fired at them. But within an hour we ran out of bullets. We went for the horses' legs and the men with knives, bayonets, scissors, stones, even our teeth. In the middle of the fighting, a woman cut a horse's leg, the rider fell on the ground, and she finished him off with a stone—and she made the mistake of crying out with joy. Suddenly the Mas' men knew who they were fighting. Shouts were heard all over the place: 'Brothers, push on! Anyone who catches a Red Bandit woman will get her as his wife!' Many of them jumped off their horses and tried to catch us alive. In the end, there were too many of them. We were overwhelmed. More than 500 women died, but I knew we had given time for the headquarters staff and the core of the army to escape." What Wang did not know was that only 400 of them managed to get away.

Operator Zhong and Ma Fucai escaped into the mountains with the headquarters staff, who were broken up into three units according to priority. "I was told to smash my wireless set and run for it," Zhong recalled. Ma joined another unit. "We were told to run eastward where the enemy was," he said. "People screamed. We didn't want to go, but they pointed their guns at us. We weren't allowed to follow the others. I had no gun—I suppose we were just decoys." He and a few men circled in the woods for days. Then they were frozen and lit a fire—the smoke betrayed them.

Wang herself and half a dozen senior officers battled their way into the mountains, but they were only able to do it after a group of women, some of them wounded, begged them to go while they stood in the way of the Mas' men. They blew themselves up with a pile of hand grenades. "I cried as we left. I knew what was going to happen. We heard the explosion from a long way off up the mountain. We only lived because they died." But in the mountains their footprints on the snow gave them away.

Propagandist Wu jumped off a cliff but only hurt her ankle; the Mas' men found her and pounced on her. Ma Haidiche hid in a niche in the rock for three days and nights. Then she heard a voice calling:

"Comrades, our troops have come to help us. Don't be afraid. Please come out." "I thought I was saved and came out," she recalled with her eyes shut. "Many of us came out, and the Mas' men raped us one after another; some were killed on the spot and their bodies were stripped bare and hung on the trees." Fighter Li escaped with her battalion commander and another woman wounded in the stomach whom they tried to carry. The woman said she was too much of a burden, took opium while they were asleep, and died. Li and the commander were caught begging in a village; Li was raped then and there trying to protect her senior officer.

If the Long March is a symphony, the Western Legion is the saddest of finales. In four months, most of its men and women died or were taken prisoner: 7,000 were killed in battle; 9,200 were captured by the Mas' men—the largest number of captives the Red Army had ever suffered. Of the prisoners, 5,200 were slaughtered and 4,000 young, strong men were at first drafted into the Mas' army and later some were given to Chiang. It was the Mas' contribution to the anti-Japanese war effort. The Red Army asked for them back from Chiang, who complied now that the Communists were his allies. About 2,000 managed to escape and found their way back to their homes in Hubei, Jiangxi, and Sichuan; another 2,000 stayed on in the Northwest after their release.

Propagandist Wu, Ma Haidiche, Feng Yuxiang, and others were taken to Xining, the headquarters of the Mas. On the way, they were raped by their guards every night; anyone who resisted was brutally killed. Wu saw a woman stripped of her clothes and left to die on the ice. In Xining, they worked in a wool factory operated by the Mas. After fifteen hours' work they were given—one woman to a company—to have their way with in the night. Later, they were "awarded" to an orderly, a cook, and a groom in the Mas' army as wives. Wu was sold to a peddler by her husband who thought she was too dirty. Ma Haidiche was taken by the cook to his home village in Linxia; when he found she could not have children, he disowned her. Feng Yuxiang was bought by an opium-den owner who then gave her to his cousin, a man thirty years her senior.

Ma Fucai was drafted into the Mas' "supplemental regiment," a euphemism for labor camp. Here 2,850 Western Legion prisoners repaired roads, dug canals, built bridges, felled trees, mined the hills, cultivated wasteland, and planted fields. Barely a year later, half of them were dead. Ma still could not bear to think of their suffering. "We were worked harder than beasts of burden, on two bowls of porridge a day. People dropped off like flies. I personally buried thirty from our battalion." Some committed suicide; others tried to escape. One of his friends was caught, and had his feet crushed by rocks; he died soon afterwards. Ma survived because a camp officer chose him to be his orderly, and later gave him to his family back in Linxia.

Operator Zhong was brought to a regimental commander after his capture. He was asked where he was from and what he did. He said he was from Jiangxi and was an orderly—he knew if he revealed his true identity as a wireless operator, he would have been tortured for information about the Red Army and certainly killed. The commander looked up with interest. He had just acquired a concubine from Jiangxi and he sent Zhong with two woman prisoners to go and work in his home in Xining. The concubine took to Zhong—she thought he was really cute. She looked after him and gave him proper food. Two years later he was again called into the Mas' army, but he sneaked back and hid in the concubine's room for days. She stole a pass, gave him all the money she had, and put him in a traders' caravan that was heading for the coast. Four months later, he got home.

Woman Wang, Fighter Li, and 130 women from their regiment were brought to the prison in Wuwei. Unlike before, the guards did not abuse them, or hand out random violence in revenge for the deaths on the Mas' side. They were given enough to eat and left to themselves— the prison officers put Wang in charge of them. They were given clothes, even taken out for baths, and shown films. They seemed to be held by humans instead of monsters. They wondered why, but one day all was made clear. They were taken to the garden of Ma Buqing's house, which was packed with officers. Ma's assistant spoke: "Perhaps you are not aware that the Nationalists and the Communists have joined hands in this moment of national crisis under the flag of General Chiang. To show our sincerity, we are going to release the following prisoners." The women fell silent as the names were called out. They noticed that with each woman's name an officer stepped to her

side. It soon dawned on them that this was not a release; they were going to be wives or concubines. The women were enraged; they clung
together and shouted abuse while the officers tried to drag them off. In
the end, thirty women were taken away while the rest were sent back to
the prison.

There the 100 women, Wang and Li among them, argued about
what they should do. They knew the fate of the first thirty also awaited
them. Many spat at the very idea. "Those were the men we fought, the
men who killed and raped our comrades," Li said, still angry after seventy years. "They were animals, worse than animals. And we were going to sleep with them and serve them? We had been so close to death
so many times. This was worse than death. I would rather have died."
But Wang disagreed. "We have been through so much. The Revolution
still needs us. If we live, we can fight another day. I suggest we think
about it. If we go along with them, we'll find our chance to escape.
Always remember, you are women of the Red Army."

Wang was taken away first, given to a brigadier. Most of the rest followed her example. Li was supposed to go with a married official forty
years her senior, but when he came to take her she screamed and
kicked, and bit him. He was horrified and said he would have nothing
to do with her. "After that, no one wanted me. They thought I would
knife them in bed on the first night, so they threw me out into the
street." A peddler took pity on her, and found a Han Chinese man who
was willing to marry her. She has lived in Wuwei ever since.

She paused for a long time. Then she went on: "Remember you
asked me what I think of Wang Quanyuan. Now you know. I hate
Wang for what she did. I've never forgiven her." I think I understood.
Li had lived on, but in pain the whole of the rest of her life. "Why am
I alive, when so many of my comrades are dead?" she repeated. She
would rather have died. Nothing would change her mind about Wang.

Wang escaped from the brigadier after three years. She found her
way back to Lanzhou where there was a Red Army office. The man
there looked at her. The Party had laid down that anyone who took
three years to come back was compromised. He just said coldly: "We
cannot take anyone after so long. It's the rule."

"I cried. I did not shed a tear when I was tortured and humiliated by the enemy. But who would not cry when your own comrades don't trust you?" Wang sobbed just mentioning it seventy years later. "It was the worst moment in my life."

"Stop crying," the man said with a stony look. "I've told you, we cannot take you back. That's final. Here are five silver dollars. We know you have done something for the Revolution. This is your fare home."

Wang stared at him, tears pouring down her face. She drew herself erect and said: "Please convey to the Party that I, Wang Quanyuan, am loyal. I will belong to the Party forever."

She turned around and left.

## ★ EPILOGUE

In the early months of my journey, and especially after a hard day on the road or walking 10 miles to track down a veteran, I would often repeat to myself: "If you find it hard, think of the Long March; if you feel tired, think of our revolutionary forebears." It was comforting, and encouraged me onwards.

But by the time I reached the end after nearly a year, I saw this saying in a new light. Pursuit by the Nationalists, snow on Jiajin Mountain, eating leather in the grassland—I had been familiar with all these since my schooldays—but nothing prepared me for many of the stories told to me by the veterans: the ferocious challenges they encountered, from their enemies and from their comrades. I kept asking myself: "How could their Long March be so different? Why didn't I know?" I checked and rechecked against archive materials, memoirs, and the recollections of other veterans. I became convinced they were telling the truth and determined to tell the full story, one that would do the Marchers justice. What they achieved and what they overcame were so much greater than we had been told.

The unwavering determination they showed is almost more than I can comprehend. The hunger and the desperate searching for food; the hostility of the Tibetans; the fate of so many of the women; arriving at what they thought was the destination, only to discover there was more pain ahead; the promised land that was not as promised. Through all these and more, they kept going. If they had doubts, they conquered them. They knew of the purges, they knew of the desertions, but they stayed loyal, they kept on going. I could see from these people how the Revolution itself succeeded. They went through the furnace and emerged as men and women of steel.

Mao said that the Long March was not an end but a first step. That too was something I came to understand differently. In the course of the March, Mao regained his supremacy, and held it till the end of his life. The new long marches he drove the Chinese people on for the next forty years were longer and more painful than the March itself. We suffered in part because we never knew why they had to go on the original March in the first place: the real reasons why the Red bases collapsed. The lessons of the March were eclipsed by the glory that was heaped on it. That remains true to this day.

Sadly, all but a few of the survivors went on to experience torments unlike anything before. Senior commanders, Party members, rank and file—virtually everyone mentioned in these pages fell foul of the seething politics of the day. For the most part it is a dreadful litany.

After her dismissal from the Red Army office, Woman Wang spent the next fifty years on an agonizing pilgrimage back to the Party. In between, accusations were hung round her neck—sometimes literally: traitor, Nationalist spy, concubine of an officer of the Mas—but nothing could crush her. Fighting injustice was in her soul. In 1989, she was finally conceded a pension, and restored to Party membership—though only from 1949. I asked her how she could be so loyal after all that had happened. "The Party are my parents. How could I not love them?" she said. Wang was one of the few who went through every phase of the March, with the 1st, the 2nd, and the 4th Armies, and the Western Legion. Her extraordinary life mirrors almost all of China's history of the last seventy years; more than this book can contain.

Soldier Huang was made an officer after the March. A peasant through and through, he gave up his commission and returned to his village. He toiled for thirty years, striving to keep his family fed. Life became brighter in 1979 when the peasants were given their own land. "I am like a landlord of the old days," he said happily. His aim is to live to 100 so he can enjoy the life he always yearned for.

Orderly Liu regretted he did not finish the March. "Otherwise I could be a big man in Beijing, with my bodyguards and a car. Instead I'm stuck in this village." I am not so sure. I think he saw the rewards, not what the Marchers had to do to earn them—they risked everything.

I have a suspicion he ran away when the going was tough on the Xiang River. He was the sand, not the gold.

Hygienist Chen spent his entire life in the army medical corps. He has Mao's *Little Red Book* on his desk which he still reads every day. He said we could find answers to all our problems in there. He did. The Red Guards accused him of bourgeois expertise; they poured water over him and made him stand in the freezing cold. He just remembered Mao's words: "The masses might go to extremes once agitated, but their intentions are good." He told the Red Guards, "There is nothing you can do to me. I've been through the Long March."

Operator Zhong put a pile of letters in front of me when I sat down with him. They were copies of what he sent to every government office or to people he thought might help clear his name. For years, even before the Cultural Revolution, he was the object of almost daily derision and humiliation, with his wife and children by his side. "They asked again and again how I escaped from the Mas' men. Where did I get my money to come back home? Was it from the concubine? Did I sleep with her? On and on it went." At long last, his commanding officer, who later became the President of China, saw one of his letters and intervened. Zhong often takes his son to the Martyrs' Memorial Museum in Xingguo and walks in its garden. "I could have been one of the martyrs. I'm lucky to be alive."

For seventeen years after the Revolution, Propagandist Wu was accused of being a traitor and deserter just because she had been in the Western Legion. When the Cultural Revolution started in 1966, she had had enough and took things into her own hands. She joined the Long Marchers' Rebel Corps, and stormed the provincial welfare office to demand justice. They tied up the Party chief there and beat him. "We wanted revenge for the way we'd been treated." She thought he was embezzling her pension and using the accusations against her as an excuse. "I had no idea he was carrying out orders from above." She was not recognized as a Long Marcher, nor did she get her pension until 1986, half a century after the Western Legion's demise.

Sangluo is the most contented of all the Marchers I met. I found it hard to believe he was ever on the March. He became one with the

Tibetans, with the life of the grassland. Where the Red Army suffered so much and was hated so much, he was loved—for his kindness, his honesty, his tolerance, his freedom from prejudice. He has transcended all his loss, all his pain.

Fighter Li, so abused by the Mas' men and so fiercely resistant, was the worst treated of all the veterans I met. As another "traitor and deserter," she never had a job and fed herself and her children on vegetable refuse. In the Cultural Revolution, she was whipped and beaten, every day, hour after hour. "The Red Guards were worse than the Mas' men. They really wanted me dead. I kept arguing with them, saying I was a Long Marcher, they had no right to treat me like that," she said indignantly. "But they said they were following Mao's orders, so I stopped resisting their torture. So many times, I wanted to kill myself. Death was so tempting, so near. But I couldn't bring myself to do it. After all I had been through, how could I die for nothing?" She too was only rehabilitated in 1986.

Feng Yuxiang, Ma Haidiche, and Ma Fucai are the poorest of the lot. Feng Yuxiang just moved into her new house, after a life in stables and run-down huts. It was not much of a house, just four walls and a leaky roof. Ma Haidiche was too poor to give her adopted daughter any dowry. Ma Fucai had to save for thirteen years just to get enough money to dig a well. Out in the villages, even if you are entitled to a pension you are lucky to get a fraction of it. For fifty years they did not have one, yet their material deprivation was nothing to them compared with their struggle to be recognized. As respected Marchers they could have held their heads high, but like so many others they were persecuted, and denied their status. "Didn't the sky have eyes to see the injustice?" Feng asked me.

Like most of the veterans, Ma Fucai felt no bitterness. He compared himself with the senior officers, the generals, and the Party leaders. "I got off lightly. They led us to victory but they were all punished. All except Mao and Zhou Enlai. How could I complain?" He went on: "Look at all the commanders who led the three armies through the Long March. They all reached the top and then fell. Zhu De, the Commander-in-Chief of the whole Red Army—the Red Guards called him a warlord general. Our commander and commissar, Xu Xiangqian and Chen Changhao—one was exiled, the other killed himself during the Cultural Revolution, all because they were Zhang Guotao's men. Look at Peng Dehuai, he criticized Mao and was tortured to death. Look at He Long, he had diabetes and they fed him glucose and he died. Look at Xiao Ke, years in a labor camp."

Ma Fucai could have added many other senior leaders' names who fought side by side with Mao and came so far, only to be disgraced. Zhang Wentian and Wang Jiaxiang, who helped Mao to return to power at Zunyi; Liu Shaoqi, who later became the President of China; Yang Shangkun, another President of China; Deng Xiaoping, who rose and fell three times and eventually changed China for good; Liu Bocheng, the Chief of Staff; Wang Shoudao, Woman Wang's husband on the Long March and later the governor of Hunan Province and Party Secretary of Guangdong. The list goes on and on. Thankfully, those who were still alive after Mao's death were rehabilitated; they went on to run China.

There were two major exceptions: Zhang Guotao and Lin Biao. After his battles with Mao, Zhang Guotao knew what awaited him and went over to the Nationalists. He ended up in Toronto, where he died alone and in poverty in an old people's home. Lin Biao was appointed Mao's heir apparent. But he opposed Mao and may have plotted Mao's assassination after losing trust. He was killed in a plane crash in 1971 when he tried to flee to the Soviet Union.

As for the three foreigners in this book, Otto Braun was told to leave China in 1939, and keep quiet about what he had done. He went first to the Soviet Union; once the Russian plane came for him, he rushed on board and would not move until it took off. He returned to East Germany in 1954 and published a memoir ten years later, including vitriolic passages about Mao.

Even after Rudolf Bosshardt was thrown out, he remained passionately involved in China. He felt that he had not worked in vain. He left his congregation in the hands of his faithful helper Pastor Tang, who later became chair of the Guizhou Christian Council and trained many Christian leaders in the province. Back in Manchester, his home city, he worked for the Manchester Chinese Christian Church. When he died in 1993, General Xiao Ke, the man who held him hostage, sent his family a message of condolence, describing him as "an old friend of the Chinese people."

Edgar Snow's *Red Star over China* was suppressed in China after the Revolution. Despite all he had done for the Communists, the occasional critical remarks in his book about Mao and the Red Army were too much for the new leader's comfort. Decades later, Snow was wheeled out again: he was invited to Beijing and stood next to Mao on the Tiananmen Square podium for the National Day parade in 1970. Mao was using Snow once more, this time to send a signal of rapprochement to Nixon. Two years later, Mao dispatched a Chinese medical team to attend at Snow's deathbed in Switzerland.

The Long Marchers persevered, fought, starved, despaired, and endured. Thousands upon thousands rose to their challenge with a bravery and self-sacrifice unsurpassed in China's or anyone's history. Had they been allowed, the survivors could have achieved anything. The Marchers' courage, their idealism, optimism, and faith were all drilled into us, held up to us for inspiration. They inspire me still. But as well as their example, we need to hear the rest of what the March has to tell us. That is what the Marchers would have wanted.

# ★ BIBLIOGRAPHY

Benton, Gregor, *Mountain Fires: The Red Army's Three-Year War in South China, 1934–1938*, University of California Press, Berkeley/Oxford, 1992.

Bosshardt, Rudolf A., *The Restraining Hand*, Hodder and Stoughton, London, 1936.

Braun, Otto, *A Comintern Agent in China 1932–1939*, translation of *Chinesische Aufzeichnungen (1932–1939)* by Jean Moore, C. Hurst, London, 1982.

Cai Tingkai, *Cai Tingkai zizhuan [Cai Tingkai Autobiography]*, Heilong-jiang renmin chubanshe, Harbin, 1982.

Cai Xiaoqian, *Jiangxi suqu, hongjun xi cuan huiyi [The Jiangxi Soviet: Reminiscences of the Red Army's Flight West]*—Communist China Research Magazine, Taibei, 1970.

Cao Boyi, *Suweiai zhi jianli jiqi bengkui, 1931–1934 [The Founding and Collapse of the Soviet, 1931–1934]*, National University of Politics, Taibei, 1969.

Central Archive, *Guomingdang jun zhuidu hongjun changzheng dangan ziliao xuanbian [Selected Documents on the Nationalist Pursuit and Attacks against the Red Army]*, 2 Vols., Archive Press, Beijing, 1987.

Central Archive and Jiangxi Provincial Archive, *Jiangxi geming lishi wenxian huiyi 1933–1934 [Collection of Jiangxi Revolutionary History Documents 1933–1934]*, Nanchang, 1992.

Chen Bojun, *Diary 1933–1937*, Renmin chubanshe, Shanghai, 1987.

Chen Bojun, Tong Xiaopeng, Wu Yunpu, and Zhang Ziyi, *Changzheng riji [Long March Diaries]*, Wenxian chubanshe, Beijing, 1986.

Chen Jin, *Chongzheng xunsi lu [Thoughts on Retracing the Long March]*, unpublished, 1990.

Chen Ronghua and He Youliang, *Zhongyang suqu shilue [Brief History of the Central Soviet]*, Shanghai sheke chubanshe, 1992.

Chen Yungfa, *Zhongguo gongchandang geming qishi nian [Seventy Years of Chinese Communist Revolution]*, Lianjing Press, Taibei, 2001.

Cheng Zhongyun, *Zhang Wentian zhuan [Biography of Zhang Wentian]*, Dangdai chubanshe, Beijing, 2000.

Chiang Kaishek, *Lushan xunlian ji [Collected Essays on Lushan Training]*, New China Publishing House, Nanjing, 1947.

Chiang Kaishek, *Xian zongtong jiang gong sixiang yanlun zongji [Complete Collection of the Late President Chiang's Thoughts and Speeches]*, Vol. 112 History Committee of the Central Committee of Kuomingtang, Taibei, 1984.

Chinese Communist Party History Documents Collection Committee and
    Central Archive, *Zunyi Wenxian [Documents on Zunyi]*, Renmin
    chubanshe, Beijing, 1985.

Cultural Departments of Sichuan, Yunnan, and Guizhou, *Chuan qian dian bian
    hongse wuzhuang wenhua shiliao xuanbian [Selected Documents of Red
    Forces in Sichuan, Yunnan, and Guizhou]*, Guizhou renmin chubanshe,
    Guiyang, 1985.

Dai Xiangqing and Luo Huilan, *Futian shibian shimo [The Beginning and
    End of the Futian Incident]*, Henan renmin chubanshe, Zhengzhou,
    1994.

Dong Hanhe, *Xilujun chenfu lu [The Collapse of the Western Legion]*, Gansu
    renmin chubanshe, Lanzhou, 1995.

Dong Hanhe, *Xilujun nuzhanshi mengnan ji [Stories of Women of the Western
    Legion After Their Capture]*, Jiefangjun chubanshe, Beijing, 2001.

Farnsworth, Robert, *From Vagabond to Journalist: Edgar Snow in Asia
    1928–1941*, University of Missouri Press, Columbia/London, 1996.

Fei Peiru, *Zhongguo gongnong hongjun di yi fangmian jun changzheng shishi
    rizhi [Record of Daily Events of the 1st Army]*, Guizhou renmin chubanshe,
    Guiyang, 1999.

Fenby, Jonathan, *Generalissimo: Chiang Kai-shek and the China He Lost*, Free
    Press, London, 2005.

First Army Political Department, *Zhongguo gongnong hongjun di yi fangmian jun
    changzheng ji [First Army Records of the Long March]*, Renmin chubanshe,
    Beijing, 1955.

Fourth Army History Committee, *Zhongguo gongnong hongjun disi fangmianjun
    zhanshi ziliao xuanbian [Selected documents on the history of the 4th Army
    of the Red Army]*, Jiefangjun chubanshe, Beijing, 1992.

Gao Enxian, *Zhongguo gongnong hongjun weisheng gonzuo lishi jianbian,
    [History of health work in the Chinese Red Army]*, Renmin junyi chubanshe,
    Beijing, 1987.

Geng Biao, *Geng Biao huiyilu [Memoirs of Geng Biao]*, Jiefangjun chubanshe,
    Beijing, 1991.

Gong Chu, *Gong Chu jiangjun huiyilu [Memoirs of General Gong Chu]*, Ming
    Bao Monthly Press, Hong Kong, 1978.

Griffin, Patricia, *The Chinese Communist Treatment of Counter-revolutionaries,
    1924–1949*, Princeton University Press, Princeton, 1976.

Guizhou Party History Office, *Hongjun changzheng he dangde minzu zhengce
    [The Long March and the Communist Party's Nationality Policy]*, Guizhou
    minzu chubanshe, Guiyang, 1993.

Guo Chen, *Teshu liandui [A Special Company]*, Nongcun duwu chubanshe,
    Beijing, 1985.

Guo Dehong and Zhang Shujun (eds.), *Hongjun changzheng shi [History of the
    Long March]*, Liaoning renmin chubanshe, Shenyang, 1996.

Guo Menglin, *Xilujun, xuezhu de fengbei [The Western Legion-Monument Built
    with Blood]*, Gansu renmin chubanshe, Lanzhou, 2002.

He Changgong, *He Changgong huiyi lu [Memoirs of He Changgong]*, Jiefangjun
    chubanshe, Beijing, 1987.

He Chengming and Zhu Yongguang, *Zhongguo gongnong hongjun xilujun wenxian juan [Archive Documents on the Western Legion of the Chinese Red Army]*, 2 Vols., Gansu renmin chubanshe, Lanzhou, 2004.

He Youliang, *Zhongguo suweiai quyu shehui biandong shi [History of Social Changes in the China Soviet Areas]*, Dangdai chubanshe, Beijing, 1996.

Huang Daoxuan, "Di wuci fan weijiao shibian yuanyin taixi [Reasons for the failure against the 5th Campaign—Analysis of nonmilitary factors]," *Jindaishi yanjun [Modern History Studies]*, No. 5, 2003.

Huang Daoxuan, "Di wuci fan weijiao zhonggong junshi zhengce zai lijie [Another look at Communist military strategy against the 5th Campaign]," *Lishi Yanjun [History Studies]*, No. 1, 2006.

Huang Guozhu et al. (eds.), *Wo de changzheng [My Long Marches]*, 2 Vols., Jiefangjun chubanshe, Beijing, 2005.

Huang Jijie and Chen Fulin (eds.), *Xin guixi shi [History of the New Gui Warlords]*, Guangxi renmin chubanshe, Nanning, 1991.

Huang Kecheng, *Huang Kecheng zishu [Huang Kecheng Tells His Story]*, Renmin chubanshe, Beijing, 1994.

Jiangxi Provincial Archive, *Zhongyang geming genjudi dangan ziliao xuanbian [Selected Archive Materials from Central Revolutionary Base]*, Jiangxi renmin chubanshe, Nanchang, 1982.

Jung Chang and Jon Halliday, *Mao: The Unknown Story*, Jonathan Cape, London, 2005.

Kampen, Thomas, *Mao Zedong, Zhou Enlai, and the Evolution of the Chinese Communist Leadership*, Nordic Institute of Asian Studies, Copenhagen/Curzon Press, Richmond, 1999.

Kampen, Thomas, "The Zunyi Conference as One More Step in Mao's Rise to Power," *China Quarterly*, No. 117, 1989.

Kuo, Warren, *Analytical History of the Chinese Communist Party*, 4 Vols., Institute of International Relations, Taibei, 1968.

Lee, Lily Xiao Hong, and Sue Wiles, *Women of the Long March*, Allen and Unwin, St. Leonards N.S.W., 1999.

Li Anbao, *Changzheng yu wenhua [The Long March and Culture]*, Dangian duwu chubanshe, Beijing, 2002.

Li Xing, "The Grain Issue Faced by the Red Army in the Grassland," *Tibet Studies*, No. 1, 2003.

Li Yimang, *Mohu de yingping: Li Yimang huiyilu [Blurred Screen: Li Yimang's Memoirs]*, Renmin chubanshe, Beijing, 1992.

Liang Zheng, "Tucheng zhanyi" ["Tucheng battle"], in Guizhou Party History Office, *Hongjun zai Guizhou [Red Army in Guizhou]*, Guizhou renmin chubanshe, Guiyang, 1984.

Liu Tong, *Bei Shang [March North]*, Jiangxi renmin chubanshe, Nanchang, 2003.

Liu Ying, *Zai lishi de jiliu zhong [In the Torrent of History]*, Dangshi chubanshe, Beijing, 1992.

Lyall, Thomas Leslie, *A Passion for the Impossible: The China Inland Mission, 1865–1965*, Hodder and Stoughton, London, 1965.

Ma Xuanwei, *Sichuan junfa hunzhan [Wars of the Sichuan Warlords]*, Sichuan shekeyuan chubanshe, Chengdu, 1984.

Mao Zedong, *Mao Zedong nongcun diaocha wenji [Collected Writings on Rural Investigations]*, Renmin chubanshe, Beijing, 1983.

Mao Zedong, *Mao Zedong Xuanji [Mao Zedong Selected Works]*, Renmin chubanshe, Beijing 1965.

Ministry of Culture, *Changzheng zhong de wenhua gongzuo [Cultural Work during the Long March]*, Beijing tushuguan chubanshe, Beijing, 1998.

Mo Wenhua, *Mo Wenhua huiyilu [Memoirs of Mo Wenhua]*, Jiefangjun chubanshe, Beijing, 1994.

People's Liberation Army Arts Academy, *Zhongguo renmin jiefangjun wenyi shiliao xuanbian (hongjun shiqi) [Selected Arts Materials of the People's Liberation Army (Red Army Period)]*, Jiefangjun chubanshe, Beijing, 1986.

Peng Dehuai, *Peng Dehuai zishu [Autobiographical Notes of Peng Dehuai]*, Renmin chubanshe, Beijing, 1981.

Research Office, Chief-of-Staff's HQ, Communications Dept., People's Liberation Army, *Hongjun de ermu yu shenjing [Ears and Nerves of the Red Army]*, Military Academy, Beijing, 1991.

Saich, Tony, and Hans van de Ven (eds.), *New Perspectives on the Chinese Communist Revolution*, M. E. Sharpe, Armonk, NY, 1995.

Salisbury, Harrison, *The Long March: The Untold Story*, Macmillan, London, 1985.

Schram, Stuart, *Mao Zedong*, Penguin, Harmondsworth, 1966.

Second Army History Committee, *Zhongguo gongnong hongjun dier fangmianjun zhanshi ziliao xuanbian [Selected documents on the history of the 2nd Army of the Red Army]*, Jiefangjun chubanshe, Beijing, 1991.

Smedley, Agnes, *China's Red Army Marches*, Lawrence & Wishart, London, 1936.

Smedley, Agnes, *The Great Road: The Life and Times of Chu Teh*, Monthly Review Press, New York/London, 1972.

Snow, Edgar, *Red Star over China*, Victor Gollancz, London, 1937.

Snow, Edgar, *The Long Revolution*, Hutchinson, London, 1973.

Su Yu, *Su Yu zhanzheng huiyilu [Su Yu's Memoirs of the War Years]*, Jiefangjun chubanshe, Beijing, 1988.

Thomas, S. Bernard, *Season of High Adventure*, University of California Press, Berkeley/Los Angeles/London, 1996.

Tong Xiaopeng, *Fengyu sishi nian [Forty Years of Wind and Rain]*, Zhongyang wenxian chubanshe, Beijing, 1994.

Van de Ven, Hans, *War and Nationalism in China 1925–1945*, RoutledgeCurzon, London, 2003.

Wang Jianying, *Zhongguo gongnong hongjun fazhan shi jianbian (1927–1937) [Introduction to the History of the Development of the Chinese Red Army (1927–1937)]*, Jiefangjun chubanshe, Beijing, 1986.

Wang Ping, *Wang Ping huiliyu [Memoirs of Wang Ping]*, Jiefangjun chubanshe, Beijing, 1992.

Wang Tingke, *Hongjun changzheng yanjiu [Research on the Long March]*, Sichuan shehui kexue chubanshe, Chengdu, 1985.

Wang Xingjuan, *He Zizhen de lu [Biography of He Zizhen]*, Zuojia chubanshe, Beijing, 1988.

Watson, Jean, *Bosshardt—a Biography: The Story of a Christian Missionary Caught Up in Mao's Long March*, Monarch Books, Great Britain, 1995.

Wei, William, *Counterrevolution in China: The Nationalists in Jiangxi during the Soviet Period*, University of Michigan Press, Ann Arbor, 1985.

Wu Xiuquan, *Wangshi cangsang [My Turbulent Past]*, Shanghai wenyi chubanshe, 1992.

Xinghuo Liaoyuan Editorial Committee, *Xinghuo liaoyuan congshu [A Single Spark Can Light a Prairie Fire—Series]*, Jiefangjun chubanshe, Beijing. 1986.

Xu Xiangqian, *Lishi de huigu [Look Back on History]*, Jiefangjun chubanshe, Beijing, 1998.

Xue Yue, *Jiaofei jishi [Accounts of Eliminating the Bandits]*, Wenxian chubanshe, Taibei, 1962.

Yan Daogang, "Jiang Jieshi zhuidu changzheng hongjun de bushu jiqi shibai [Chiang Kaishek's plans for pursuit and attack against the Red Army and his failure]," in *Wenshi ziliao xuanji [Selected Historical Accounts]*, No. 62, Wenshi ziliao bianjibu, Beijing, [no date].

Yang, Benjamin, *From Revolution to Politics: Chinese Communists on the Long March*, Westview Press, Boulder, San Francisco/Oxford, 1990.

Yang, Benjamin, "The Zunyi Conference as One Step in Mao's Rise to Power: A Survey of Historical Studies of the Chinese Communist Party," *China Quarterly*, No. 106, 1986.

Yang Kuisong, *Mao Zedong he Mosike de enen yuanyuan [Mao and his Love-Hate Relationship with Moscow]*, Jiangxi renmin chubanshe, Nanchang, 2005.

Yang Kuisong, *Xian shibian xintan [A New Inquiry into the Xian Incident]*, Dongda tushu gongsi, Taibei, 1995.

Yao Jinguo, *Zhang Guotao zhuan [Biography of Zhang Guotao]*, Renmin chubanshe, Xian, 2000.

Young, Helen, *Choosing Revolution: Chinese Women Soldiers on the Long March*, University of Illinois Press, Urbana, 2001.

Yuan Lishi, *Xue se liming [Bloodstained Dawn]*, Jinling chuban gongsi, Hong Kong, 2002.

Zeng Zhi (ed.), *Changzheng nuzhanshi [Women Warriors on the Long March]*, Vol. 1, Beifang funu chubanshe, Changchun, 1986.

Zeng Zhi, *Yige geming de xingcunzhe [A Survivor of Revolution]*, Guangdong renmin chubanshe, Guangzhou, 2000.

Zhang Guotao, *Wo de huiyi [My Memoirs]*, 2 Vols., Dongfang chubanshe, Beijing, 2004.

Zhang Xueliang, "Penitent Confession on the Xian Incident," *Chinese Studies in History*, Spring 1989.

Zhou Wenqi and Zhu Liangru, *A Special and Tricky Subject: The Chronology of the Relationship between the Comintern, the Soviet Union, and the Chinese Communist Party 1919–1991*, Zhongyang wenxian chubanshe, Beijing, 1993.

## ★ NOTES

This book employs the pinyin system for transliteration from the Chinese, except for familiar names such as Canton, Chiang Kaishek, etc.

CHAPTER 1

1   Kuo 1968, Vol. 2, p. 614
2   Mao 1983, p. 351
3   Jiangxi 1933, Circular 4
4   He 1987, p. 191

CHAPTER 2

1   Kuo 1968, Vol. 2, p. 438
2   Liu Shaoqi, *Struggle*, No. 53; March 3, 1934
3   Smedley 1972, p. 239
4   Cai 1982, p. 245
5   Huang 2003, pp. 80–113
6   *Ibid.*
7   Wei 1985, pp. 112–116
8   Cai 1970
9   Chen 1987, p. 304
10  Central Archive and Jiangxi Provincial Archive 1992, p. 107
11  Salisbury 1985, p. 44
12  Chiang 1947, p. 18.
13  Zhou and Zhu 1993, p. 241
14  Braun 1982, p. 46.
15  Huang 2006
16  Braun 1982, p. 68
17  *Red Star*, No. 33, April 22, 1934
18  *Red China*, No. 240, October 3, 1934, p. 16
19  Geng 1991, p. 129

CHAPTER 3

1   Gong Chu 1978, pp. 395–399
2   *Ibid.*
3   Yang 2005, p. 29
4   *Ibid.*, p. 40
5   Dai and Luo 1994, pp. 114–119

6   As quoted in Jung and Halliday 2005, p. 98
7   Smedley 1972, p. 261
8   Fenby 2005, p. 256
9   Huang 1994, p. 100
10  Chen 2001, p. 286
11  Jiangxi Provincial Archive 1982, p. 320
12  Griffin 1976, p. 34
13  *Struggle*, No. 39, December 19, 1933
14  Gong 1978, pp. 431–443
15  *Ibid.*, p. 449
16  Liu 1992, p. 56

CHAPTER 4
1   Huang and Chen 1991, pp. 313–317
2   *Ibid.*
3   Yan (no date), p. 15
4   Cai 1970, p. 210
5   Chen 1987, pp. 325–326
6   Cai 1970, p. 216
7   Liu 2003, p. 9
8   Second Army History Committee 1991, p. 140
9   Guo and Zhang 1996, p. 93
10  Alan Bennett, *The History Boys*
11  Mo 1994, p. 246
12  Salisbury 1985, p. 101
13  Chen and He 1992
14  Braun 1982, p. 90

CHAPTER 5
1   Chen 1990, p. 135
2   *Ibid.*, p. 56
3   Bosshardt 1936
4   *Ibid.*, p. 91
5   *Ibid.*, p. 251
6   *Ibid.*, p. 252
7   *Ibid.*, p. 120
8   Xiao Ke 1989, preface to Chinese translation of Bosshardt 1936
9   Second Army History Committee 1991, p. 137
10  Lyall 1965
11  Bosshardt 1936, p. 287
12  *Ibid.*, pp. 76–78
13  *Ibid.*, p. 272
14  *Ibid.*, pp. 272–273
15  *Ibid.*, p. 234
16  Xiao Ke 1989, preface to Chinese translation of Bosshardt 1936

CHAPTER 6

1   Cai 1970, p. 296
2   Benton 1992, p. 68
3   Salisbury 1985, p. 120
4   Zhang Wentian, speech, Chinese Communist Party, p. 78
5   Salisbury 1985, p. 111
6   Liu 2003, p. 88
7   Salisbury 1985, p. 123
8   Snow 1937, p. 392
9   Cheng 2000, p. 78
10  Interview with Huang, p. 194
11  First Army 1955, p. 23
12  Liang 1984, pp. 27–35
13  Research Office 1991
14  Guo 1985, p. 202
15  Liang 1984, p. 38
16  Braun 1982, p. 114
17  Selected Archive Materials from the 2nd Revolutionary War Period, cited by
    Liu 2003, p. 9
18  Braun 1982, p. 144
19  Cheng 2000, p. 220
20  Kampen 1989, p. 134

CHAPTER 7

1   Young 2001, p. 111
2   *Ibid.*, p. 39
3   *Ibid.*, p. 33
4   Zhang 2004, Vol. 2, p. 275
5   Fenby 2005, p. 200
6   Yao 2000, pp. 186–187
7   He Libo, *Earth Magazine*, No. 22, 2002
8   Salisbury 1985, p. 80
9   Zhang 2004, Vol. 2, p. 202

CHAPTER 8

1   Lee and Wiles 1999, p. 97
2   Snow 1937, p. 194
3   He 1987, p. 347
4   Interview with Ma Xuanwei, author of *Wars of the Sichuan Warlords*
5   *Ibid.*
6   Snow 1937, p. 196
7   Salisbury 1985, p. 224
8   Notes of interview with General Li Jukui, Sichuan provincial archives
9   *Ibid.*
10  Yuan 2002, p. 459
11  Diary of Tong Xiaoping in Chen et al. 1986, p. 131
12  Braun 1982, p. 123

13 Zhang 2004, Vol. 2, p. 135
14 *Ibid.*, p. 310
15 *Ibid.*, pp. 321–322
16 Liu 1992, p. 79
17 Braun 1982, p. 168
18 Fourth Army History Committee 1992, p. 139
19 Liu 1992, p. 83
20 Xu 1998, p. 453
21 Wu 1992, p. 137
22 Cai 1970, p. 377
23 Zhang 2004, Vol. 2, p. 268
24 Zhu Yu, *Issues on the Secret Telegram Debate*, unpublished paper
25 *Ibid.*

CHAPTER 9

1 Guizhou Party History Office 1993, pp. 289–290
2 *Ibid.*, p. 288
3 *Sichuan and Tibet Frontier Quarterly*, May 1935
4 Braun 1982, p. 126
5 Li 2003, p. 87
6 Wang 1992, p. 109
7 Chen 1987, pp. 146–147
8 Liu Zhong, unpublished memoirs
9 *Ibid.*
10 Diary of Tong Xiaopeng 1986, pp. 142–145
11 Second Army History Committee 1991, p. 156
12 Salisbury 1985, p. 270
13 Diary of Tong Xiaopeng 1986, p. 148
14 Huang et al. 2005, Vol. 1, p. 91
15 *Ibid.*, Vol. 2, p. 656
16 Luhuo County Archives
17 Li 2003, p. 90
18 *Ibid.*

CHAPTER 10

1 Braun 1982, p. 148
2 Wang 1992, p. 142
3 Liu 2003, p. 166
4 Peng 1981, p. 211
5 Mao Zedong 1965, Vol. 1, pp. 256–257
6 People's Liberation Army 1986, p. 576
7 *Red Star*, No. 3, November 11, 1934
8 *Ibid.*
9 Ministry of Culture 1998, p. 99
10 *Ibid.*, p. 79
11 Cai 1970, pp. 129–131
12 Su Yu 1988, p. 111

13   Snow 1937, p. 120
14   Thomas 1996, p. 80
15   Jung and Halliday 2005, p. 137
16   Thomas 1996, p. 137
17   Snow 1937, p. 81
18   Jung and Halliday 2005, p. 199
19   Thomas 1996, p. 147
20   Farnsworth 1996, p. 311
21   *Ibid.*
22   Thomas 1996, p. 1
23   *Ibid.*, p. 189
24   Jung and Halliday 2005, p. 139

CHAPTER 11

1    Fourth Army History Committee 1992, p. 666
2    Liu 2003, p. 211
3    Xu 1998, p. 494
4    Yang 1995
5    *Ibid.*, p. 96
6    Yuan 2002, p. 52
7    Liu 2003, p. 285
8    Yang 1995, p. 238
9    Liu Xuezhi, *Before and After Demobilisation*, in Xinghuo Liaoyuan Editorial
     Committee 1986, Series 5, p. 303
10   Yang 1995, p. 235
11   Li 1992, p. 241
12   Yang 1995, p. 227
13   Jung and Halliday 2005, pp. 187–188
14   Zhang 2004, p. 391
15   Yang 1995, p. 355
16   Fenby 2005, pp. 12–13

CHAPTER 12

1    Dong Hanhe, *Draft History of the Western Legion*, unpublished, p. 422
2    Liu 2003, p. 101
3    Guo 2002, p. 38
4    Yuan 2002, pp. 243–244
5    Liu 2003, p. 345
6    Yuan 2002, p. 367
7    Xu 1998, p. 391